FOOTLOOSE IN ITALY

Footloose

IN ITALY

by Horace Sutton

WITH PHOTOGRAPHS MOSTLY BY
THE AUTHOR

RINEHART & COMPANY, INC.

NEW YORK · TORONTO

FOREWORD

As you've no doubt heard, Italy is probably the biggest museum in the world. And when it comes to churches, nobody has more of them. There isn't any other handy corner of the earth whose history is commemorated by so many ruins.

Art, ruins and history are a combination which most people find as exciting as lemon junket. And yet Italy is an exciting country. To preserve the native excitement and keep the somniferous effect as low as possible, this book acknowledges the presence of art in Italy, but it leaves art appreciation to the connoisseur. It records the famous churches of Italy, but it avoids filibustering among the naves and atriums. It visits the ruins, and even recalls some appropriate history, but it is no substitute for a history book. Often it is more occupied defining the difference between a *palazzo* and a *pizza*, telling you which you ought to visit, and which you ought to eat.

Since Italy was until recently no less Greek to me than Athens, I find myself indebted to many people, Italians and Americans, who charted my course, eased my path and sometimes took me by the hand. To be perfectly honest this book could not have been written without the ceaseless efforts both here and in Italy, of Manolita T. Doelger, director of the Italian National Tourist office in the United States. My further thanks are due to the members of her staff in New York, particularly to Piero Bonelli. Also to Pierre Rousselle and Ellis Reed of Air France; Bob Matthews and Jim MacArthur of the American Express Company; to Rodolfo Rueck of Venice, publicity director of the Compagnie Italiana dei Grandi Alberghi; and to Edith Turner, representative of that company in New York. To the people of CIAT, the Compagnia Italiana

v

FOREWORD

Autoservizi Turistici, notably Comm. Enrico Linzi, Giovanni Galleni and Giuseppe Tieri, its manager in the United States.

Along the length and narrow breadth of Italy I owe a vote to these Italians who showed me their country, always making me feel that their region was even more delightful than the one I had just left. They are: In Rome, Eugene Saroli and Magda Stringher; along the Road North, R. L. Quercetani and Prof. Tealdo Tealdi of Florence, and Alvas Sternieri of CIAT in Bologna and the Romagnola; in Venice, Rodolfo Rueck, Comm. Giovanni Rodano and Count Ottavio Zasio of the United Press. There is no better guide to the Dolomites than F. Terschak of Cortina d'Ampezzo. In the Lake country I am indebted to Willy Dombré of Cernobbio, Franco Maresca of Stresa and Liugi Nancio of Gardone; along the Riviera to, Aldo Zoli and Edoardo Morandi of San Remo, and Giulio Tobino of Genoa; on the Road South, to Augusto Cesareo of Naples and Mario Massimo of Capri; and in Sicily, to Lucia La Rosa. Suggestions of what to eat in each region and "How to Eat in Italy" were prepared by Raffaele A. Masprone, manager of the Gritti Palace in Venice, and his chef de cuisine, Giuseppe Gatti, formerly personal cook to Mark Clark. The section on the Vatican was prepared with the help of Franklin C. Gowan, special assistant to the President's personal representative to the Pope.

Except where otherwise credited, the photos were taken by me during the summer and fall of 1949 on a Rolleiflex camera, Schneider Xenar 3.5 lens and were developed and printed by Paul Anderson in New York. The book was edited with love and care by Bill Raney of Rinehart, than whom there has never been a more fervent Italophile. Not even Garibaldi.

H. S.

New York City
January 1950.

CONTENTS

For

B. C. S.

my champion, my critic,
my Eastern sales manager, my mother.

THE FACTS
OF LIFE

I. THE FACTS OF LIFE
... in Italy

For a nation whose land was used as a battlefield in a slow, sloppy, prolonged war of attrition, the south beset by an invader, the north in the grip of an erstwhile ally turned captor, Italy has bounced back with tremendous vitality. Cities mangled beyond identification in the conflict have been abandoned and built anew. Bombed hotels have been reconstructed, new ones built. The roads are excellent. The work has gone ahead ploddingly, ceaselessly. There is none of the frenzied American stress for continual improvement. One senses that the country would like to get back where it was before the shooting started, but not necessarily farther. The shops and offices in most cities, during the warm season, are open from nine until noon, and again from four until eight. Between times Italians talk politics, dawdle over an *apéritif* at an outdoor cafe, eat, sleep and propagate.

Outside of a hot dog and roll there is little in Italy that you can't get. For the tourist, certainly, there is no shortage in any commodity, and Americans will find prices about twenty percent lower than the big city cost of living at home. Italy's poverty becomes more evident as one travels south from Rome, and it reaches a high, or low, in Sicily. Basically the country's economic problem results from the double disadvantage that it possesses virtually no mineral resources of its own, and that its population is increasing at the incredible clip of 500,000 every year. The overpopulation necessitates creating jobs, especially government jobs, where none is necessary. In takes four customs clerks to do the work one efficient man could accomplish without straining, and each feels a certain responsibility to impress upon whoever is handy at the time, his true importance. I still have $28.40 worth of film and flashbulbs, flown across the Atlantic at a cost of $6.50 imbedded in Italian customs. I put up what I considered a good fight, but succumbed to overwhelming odds.

In dealing with street beggars, whom you will find in Venice, in Genoa, in Rome and all points south, some Americans bestow lavish tips on all comers as an execution of a personalized Marshall Plan. (In turn bits of chocolate go to all children, and pats on the head to all local dogs.) The presence of beggars embarrasses most Italians, and those who are latent apologists for the late Fascist regime will say that at least during those times one didn't have this kind of a situation on the streets. Most Italians recognize beggars as part of an organized racket, and get rid of them by giving them five-lire notes worth about seven-tenths of a cent. It is said that the sleeping babies so frequently carried by alms-seekers often are rented to them, and sometimes the baby is drugged.

Generally you will find Italians to be suave, sentimental and sincere. They are the hand-kissingest men this side of Rudolph Valentino. When they are particularly glad to see each other, Italians will indulge in a kissing operation that involves both cheeks of both parties. Women kiss women, men kiss men, and sometimes they do it with one of each.

with tremendous vitality

American women, particularly blondes, seem to develop the flutters over dark Italian men. The favor is wholeheartedly returned. Janis Paige, a Hollywood lady, spent five months in Rome and told the reporters when she arrived back home that Italian wolves use hand signals instead of whistles. If an Italian man sees a pretty girl he presses his forefinger into his cheek and smiles, Janis said. If the girl is simply stunning he pokes a forefinger in each cheek and rolls his eyes. This, ladies, is the Roman call to arms as reported by Miss Janis Paige who would have more reason to know than I.

When they are happy Italians will sing, and when they are sad they are sour. They have a rather low boiling point, and when they get angry it is best to stand clear of flying gesticulations. On

between times Italians talk, dawdle, propagate . . .

the other hand they are easily disarmed with a smile. They get along well with Americans, and feel neither a personal humiliation about the war, nor an embarrassment about postwar American assistance. As far as the war is concerned they feel they were badly led. They are not resentful of Marshall Plan aid, first because they recognize that they sorely needed the help, and secondly because they are confident they are making excellent use of United States money and materials.

The Italian language, like the Italian nature, follows the pleasant lines of least resistance. The words are musical, often sound like their meaning. *Adagio* means slow, *piccolo* means small and *piano* can mean floor or smooth, or softly. To make the water warmer turn the faucet marked *calda.* When answering the phone say *pronto,* which means hello, or literally, ready. *Presto* is the word for hurry.

Most words end in "o," "a," "i" or "e." If you want a telephone, look for a *telefono.* If you want a husband, look for a *sposo.* If you want a drink ask for *scotchi.* Italians also drop their "h's." The letter hardly exists in the language. If you are bound for the race track, follow the signs that point to the *ippodromo,* and if you should lift something heavy, what you are in for is an *ernia.*

You need have no fear of intellectual starvation in Italy. You'll find a broad selection of popular American and British books both in paper and cloth bound editions. Newsstands in the big cities carry virtually every American magazine, a little late and a little higher in price, but welcome for all that. The continental edition of *Time* and *Newsweek* is available on schedule in all but the most remote parts of the country. The *Rome Daily American,* published since the war by a staff of former Stars and Stripers, is a four- to six-page tabloid containing such bits of Americana as a gossip column, ball scores, Blondie and Billy Rose. It is on the stands in Italy several hours ahead of the Paris edition of the *New York Herald Tribune.*

There is one movie theater in Rome which shows English language pictures, but you will have more fun seeing such American films with dubbed-in Italian voices as "i Volontari del Texas" with William Boyd. Wild West adventures in the Italian comic books, however, have recently incurred official displeasure. Buffalo Bill has been banned, but still riding high is "Le Meravigliose Avventure di Kit Carson." And when *The Outlaw,* starring Jane Russell was prepared for Italian exhibition its name was changed to *Il Mio Corpo Scaldera,* or *My Body Will Warm You.*

Italian bread is white, but you will see it only rarely. Restaurants serve hard, doughy rolls that taste something like the bloated

population is increasing at an incredible clip

pretzels sold on pushcarts on New York's lower East Side. You'll also find *grissini*, one meter long, there being 39.37 inches in each meter. There is plenty of butter around. Sometimes it appears automatically, other times you have to ask for it, and occasionally you are charged extra for it.

The lightest thing you can eat in Italy is breakfast which, after the Continental manner, consists of the usual rolls, butter, jam and coffee with hot milk. If hot milk does the same thing to your appetite it does to mine, and you still want to dilute the coffee you can cut it with hot water. Continental breakfasts served in your room will cost about fifty cents in the best hotels. You may feel better, if you plan to hike the ruins, or tramp the museum corridors,

Blondie and Billy Rose

with something heartier aboard. You can get orange juice and bacon
and eggs which will run your bill up to $1.25.

What they don't eat at breakfast Italians make up for at lunch
and dinner. Italy is full of *pasta*, and it is inevitable that if you visit
the country you will be too. *Pasta* is a combination of flour, water
and eggs, and it comes in at least fifty-seven varieties. Spaghetti
is *pasta* and so are noodles, Italian cooking varies with the sauce
which one drapes over the *pasta*. In Bologna the Bolognese eat it
with meat sauce, in Genoa, the Genoese eat it with *pesto*, a kind
of green herb. Up in the north country the starch staple is rice,
gnocchi (a mixture of wheat and potatoes), and *polenta* (a ballast
made of corn meal). The *pasta*, rice, or *gnocchi* is served as a sort

of appetizer. Since they give you — as one Englishman recently reported — enough spaghetti to knit a pullover it often isn't necessary to plunge deeper into the menu. Veal is the national meat in Italy like roast beef in England and steak in the United States. It comes smothered in cheese, breaded, grilled, mixed with peppers, sautéed with flavorsome leaves, or cold in a sandwich. Should you see beefsteak on a menu, don't order it with visions of a two-pound porterhouse. It comes razor thin, like the veal. Most hotels, however, serve an *entrecote* or a *filet*.

When it comes to dessert Italians have the French penchant for fruit and cheese. Italy, after all, is the mother of Bel Paese and Gorgonzola. The fruit is rich and oversized, and the grapes grow like the weeds in Hogan's sandlot. Italians don't attach the same importance as the French do to wine labels and years. One merely asks for white or red, and if you ask for none the *sommelier* doesn't have a heart attack on the spot. The whites come in a variety of tastes, but the reds tend to be heavy and heady. One year's vintage, however, seems to be quite as good as the next or the last, the weather being considerably steadier than the politics.

Travelers who stick to bottled table water can ask for Fiuggi, which is still; Pellegrino, which is slightly gaseous; or Recoaro, which is super-bubbly. There are other brands, of course, but a mention of preference indicates the degree of effervescence you desire.

It is, of course, as in most Continental countries, virtually impossible to have coffee and dessert arrive, after the American custom, at the same time. What makes such a coincidence even more improbable in Italy is the Italian custom of having coffee in a different place from the one in which you had dinner. Some hotels only serve coffee at the bar. Then there are bars which specialize in coffee. The new postwar coffee houses are bright, shiny and modernistic, where, since there are no seats, you take your coffee standing up. All bars are equipped for the manufacture of coffee, with

grapes grow like weeds in Hogan's sandlot

a contraption of valves, pipes, dials and gauges doubtlessly patterned after the boiler room of Fulton's Folly. After a considerable amount of huffing, coughing and spitting the machine grudgingly gives up a thimbleful of coffee you could put in your eye. Don't! It is stronger than moonshine, as black as tar and just as tasty.

Italians are in the habit of dropping by the bars or the cafes (called *caffès*) and drinking perhaps half a dozen cups of coffee an evening. And there are those who claim that the local coffee habit is the whole key to the Italian disposition. If you think that Italians are naturally excitable it's just that the country has coffee nerves on a national scale.

Since the working day doesn't end until eight, the fashionable dinner hour begins at nine. At resorts and big city hotels there is

a long and interesting cocktail hour which runs from about seven until nine. You can find American whiskey and Scotch just about everywhere at $1.00 to $1.25 a drink. Martinis and Tom Collinses made with Gordon's gin — they make a point of asking you — costs about eighty cents in the big cities, and just about half that in the hinterlands. If you want to drink native there is always vermouth and soda which is light and as nonalcoholic as you can get without ordering an orange crush. An *Americano,* which bears no relation to anything American, is vermouth, soda and *campari* — a scarlet-colored bitters. I have it on good authority that an *Americano* is called an *Americano* because it is a mixed drink, a bit of alcoholic chemistry for which the Americani are apparently well noted abroad. For more formidable fortification try a *Negroni* — vermouth, *campari,* seltzer and gin — or a *Cardinale* — a Martini with *campari* which turns it red.

For the most part Italy's restaurants have an excellent selection of food at prices Americans will not find high. It is possible to have a dinner for $4, but you would have to look for a restaurant with a bill of fare that high. Lunch and dinner in most of the better hotels costs the same, about $2, *prix fixe,* which is fairly high for lunch, and rather inexpensive for dinner. American plan rates in the resort hotels are well below comparable establishments in the United States. Restaurants all over the country are *à la carte,* but you can get by nicely for $1.50 to $2.50 in the nicest places, a dollar or so more if you want wine. With rare exception, ten to fifteen percent service is figured into the bill by the time you get it. If you've been pleased with the service you may indicate it by leaving the waiter the breakage from your change or one- or two-hundred lire notes in addition to the automatic tip which has already been extracted from your pocket. The music you hear in restaurants is usually contributed by street musicians who make the rounds and pass the plate. Fifty lire or less

you take your coffee standing up

is sufficient unless you've asked the boys to put on a four-star production of the score from *Aida* just for you.

In summer the restaurants spread their tables all over the sidewalks, the gutters and out into the squares. It's rather a pleasant custom and gives one a feeling of being part of the community. Not only are you serenaded by strolling musicians, but you are solicited by newsies, by blackmarket cigarette salesmen, and often by beggars. Two cartons of American cigarettes were all the Italian customs would allow when this was written, but there was official pressure to increase the allowance. American cigarettes legitimately purchased in the hotels and the *tabbacchi* shops cost fifty cents a pack. The blackmarket vendors, who for some reason sell furtively at the restaurants and wide open in the big city markets, charge about thirty cents a pack, get their supply from sources on the ocean liners or U. S. Navy ships. Some American cigarettes filter through employees in tax-free Vatican City. I hope you will pardon me if I refer to them as holy smokes.

Italian hotels follow the European custom of exacting an automatic fifteen, and in some cases eighteen, percent of the total bill for service. Add to that a *taxe de séjour* and a few inevitable local levies and you can count on your bill being twenty percent higher than the straight room or room-with-meals quotation. Except for Rome and some of the flashier establishments in Venice, hotel prices are a good deal less than comparative accommodations in the United States, the extra twenty percent included. You may not find the obligatory service charge to your liking, but the hotel workers' unions in Europe have insisted on it, and I'm afraid it is here to stay. On the question of how to tip in view of the obligatory charge there are a number of divided schools. Some people say that service and other additional automatic charges should be viewed as part of the regular rate, and that one should start tipping from there. As far as I am concerned that is an extreme view. Others insist that they are paying fifteen percent of their bill for service, and refuse to tip beyond that. I feel that's going a little far, too. For my lire the most sensible plan is to tip, lightly and politely, for extra services rendered by pleasant people. The hundred-lire note is the basic currency for tipping — one, two or three — those who call taxis, carry your baggage, obtain tickets or have your clothes pressed.

Virtually any question you can compound can be answered by the hotel concierge, a gentleman who wears a frock coat with crossed keys on the lapels. You will find him standing behind a desk in the lobby. The better the hotel the more languages he speaks. (For a story about one of Italy's best and busiest concierges, see the chapter on Rome.)

In the better hotels you will be shown to your room by an assistant manager who might be insulted if you gave him a tip. Your baggage will be brought upstairs by a baggage porter who certainly would be insulted if you didn't. There are no bellboys, as we know them, in Italy.

As far as I can determine, marble is about as cheap as beaverboard, and you may, in the normal course of things, get a bathroom that makes the War Memorial of Waukesha Falls look sick. Although many bathrooms have showers I have never seen a shower curtain in Italy. According to Continental custom every bath has a *bidet,* Europe's contribution to the furtherance of female hygiene. Most baths are stocked with immense terry cloth towels, or with fluffy terry cloth robes which are hung, when not in use, over heated towel racks. If, after returning from Italy, a normal American towel seems about as adequate as drying yourself with a washrag, Lord and Taylor and Gimbel's in New York have the terry cloth numbers at about $10 apiece. Every hotel bathroom has toilet paper, but you'll do well to keep some flat-packed tissue in pocket or purse for the public lavatories which are usually without. Although you can buy all the soap you want at prices only slightly higher than stateside, not one hotel provides a bar. If you are going to be unhappy without your favorite brand, better bring your soap, and a soap dish, from home.

Don't be distressed by the public urinals which are as much a part of the city street corner as the lamppost. What you called a *pissoir* in Paris is an *orinatoio* or *vespasiano* here. Macy's window couldn't be more public.

Doubtless the biggest bargains in the boot are in the beauty parlors and the barber shops. I have it on what I take to be un-impeachable feminine authority that a wash, set and manicure — a bit of dalliance that might have run up a tab of $7.50 at An-toine's — came to the equivalent of one buck fifty in the coiffeur

if you want to drink native ...

of the best hotel in Rome. Similarly a haircut and a shampoo set me back a total of seventy-five cents. I would advise gentlemen, unless they don't mind smelling like the inside of a Shanghai house of pleasure, to avoid so-called hair tonics in the barber shops. They are all alcohol and eau de cologne.

In spite of the fact that gasoline runs about a dollar a gallon there are hordes of Americans driving their own cars. The sight of a 1950 convertible Studebaker with an Indiana license plate parked in front of Caesar's Forum is not an incomprehensible sight. You'll find modernistic new Esso stations and Shell pumps all over the country.

There are some flashy Fiats on the avenue, but most Italians drive either Vespas, *topolinos,* or bicycles. A Vespa, which means wasp, is the name given to the rakish little motorized scooter bikes which have made a tremendous hit because they are cheap, fast and racy looking. A *topolino,* which is a little mouse, is the name for Fiat's tiny two-passenger automobile. Italians drive their vehicles according to the Latin, or horn-of-plenty system. Car drivers blow their horns almost incessantly because the streets are narrow, the bicycle traffic is undisciplined, there are few traffic lights, and also because they like to blow their horns. If you are a pedestrian and you encounter an oncoming Vespa, *topolino,* bicycle, or unclassified velocipede, the man on wheels has the right of way. If you would like to contest that fact you will shortly be contemplating the blue Italian sky from a recumbent position in the Italian gutter. Car drivers, regardless of nationality, driving proficiency, or previous condition of servitude, will find themselves obliged to pay for parking in certain large cities. An attendant who wears a cap emblazoned with the insignia of some auto club will come around to extract the fee from you. I was never quite able to determine why certain clubs have shake-down franchises on certain corners. Theoretically if you belong to the club in question, for you the right to park in the city streets is free.

But with the exception, possibly, of the gondoliers in Venice who seem to suffer from the same dyspepsia that afflicts the cab drivers of Paris, even the most hair-raising financial extraction is done with *politesse* and charm. The curbstone bankers who deal in dollars and hang around in front of American Express offices approach you with a discreet, "Change your money, sir?" The sidewalk jewelry salesmen who corner you with an armful of trays are more poetic. They say, "Hello, cameo?" Four years after the war and two years after the occupation, it is surprising to hear the prostitutes sitting at the cafes open the bidding with the familiar, "Hey, Joe, gotta cigarette?" Ask at the hotel desk for the nearest phone booth, and an attendant ushers you there,

ALBERGO QUIRINALE - ROMA

Sig. MR. AND MRS. John Smith

App. 229   A. 2   B. ____   D. ____

Mese Sept. 1949	7th	8th	9th	10th
OMNIBUS E BAGAGLIO				
APPARTAMENTO	4000	4000	4000	
PENSIONE				
BAGNI				
RISCALDAMENTO				
PRIMA COLAZIONE		600	600	600
COLAZIONE	1200	2400	2400	
PRANZO	2600	2600	2600	
EXTRA				
UOVA		300	600	600
SUGHI DI LIMONE E ARANCIO		300	300	300
TE, CAFFE, LATTE, ecc.				
FRUTTA				
BISCOTTI				
VINO	700	700	700	
LIQUORI				
BIRRA		360	180	
ACQUA MINERALE	170	170	170	
SPUMANTE				
BAR				
BIANCHERIA		1200		
STIRERIA				
TELEFONO		50	40	
TOTALE DEL GIORNO	8670	12680	11690	1500
RIPORTO		8670	21350	33040

AMMONTARE DELLA NOTA L. ____ 34540

SERVIZIO 18 % ____ 6220

IMPOSTA ENTRATA 3 % ____ 1040

BOLLO ____ 40

TOTALE L. ____ 41840

Italian hotel bill

don't be distressed

dials the number himself, and when your number is ready he wipes the receiver and hands it to you. Ask the doorman at Rome's open-air opera for a taxi and he is off over the hills like Paavo Nurmi with a hotfoot. Italy is anxious to please. One hotel manager who had greeted me with a bow and handshake implored me to ask him for any favor. "If there is anything I can do for you, sir," he said, bending in half, "please dispose of me."

❦ How to Get There

If you have the cash, the time, and the inclination to go abroad, all you need now is Uncle Sam's permission. If you are a native-born or naturalized American citizen present yourself before a clerk of a Federal court, or a state court which has been authorized to naturalize aliens, or before an agent of the Department of State. In New York, passport agents of the State Department can be found in the Subtreasury Building on Wall Street, or on the mezzanine of 630 Fifth Avenue in Rockefeller Center. In San Francisco, Chicago, and Boston, offices are located in the Federal Post Office building; anybody in Washington may file directly with the Passport Division, State Department.

You must come equipped with:

1. Two photographs, full face, against a light background, printed on thin paper, size no larger than three by three inches, nor smaller than 2½ x 2½.

2. For native-born citizens, a birth certificate or old passport. For naturalized citizens, naturalization papers, or previous American passport.

3. An informal note telling when, where, and how you are traveling.

4. If traveling on business, a letter from your employer addressed to the Secretary of State, describing the purpose of your trip, the destination and the anticipated duration of your stay.

5. One witness who has known you for two years who is himself a United States citizen, and who will appear with you in person to file your application.

6. $10.

File early, for the lines get longer as the days get warmer.

Visas aren't required in Italy any more, unless you plan to stay for longer than six months, in which case they are issued free by an Italian consulate upon presentation of your passport, and two extra passport photos. The abolition of visas for tourists is a sign of progress only obviated by the fact that hotels are required to register you with the police when you apply for lodging.

You must surrender your passport when you are assigned a room. Should you live with friends in Italy you must register at the police station in each city you visit within three days after your arrival there. Should you stay less than three days it is not necessary to register. Tourists without a visa who decide to stay in Italy longer than ninety days must apply for a ninety-day extension which is automatically granted.

You are allowed to bring into Italy 400 cigarettes, or two cartons. There is some pressure now to increase the allowance by another five packs. One portable radio per person may be brought to Italy duty free, but a license must be obtained at a post office if you want to be legal about using it. Radio is a government monopoly and the treasury collects a listening fee from all owners of sets.

If you are bringing in your own car, better check the International Travel Department of the American Automobile Association, 25 Broad Street, New York City.

The lire isn't what it used to be, but it did rally strongly after the devaluation of the pound. Hotels in Italy will very often give you the official rate of exchange which might be considerably lower than the free rate which is available in the back rooms (and often in the front rooms too). Since the free rate fluctuates, it's a good idea to exchange your currency as you need it. You can enter Italy with 10,000 lire, no questions asked. You can obtain a favorable rate before leaving New York from Foreign Currency Exchange, 1472 Broadway, or Perera, 10 Broadway, or 636 Fifth Avenue, all in Manhattan. Once abroad you will get the best rate if you exchange hard cash. American Express will cash its own traveler's checks for lire at the prevailing legal rate. However, it deducts a fee for cashing its own checks for dollars in any of its foreign offices. Letters of credit are often a headache.

An Italian rule permits you to export $500 worth of goods

purchased in Italy provided they are souvenirs, and essentially products of the Italian handicraft industries. A clause specifically precludes the purchase of works of art or antiques which may not be exported from art-happy Italy without the specific permission of the government's Fine Arts Commission.

The $500 rule matches the U. S. regulation which permits American tourists to bring home $500 worth of merchandise.

Arriving in the United States, you'll clear customs quicker if you itemize every last souvenir you bought on the customs declaration. You can, of course, back the declared value of merchandise with bills of sale, but an ornery inspector might render his own appraisal if your estimate looks a little light. If your camera is of foreign make register it with American customs before leaving the country, and surrender the affidavit to customs when you arrive home. And unless you want to be greeted back to the U.S.A. with a shot in the arm, bring a signed statement from your physician which says that you were vaccinated within the last three years.

❧ Air Road to Rome

About the easiest way to get to Europe, short of joining the army, is to eat and sleep your way across in half a day. Nobody accomplishes the transition from Manhattan to Montmartre in more sumptuous style than Air France. Its sky road to Rome lies via New York, Boston, Gander and Paris. Sometimes when the winds are right the Constellations fly direct from Boston to Paris in twelve hours. In the height of the summer season there are three direct connections out of Paris for Rome. In off-season there is at least one through flight a week from Idlewild Field, New York, to Ciampino Field, Rome.

As I say, eating and sleeping are the chief forms of distraction en route. If you're hungry when you land you've got the appetite of Humphrey Pennyworth. Air France serves its meals course by course, a fastidious air-borne custom which probably has come to your attention ere now. An inventory of the typical first tray, brought by the steward, not the hostess, might include the following: *Terrine de Foies de Volaille Bressane,* which is to say, *paté;* white bread, a split of champagne (not California); a jigger of Cognac Hine V.S.O.P.; *Medaillon de Langouste Venitienne,* or lobster salad; a pear cushioned in lettuce leaves; pastry wrapped in cellophane; and cheese. At the risk of jeopardizing Clementine Paddleford's job, let me explain that the steward then serves each passenger *Poulet en Fricassèe à l'Ancienne* (which you may recognize as chicken fricassee), not to mention *riz pilaw* and *haricots verts.*

This total combination is destined to put you to sleep quicker than a travelogue. Since you are flying into the dawn — gaining hours are as you head east — you will probably awake with the first streaks of light out of the Irish Coast. The commissary finds that an occasion to serve *croissants* and coffee.

The men's room has adequate shaving room, washbasins, a collapsible chair, chemical toilet, and free Lentheric eau de cologne. The ladies room, a female agent informs me, is suitably pink, has dressing tables and mirrors, chemical toilet, chaise longue, and a jumbo bottle of chic French perfume.

Passengers for Rome need not go through customs in Paris if they remain at the airport while changing planes. Paris to Rome direct takes four hours. There are other Air France flights for Rome via Lourdes in Southern France, and Milan.

Among the other airlines connecting the United States with Italy are TWA, the only American flag line flying direct to Rome; Pan American which offers connections with Panair to Brazil either at London or Madrid; Sabena, the Belgian line which flies via Brussels and continues beyond Rome to Naples; and **KLM** the Royal Dutch Airlines, flying via Amsterdam.

The international fleet has lately been joined by **LAI**, Linee Aeree Italiana, an Italian line forty percent owned by **TWA**. It flies New York-Milan-Rome-Naples-Palermo. Its continental Italian service includes connections between Rome, Palermo, Venice, Milan, and Naples. The domestic service employs DC-3's.

Alitalia, an independent Italian line flies Rome to Catania (for Taormina); Rome-Nice-Geneva; Rome-London; and Rome-Nice-Paris. It uses DC-3's, British Lancastrians, and Douglas Dakotas.

❧ *Italy by Sea*

Italian Line. The old *Rex* which once held the blue ribbon of the Atlantic was sunk in the shallow waters southwest of Trieste. Much of its hulk has since been salvaged by Yugoslavia. The *Conte di Savoia*, somewhat smaller than the *Rex,* once cam-outflaged as a Venetian island during the late war, was sunk in the lagoon between Venice and the Lido. The old *Roma*, which Mussolini started to transform into an aircraft carrier, was sunk long before it launched a plane in the harbor of Genoa.

That unhappy casualty list leaves the Italian line with the *Saturnia* and the *Vulcania,* prewar sister ships, and the *Conte Biancamano* which are now maintaining a schedule between New York, Gibraltar, Palermo (10 days), Naples (11 days) and Genoa (12 days). Occasional stops are made at Cannes. Both are motor vessels, and carry first, cabin and tourist class. American Export Lines are general agents for the Italian Line in the United States.

Home Line. A new company backed by Greek and Swedish capital, flying the Panamanian flag, staffed by Italian crews, serving Italian cuisine. Their ships are the *Atlantic*, nee the *Matsonia* which plied between San Francisco and Honolulu; and the *Italia*, formerly the *Kungsholm*, a stout ex-Swedish American liner which functioned as a U. S. Army transport. The *Atlantic* sails for Barcelona, Cannes, Genoa and Naples which it reaches ten days out of New York. The *Italia* touches at Lisbon, Palermo, Naples and Genoa where it arrives in twelve days from New York.

American Export Lines. An American flag carrier, it specializes in Mediterranean service. The *Four Aces — Excalibur, Exochorda, Exeter* and *Excambion —* are small, one-class ships of 9,644 tons, sailing between New York, Marseilles, Naples, Alexandria and Bayreuth; and returning via Leghorn, Genoa, Boston and New York. The *LaGuardia*, a former Army transport of 18,000 tons, carries first and tourist class. It sails to Gibraltar, Palermo, Naples, Piraeus (Greece), Haifa, and return.

Gdynia-American Line. A Polish line, which like Poland, comes under the Soviet sphere. There is some Italian staff on the ship because it sails to Italian ports, but passengers who have taken the line's *M.S. Sobieski* insist the crew includes a political commissar. There is first and cabin class aboard the *Sobieski* which puts in at Gibraltar, Cannes, Genoa and Naples.

❦ *Inside Italy*

Unless you have your own car, the best way to see Italy is aboard the CIAT bus system. CIAT's huge new buses, built since the war, were expressly designed for tourist travel. They have a sliding roof, a radio, a bar serving Coca Cola, mineral waters and vermouths. Press a button and a desk unfolds in your lap from the seat in front of you. Two drivers, dressed in tan coveralls and blue kerchiefs, take turns at the wheel. A hostess who speaks English, French, Italian, and often German, points out the sights in a variety of languages, brings you maps and drinks, and sees that you get in the right restaurants when the bus stops for lunch.

Departing from a city in the morning, CIAT picks up each passenger at his hotel. Arriving at a destination each passenger is deposited at his hotel. Baggage is carried in a trailer. Sixty-six pounds goes for free. Each bus carries thirty passengers, and seats must be reserved in advance. Your hotel concierge will relieve you of that chore.

The short distances between cities in Italy tend to make each day's routing more of an excursion. North from Rome, CIAT buses connect with Florence either via Siena or Assisi and Perugia. From Florence they travel northwest via Pisa, the eastern Riviera and Genoa, then north to the Lake Country, and east to Venice. Another route from Florence touches Bologna — with an optional side-visit to Ravenna, Rimini and San Marino — and on to Venice. South from Rome, buses roll to Naples via Cassino or the seacoast route, and there are excursions to Pompeii, Amalfi and Sorrento. All services travel in both directions. During the winter season there are complete circuit tours of Sicily. For an idea of the rates aboard CIAT, the trip from Rome to Florence, a distance of 230 miles, costs $5.60 figured at the official rate of exchange.

Similar bus service is operated by Linjebuss, a Swedish company, which sends its modern buses all through Europe from its origin point in Scandinavia. In Italy the Linjebuss routes cover the Riviera, the Lake Country, Venice, Florence, Pisa, and south to Rome. Fares include meals and hotel accommodations.

At the war's end the government-owned Italian State Railways looked themselves over, and figured their entire system was ten percent operational. What stock hadn't been bombed by the Allies had been stolen by the Germans. Tracks were torn up the length and breadth of Italy, stations were bombed-out wrecks, railroad bridges were out. By the time the Holy Year of 1950 began the railway system, if not sparkling and modern, was at least ninety-eight percent operational. Americans can look for no vista domes, pneumatic doors, nor trains that show movies. The cars are old, and they are often crowded. In the diners, according to the Continental system, there is a standard menu which is served to everyone. It always includes *pasta*. Wines, mineral waters, coffee, liqueur and extra desserts are optional.

Paris to Rome takes about twenty-four hours, and should you come by way of Switzerland, you will know when you are in Italy when the orderly, manicured countryside suddenly, in the course of a kilometer, becomes sloppy, homey, and lived-in. The *Simplon Express* heads for Rome by way of Stresa, Milan, Bologna and Florence. The *Orient Express*, originating in London, and bound for Istanbul, stops in Milan, Mestre (for Venice) and Trieste. The *Calais-Mediterranean Express,* known in some circles as the *Blue Train*, runs through Marseilles, then skims the Riviera, stops at Genoa, and finally, Rome. The *Rome Express* comes by way of Chambery, Modane, Turin, Genoa, and Rome.

In spite of the extreme shortages of all railroad equipment you still have your choice of four types of trains.

RAPIDO

the fastest route; makes no intermediate stops; carries first class, and occasionally first and second class; small supplemental charge.

DIRETTISSIMO

fast, but not as fast as the *rapido;* makes some intermediate stops; small supplemental charge.

DIRETTO

still an express train, but making more stops than either the *rapido* or the *direttissimo.*

ACCELERATO

despite its name, it is a downright local, making all the whistle stops.

American travelers will be startled at the inexpensive railroad in Italy. Rates for a hundred-mile trip would come to this:

			extra tariff for rapido
First class	—	$2.95	.80
Second class	—	$1.95	.25
Third class	—	$1.15	x

From New York to Philadelphia, a distance of ninety miles, the Pennsylvania Railroad charges $3.52 in coaches, $5.55 in parlor cars, seat and tax included.

❧ *How to Find an Italian Restaurant*

Since things, especially in foreign lands, are not always what they appear to be, the following capsule directory will tell you which is a bar and grill and which is an automat.

biereria	— beer and wines only
osteria	— a saloon, probably the town tavern

trattoria	— a middling restaurant which also serves drinks
trattoria con alloggi	— an inn with rooms
ristorante	— better class restaurant
albergo	— hotel

❦ *How to Eat in Italian*

You may be thoroughly conversant with the American version of such Italian finery as antipasto, pizzas, spaghetti and ravioli. Elementary, my dear Watsono! In Italy things really get complicated. To avoid having the waiter show up with an order of calf's brains when what you really wanted was a bowl of jello, herewith are 193 possible items which you are likely to find on Italian menus and their equivalent in English. Suggested regional fare is noted and analyzed in each chapter.

abbacchio	young lamb
acciughe	anchovies
aceto	vinegar
acetosella	soup greens
acqua	water
agnello	lamb
albiococche	apricots
allodola	lark
alosa	shad
alzavola	widgeon (wild duck)
ananasso	pineapple
anatrotto	duckling
anguilla	eel
anguria	watermelon

animella	sweetbreads
anitra selvatica	wild duck
antipasto	hors d'oeuvre
aragosta	crawfish
arancia	orange
arrosto	roast
arselle	clams
aringa	herring
asparagi	asparagus
astice	lobster
avena	oats
baccala	codfish
banana	banana
beccaccia	woodcock
beccaccino	snipe
bistecca	steak
bollito di bue	boiled beef
bue	beef
burro	butter
cappone	capon
capretto	kid
capriolo	venison
carciofi	artichokes
carpione	carp
carote	carrots
castagne	chestnuts
cavolfiore	cauliflower
cavoli nani	Brussels sprouts
cavolo	cabbage
cavolo rosso	red cabbage
cetrioli	cucumbers
cicoria	chicory

ciliege	cherries
cipolla	onions
composta di frutta	stewed fruits
cosciotto d'agnello	leg of lamb
cosciotto di montone	leg of mutton
cosciotto di vitello	leg of veal
costolette d'agnello	lamb chops
costolette di maiale	pork chops
costolette di montone	mutton chops
costolette di vitello	veal chops
crauti	sauerkraut
crescione	watercress
crespelli	pancakes
crostatine di frutta	tartlets
datteri	dates
dattero di mare	mussels
endivia	endives
estragone	tarragon (seasoning)
fagiano	pheasant
fagiolini	string beans
farina	flour
fagioletti	kidney beans
fave	beans
fegato	liver
fettuccine	thin noodles (eggs & flour)
fichi	figs
filetto	steak (filet)
filetto di bue	filet of beef
finocchio	fennel
fragole	strawberries
frattaglie	giblet
frittelle	fritters

frumento	wheat
frutti di mare	shellfish
funghi	mushrooms
gallo di montagna	grouse
gamberetti	shrimps
gamberi di fiume	crawfish (river)
gallina faraona	guinea hen
gelato	ice cream
ghiaccio	ice
granturco	corn
graticola (alla)	broiled
insalata	salad
intingolo d'agnello	lamb saute
intingolo di bue	beef saute
intingolo di montone	mutton saute
intingolo di vitello	veal saute
lardo	lard
lasagne verdi	large green noodles
lattuga	lettuce
lavareto	lavaret
lenticchie	lentils
lepre	hare
limone	lemon
lonza	sirloin
luccio	pike
mandarino	tangerine
mandorle	almonds
marrone	chestnuts (big)
mela	apple
melanzane	eggplant
melone	melon
merlano	whiting

merlo	blackbird
merluzzo	scrod
mirtillo	blueberries
nasello	smelt
nespole	medlars (European)
nocciole	hazlenuts
noci	walnuts
oca	goose
olio	oil
olive	olives
origano	origan
passerino	flounder
pancetta	bacon
patate	potatoes
pavoncella	plover (bird)
pepe	pepper
peperoncini	small peppers
peperoni	peppers
pere	pears
pernice	young partridge
pesce persico	perch
pesche	peaches
piccioncino	squab
piselli	green peas
pizza napolitana	pie
polenta	maize meal pudding
pollo	chicken
pomodoro	tomato
pompelmo	grapefruit
prezzemolo	parsley
prosciutto cotto	ham
prosciutto crudo	raw ham

prugne	plums
pulcino	spring chicken
quaglia	quail
radica forte	horseradish
rape	turnips
ravanelli	radishes
razza	skate
ribes	currant
riccio di mare	sea urchins
riso	rice
rognone	kidney
rombo	brill (fish)
rosolato	browned
salame	salami
salmone	salmon
salsa	gravy
sardinas	sardines
scaloppine	veal cutlets
scampi	Dalmatian shrimps
sedano	celery
sella d'agnello	rack of lamb
sella di maiale	rack of pork
sella di montone	rack of mutton
sella di vitello	rack of veal
semolino	semolina
sgombro	mackerel
sogliola	sole
sorbetto	sherbert
spadini	skewered
spalla d'agnello	shoulder of lamb
spalla di montone	shoulder of mutton
spalla di vitello	shoulder of veal

spinaci	spinach
stoccafisso	haddock
storione	sturgeon
susina claudia	green gages (plums)
tagliatelle	noodles
tagliatelle verdi	green noodles
tartufo	type of mushroom
testina di vitello	calf's head
timballo	timbale (pie)
tonno	tuna
tordi	field fares (game)
triglia	red mullet
trota	trout
uva	grapes
uovo	egg
vino	wine
zucca	pumpkin
zucchero	sugar
zucchini	small squash

❦ *Italian Geography Made Easy*

ITALIAN	ENGLISH
Dobbiaco	Doblack
Firenze	Florence
Genova	Genoa
Livorno	Leghorn
Milano	Milan
Napoli	Naples
Padova	Padua
Roma	Rome

Siracusa	Syracuse
Tevere	Tiber
Torino	Turin

. . . and as the Italians see the rest of the world:

Anversa	Antwerp
Cina	China
Danimarca	Denmark
Olandese	Dutch
Egitto	Egypt
Inghilterra	England
Francia	France
Francese	French
Germania	Germany
Tedesco	German
Gibilterra	Gibraltar
L'Aja	The Hague
Olanda	Holland
Ungheria	Hungary
Paesi Bassi	Netherlands
Parigi	Paris
Scozia	Scotland
Svizzera	Switzerland
Tamigi	Thames
Stati Uniti	United States
Galles	Wales

❧ *Facts and Figures in Italy and America*

	AMERICAN	ITALIAN		AMERICAN	ITALIAN
Men's	14	36	Dress	12	38
collar	14½	37	sizes	14	40
sizes	15	38		16-34	42
	15½	39		18-36	44
	16	40		38	46
	16½	41		40	52
	17	42			

Temperature

	AMERICAN	ITALIAN	FAHRENHEIT	CENTIGRADE
Women's	4	37	101	38.3
shoe	5	38	100	37.8
sizes	6	39	99	37.2
	7	40	70	21.1
	8	41	60	15.6
	9	42	32	0
			0	—17.8

ROME

Caesar's legions and soldiers from Deer Lodge

2. ROME

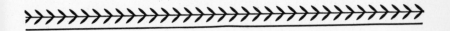

The timeless city to which all roads lead has emerged from the late great war with hardly a scratch. There are scars on many a Roman, but few indeed on Rome. After all, with wars and the men who make them Rome has had considerable experience. The city can trace its forebears back for twenty-seven centuries and in all that time men and motives have changed very little.

You couldn't call Rome a gay city. It's too steeped in its own history, too phlegmatic in its easy habits, too somnolent in its summer sun for that. If you compare Rome with Paris — and that is an inevitable comparison — probably you will find Paris fragile, delicate, beautiful as a ballerina is beautiful; while Rome is ponderous, a bit heavy-footed, solemn with great age, dignified with great history. Here marched Caesar's legions and the Duce's blackshirts, and Mark Clark's soldiers from Kearny, New Jersey, and Deer Lodge, Montana. Rome flushes thoughts from your childhood: It is the place that burned while Nero fiddled, where Mark Anthony rose to speak at Caesar's burial, where Charlemagne was crowned. And the charm, the excitement of Rome is that you can walk where Nero fiddled, where Anthony spoke, and where Charlemagne kneeled to become emperor of the Romans. The ruins and the remnants of twenty-seven hundred years of civilization are all in the out-of-doors, as handy to the casual city stroller as a municipal park.

Rome's beginnings are traced by legend, to Romulus and Remus, a pair of twins born to Rhea Silvia and Mars. As infants they were abandoned on the banks of the Tiber and suckled by a she-wolf, a motherly act that has been reproduced in bronze all over the world. Romulus, who eventually visited fratricide on brother Remus founded Rome on what is generally credited to be the 24th of April 753 B.C., a date which is still something of a Roman holiday. The first citizens were largely shepherds, and since women were perforce only a sometime thing in the new Rome, Romulus organized a raid on the people of the Sabine hills. He brought back a number of Sabine women, an episode thereafter known in art and history as the "Rape of the Sabine Women," and Rome was off to a rousing conjugal start.

The early settlements were built on the Palatine Hill, one of the seven hills of Rome over which the village gradually expanded. The others, if you are keeping score, are named Capitoline, Quirinal, Coelian, Aventine, Viminal and Esquiline. The first of a two-hundred year succession of kings, Romulus was murdered by his senators in 735, an inauspicious beginning for the city. In 509 B.C., Tarquin the Proud was dethroned and dispatched from the city for having been an immoral tyrant. The regime of royalty ended and Rome became a republic.

After a quiet fifty years as a republic, Rome began to flex her muscles, spreading her influence over most of central Italy. But in 390 B.C. the Gauls invaded the republic, sacked Rome, and exacted a heavy ransom. The city was rebuilt and under

Appius Claudius, an early liberal, the first aqueduct was erected, and the road from Rome to Capua, known as the Appian Way was constructed. The American and allied armies rolled down the Appian Way to Rome in 1943. In the hundred years that followed, Rome again began to spread her sphere of influence over her neighboring Mediterranean countries, a process which finally enraged King Pyrrhus in Greece. His victory over the Romans at Asculum in 279 B.C. was so costly that in effect it was a stunning defeat — but from the battle we got the term *pyrrhic victory*.

Only a few years after the fight with Pyrrhus, Rome went to the mat with Carthage in the First Punic War for the domination of the Mediterranean empire. She joined forces with the King of Syracuse, conquered Agrigento, pushed the Carthaginians out of Sicily, and carried the war to Africa. In the Second Punic War, which broke out in 218 B.C., Hannibal organized a fighting force in Africa and brought it all the way to Italy by way of Spain. He was defeated and Rome ruled the Mediterranean. Having won handily in the west, she turned her hostile efforts to the east, and entered into a series of three wars with Macedonia. Within fifty years Rome's rule extended from Syria to Spain including Carthage and the northern coast of Africa. It was 146 B.C., but the empire was just beginning.

If you artfully avoided a complicated course in Roman history in school there is no good reason why you should be stuck with one here, but so many of the ruins which can still be seen in Rome begin with this period, a bare outline will make any rubberneck tour more than just a dutiful excursion.

As Rome's empire and influence expanded abroad, her troubles began to increase at home. For one thing the Patricians, the senatorial ruling families, and the citizens who had been elevated to the royalty conspired to eliminate all other classes

ST. PETER'S AND THE TIBER
a lengthwise split

from governmental positions. With Pompey, a Roman general,
and Crassus, a millionaire, Julius Caesar in 60 B.C. formed the
first of the Roman triumvirates, or coalition of three joint rulers.
Crassus was killed in Syria, and Caesar eventually upended Pompey by crossing the Rubicon and marching on Rome. Pompey
continued the tilt for power from a headquarters in Greece, but
in 45 that collapsed and Caesar was declared dictator for life. On
March 15, 44 B.C., he was assassinated. A patrician, a great general, a politician of ability, a champion of public progress, Caesar
emerges from history as something of a public hero. His tomb
and the ruins of his forum can still be seen.

Seventeen years later, in 27 B.C., Octavius, under the name

of Augustus Caesar, became the first emperor, the lord of all of Rome's vast holdings. During his reign Rome was at peace with all the world, and Augustus could concentrate on enriching the city. The Pantheon, the Porch of Agrippa, and the Theater of Marcellus were all built while he ruled.

The Roman Empire lasted until 476 A.D., and as you visit Rome today these are some of the emperors whose names you will hear and, in some cases, whose monuments still exist: 54 A.D., Nero who poisoned his stepbrother, had his mother murdered, caused Rome to be burned (blaming the Christians), killed his wife, his stepsister who refused to marry him, and the husband of his future wife and finally committed suicide; Vespasian, 69-79, who tried to restore the voice of the people; and Trajan who ruled from 97-117. Under his reign the empire reached its broadest borders, encompassing Arabia, Armenia, Asia Minor, what is now Britain, Corsica, Crete, Cyprus, Cyrenaica, Dalmatia, Egypt, what is now France, Greece, Macedonia, Sardinia, Sicily, Spain, Syria, Thrace, Tunis, the western part of Germany and the Italian mainland. Hadrian ruled from 117 to 138 and there are still magnificent ruins of his villa; Caracalla, a ruthless emperor who ruled from 211 to 217 and whose baths are now the site of Rome's open-air opera; Diocletian, 284-305; and finally Constantine the Great (306-337) who became a Christian because he saw the apparition of a cross in the sky, and who later moved the capital of the empire to Constantinople, a city he built on the ruins of ancient Byzantium. Although Constantine had afforded Christianity the right to worship freely with other religions, Julian the Apostate, who took over in 361, renounced Christianity and again opened the heathen temples. Other emperors came along, but during the century which followed Rome began to crumble from within from overtaxation and internal strife. Meanwhile, invaders began to eat away at the borders, the Visigoths in southern France, the

Vandals, Sueves, and Alans in Spain, the Vandals in Africa, and the Huns in France and Italy. Rome was sacked in 410 and again in 455. Romulus Augustus was the last emperor, and in 476 A.D. the Roman Empire which had risen from a shepherd's settlement and flourished for 1,200 years collapsed from within.

Today Rome is a great city of two million, split lengthwise by the ancient Tiber which flows into the Mediterranean fourteen miles away. A fourth of the city lies on the left bank, three quarters on the right. Rome is the national capital of Italy and the world capital of Catholicism. Except for December and January when the temperature occasionally slips below fifty, the city is sunny and mild, and in summer downright hot. In its dignity, and its penchant for pomp, Rome is often colorful. The streets are crowded with priests in black gowns, with monks in black and brown, with missionaries in from tropical outposts still wearing white robes and open sandals, with German student priests in smocks of flaming red who are known as *gamberi cotti* — boiled shrimps. There must be more cops foot-for-foot in Rome than you would be likely to find at a policeman's ball. All of them work in pairs even when directing traffic or when they are mounted on motorcycle or horseback. The traffic police dress in immaculate white uniforms, wear white pith helmets, white shoes and gloves. To the foreign observer their signals will look not unakin to setting-up exercises. I can perhaps best decipher their intentions for you — should you be enough of a daredevil to be driving your own car in Rome — by explaining that when they face you or have their backs turned to you and their arms are extended shoulder high you are supposed to stop. If they are turned sideways to you, and their arms are extended in a direction parallel to the street on which you are driving *that* is a signal to go. Should this explanation for some obscure reason be unclear to you, release the clutch and step lightly on the gas. If the policeman

THE AMERICAN EMBASSY
the card is usually hidden

blows his whistle and turns purple where his neck meets his tunic, put on the brake. I am not guaranteeing it, but more than likely if you don't understand Italian and your car has a foreign license probably he will smile, waggle his finger, go *tst! tst!* and let you drive on. So much for traffic cops. The streets are patrolled by other police who wear white peaked hats, white coats and black breeches with a purple stripe. They carry swords and march in pairs. The streets are further patrolled by the *carabinieri* who wear black Napoleonic hats, black tunics with white Sam Browne belts and red-trimmed epaulets, black trousers with white stripes. They carry swords and walk in pairs. They also get sore as hell, frequently, when tourists try to take their pictures.

If you enter the city by any means other than your own car, one of the first Romans with whom you will have contact will be the cab driver. In Paris the cabs are red and black, here they are green and black which seems to be the standard taxi color all over Italy. If you decide that your financial transactions with Rome's cab drivers must be exact to the penny you will need a perfect command of Italian, including local dialects and slang, and a dexterity of mathematical wit worthy of a Quiz Kid. Should your fare come to, say, 380 lire on the meter, and should you hand the driver a 500-lire note, you are liable to get back a flat 100 lire in change. Sometimes the driver will be extracting his own tip, but other times he hasn't the change. The lira being what it is these days, he doesn't feel it is worthwhile to run into the nearest shop and change a bill just to give you twenty lire or three cents. Sometimes, but not nearly as often, under similar circumstances he will knock ten or twenty lire off what the clock reads. In better hotels the doorman will always have change, and probably he will speak English. One of his understood duties is to act as liaison between cab driver and tourist, and to see that the tourist does not get fleeced. There are a number of complicated *supplementos* that depend on baggage, extra passengers, the time of day, and generally the condition of the driver's digestive system and the current status of his home life. The rules are posted in a number of languages inside all taxi cabs, but in case you should want to bone-up in advance here are the regulations as they are presented in English:

TILL TWO PERSONS

For the first 280 meters or for two minutes of engagement. . L.90
For the succeeding 280 meters or two minutes of engagement . L.20
From 10 pm to 6 am it is due an overprice of. L.150

VILLA BORGHESE
lovers and strollers

SUPPLEMENTAL RATE

For each person above two...........................L.10
For luggage of dimension below 50x70x30 centimeters
(with exception of umbrellas or clothes, pegsand, hand
packages) L.10

There is a rather large fleet of carriages in Rome which are
metered too. Although the drivers are supposed to display a list
of rates, the card is usually hidden under a blanket or carried
face down on the floor. The method of determining the fare of a
carriage ride is a formula known only to the carriage man and

his horse. You can expect the tariff to run about twenty-five percent more than a taxi.

Rome's big municipal park is the Villa Borghese, or officially, the Villa Umberto I. Its tall, gangling umbrella pines, bare except for a puff of evergreen on top, form a cover over the heads of the lovers who picnic on the park's sandy soil and the strollers who meander along the winding lanes. Those who come first to Rome probably will see their first umbrella pines in the Villa Borghese, but they are a trademark of Italy as are the rows of delicate poplars of France.

Inside the park is the Borghese Gallery, which houses the best collection of art in Rome aside from the Vatican galleries. The Borghese Gallery's first collection of some 255 pieces was sold to Napoleon by his brother-in-law, Prince Camillus Borghese in the face of stiff Vatican protest. The present collection was gathered together from works of art in various villas of the Borgheses and augmented by discoveries of new excavations. It includes a number of statues by Bernini, and on the first floor, over 600 paintings including the "Descent from the Cross" and the "Fornarina," both by Raphael.

Most of the city's tourist life and its better hotels are centered in a ten-block radius drawn from the southern end of the park. The main artery of the visitor's quarter is the Via Vittorio Veneto, a broad avenue that curls out of the Porta Pinciana, the park's southeast entrance. Lined with hotels, decorated with trees, paved with rows of sidewalk tables, the Via Veneto has always held a fatal fascination for tourists. When the allied armies hit the city the hotels were requisitioned by the military, and soon the fascination of the Via Veneto got under the soldier's skin too. The grassy plots were rutted with the treads of tanks, half-tracks, jeeps, and six-by-sixes, parked side by side in endless rows. Since the soldiers hung out there, the girls who were interested in the soldiers began coming too. In Italy's dirty war the back-of-the lines life was the dirtiest. There got to be so much traffic in sex under the trees of the Via Veneto that a *Newsweek* correspondent sent back a piece calling it the Via Venerio.

On pleasant, placid Sunday afternoons, now, you would hardly imagine that the Via Veneto ever had a seamy side. From the edge of the park the cafe tables run down both sides of the street as far as the Excelsior Hotel. Sometimes the sidewalk squatters are so tightly packed that only a lane is left for the gauntlet-running pedestrian. The cafes are crowded every day during cocktail hour, but on a Sunday you might see anybody — three Hindus on their way to a spaghetti dinner, a mother sipping a vermouth and nursing her child, a Belgian lady with two Chihuahuas, or the David Selznicks. Of the cafes, the Doney, because it is next door to the fabulous Excelsior, gets most of the flossy international trade. Besides liquor, ice cream and coffee which it serves throughout the day, Doney's offers a magnificent collection of breakfast pastries, far better than you will find in the best hotels. The waiter serves you a glass-covered trayful. You eat as many as you want. He keeps score.

The headquarters for the visiting royalty, the visiting press, the visiting movie stars, and anyone else who has the price and can wangle a room is indisputably the Hotel Excelsior. Even before the war the Excelsior attracted the footloose Hollywood crowd. The hotel was headquarters for the company that filmed *Ben Hur* in Rome more years ago than most anyone cares to remember. The register has been signed by Douglas Fairbanks senior and junior, by Mary Pickford, Harold Lloyd, Marion Davies and Dolores del Rio.

A special bed was installed for the visit in 1937 of fat Hermann Goering who occupied rooms 206, 207 and 208. And part of that suite occupied by Goering in 1937 was occupied by Pete

DONEY'S
the waiter keeps score

Kriendler of New York's "21" Club in the summer of 1949, such being the fortunes of war and peace and the tides of time.

Count Ciano, Mussolini's son-in-law, who was executed by the Duce, used to live at the Excelsior when his apartment was closed. When Hitler formally visited Italy in 1938, Ciano threw an elaborate dinner-dance at the hotel. In the years of the Rome-Berlin axis that followed, Himmler checked in and got suite 16, 17 and 18. Later, Von Ribbentrop used the same quarters. Goebbels lived in 111, 112 and 113. In 1943 the Excelsior was requisitioned as a headquarters for high German officers. Keitel, VonBrauschning, and most of the bigwig brass stopped there. Marshal Kesselring stayed on for some months after the Cassino

THE EXCELSIOR
"Who are you?"

battle which started on March 15, 1943. By 10 P.M. on June 4, 1944 the last of his staff left the hotel for points north. For a few minutes Rome was quiet. The hotel staff peered out of the driveway in front of the building. A squad of infantry appeared on a corner. Armando Armanni, the manager then and now, called out, "Who are you?" Said the soldiers, "We are an American patrol." Said Armanni, "Well, come in and have a drink." At one or two o'clock in the morning a jeep pulled up in front of the Excelsior and a tall man with two aides got out. "I'm General Clark," the tall man said. "Can you put me up for the night?" They gave him Kesselring's suite.

As the liberation became the occupation, the Excelsior became part of the Fifth Army Rest Center. For the troops who came back from the front there was a cabaret show every night. Pinball machines were set up, and there was a shooting gallery where a soldier could spend a busman's holiday. Like many another requisitioned Roman hotel, the Excelsior was the scene of some wild escapism. Once a girl flung herself out of a window and crashed on the sidewalk. The hilarity quieted down some after that.

But even the GIs back from the front to blow off steam failed to turn the hotel as completely upside down as did the GI wives and the GI kids who lived there in the placid days of peace that followed. Finally, on October 31, 1947, after three and a half years in American hands, the Excelsior was turned back.

When the dust of war had settled Rome emerged into the postwar peace as a movie colony. Roberto Rossellini produced *Open City*, then *Paisan*. In the states, *Shoe-Shine* was a hit, too. American producers and American actresses and actors soon got the idea. Italy's classic monuments were a big out-door set. Since they were already there, they cost nothing to build. What was more, Italian labor by California standard was cheap. The cinema activity grew important enough to be termed a "renaissance." Said Jack Begon, NBC's Rome correspondent to listeners in America, "This is Hollywood-on-the-Tiber."

The register of the Excelsior reflects Rome's new role. After the war came David Selznick and Jennifer Jones, Anatole Litvak and Danny Kaye, Binnie Barnes and her husband, Mike Frankovitch, an ex-All-American turned movie producer. Ingrid Bergman put up there when she first came to Italy. Rossellini keeps an apartment in the place all year around. Tyrone Power stayed there until he rented the Countess di Frasso's villa. After his honeymoon with Linda Christians he walked in the lobby decked out like an Austrian Alpinist. Then, since the movie colony had all trouped to Rome, there came in their wake Louella Parsons and Hedda Hopper, known on the West Coast as writers.

The downstairs bar of the Excelsior, a simple, leathery-looking room with deep chairs and sofas, has become a late-evening haunt of the American press colony, the movie producers, the actors, and the aspiring young actresses who have come from the states to break into the Italian movies. Everybody drinks coffee. The press plays gin rummy. The actresses look pretty. And the movie men sit in the corners giving the industry a good working over in deep, earnest tones. The place is known among the habitués as "The Snake Pit."

If it's peace and quiet you seek, you can with equanimity make your reservations at the Grand Hotel which is also owned and operated by the CIGA chain which runs the Excelsior. Actually ownership is the only thing the two hotels have in common. The Grand is starchy and dignified, attracts diplomats, monsignori, grande dames and ladies who travel with their dogs. In its rich, if antique appointments it is somewhat reminiscent of the Plaza in New York. It has three hundred rooms, mostly with bath, and is located a few blocks from the Excelsior, near the Piazza Esedra, convenient to the railroad station. Its rates run about two dollars less than similar accommodations at the Excelsior, even though, like the Excelsior, the Grand is officially classified as a *di lusso*, or de luxe category hotel.

Although the Grand plays host to many a United States tourist nowadays, doubtless the first American to step over its portal after the Germans left in the summer of 1944 was an American war correspondent named Mike Stern. In Rome with a pair of other journalists a day before Rome officially fell, Stern and party burst throught the front door while some Germans were apparently still packing their belongings upstairs. John Lodigiani, the Grand's headwaiter, seeking to avoid an international incident and perhaps prevent any blood spilling in the lobby rushed out to intercept the Americans. When he put up his hands to stop them, Stern pointed an incriminating finger at him and thundered, "You're under arrest!" John crumpled to the floor in a dead faint.

He has since recovered, and works winters at the Grand and summers at the CIGA chain's Excelsior Lido in Venice. Stern, of whose exploits we shall hear more anon, grew to like Rome so much he now lives there with his family. A correspondent for Fawcett Publications, he also free lances for *Esquire* and *Collier's,* and since he now speaks Italian with some fluency, he also successfully publishes Italian magazines. He is a journalist of the rough-and-tumble school who still bears scars on his face inflicted by Jack "Legs" Diamond and company because Mike revealed the gangster's hideaway. Carrying his tradition to Italy, Stern was one of the first correspondents to wangle an interview with Giuliano, the Sicilian bandit, who was hiding away in the hills. When he came back to Rome with the story, other correspondents for American newspapers and wire services, heartened by Stern's succcess, headed for Sicily to get interviews of their own. Stern was writing for a monthly magazine which goes to press months before it appears, and he realized he was sure to get scooped on his own story. To protect his beat he sent Giuliano a letter advising him that the Italian government was sending police spies to his hideaway in the guise of American newspaper correspondents. If Giuliano was wise, Stern advised him, he would refuse to see any more "so-called" American journalists.

One of Rome's newest establishments is the Mediterraneo at Via Cavour 15, near the station. Rebuilt from an old 75-room hotel, it now has 220 rooms all with bath. Its public rooms are all air-conditioned, a singularly advanced note on the Continent, and an improvement of particular necessity in Rome.

Classified as a *di lusso* hotel, the Mediterraneo charges about

$4 for single rooms, about $6 for doubles, European plan. It has an à la carte restaurant called the "21" after the number of its side-street entrance. Carlo Muzi who ran the Italian Pavilion at the New York World's Fair is the "21's" manager.

Although it opened in 1944 under requisition to the American State Department, the Mediterraneo's first guests were Irving Berlin and the soldier cast of 200 of *This Is The Army*. The hotel wasn't finished, and there wasn't a stick of furniture in the rooms, but as the sympathetic management explained, "The poor maestro had no place to go."

A hotel considered by many to be the best in Rome is the smaller Hassler-Villa Medici, or just plain Hassler. Located at Piazza Trinita dei Monti No. 6, at the end of a quiet side street, it overlooks the famous Spanish Steps that lead down to the Piazza di Spagna. The rooms are attractively furnished, the decor is new, and the restaurant has an excellent reputation.

The Palazzo e Ambasciatori, known handily as the Ambassador, sits on the Via Veneto at No. 70 opposite the American Embassy. It is especially famous for its ground-floor bar, and for its open-air terrace that hangs over the avenue. At the bottom of the Via Veneto, as it slopes down to the Piazza Barberini is the Bernini-Bristol, commonly called the Bernini. Chiefly a commercial hotel it trades in Italians and foreign businessmen rather than a strict tourist clientele.

Of Rome's first-class establishments (by the official interpretation "first-class" comes after "de luxe") the best is undoubtedly the Quirinale near the Piazza Esedra at Via Nazionale No. 7. The biggest attraction at the Quirinale is its open-air restaurant and night club. Its terraced tables illuminated by scattered lampposts, form an informal amphitheater. In the center is a marble dance floor shaded from the moon by a giant cedar tree which grows in the middle. The band does nicely with an English version of "Bali H'ai," but its *pièce de* linguistic *résistance* is its rendition of the now virtually extinct "The Trolley Song," ("Clan, Clan, Clan wen da trollee!")

Among other recommendable first-class-category hotels are the Eden, Via Ludovisi No. 49, a short walk from Via Veneto, and the Flora which is on Via Veneto, right next to the Villa Borghese.

In any hotel in Italy the all-purpose, triple-threat, answer man is the concierge who operates on his feet behind a counter in the lobby. One of the most famous concierges on the Continent is the Excelsior's Albert Pinto who is suave, goateed, and excruciatingly polite in half a dozen languages. The questions which may be thrown at Signor Pinto in the course of a day might be these: How much do taxis cost? How do I see the Pope? What is the condition of the road to Naples? What are the best hotels in Capri? What's the best restaurant in town? What's the current exchange between lire and pengos?

It is Pinto's duty to catch all these questions in the language in which they have been pitched, and to return the answer spontaneously, correctly, politely in the same language it was asked. It is also Pinto's prime duty to obtain railroad tickets, wangle opera tickets, locate a doctor in a hurry, and show *m'sieu* the shortest route to the American Express Company.

To keep things humming in the hot corner at the Excelsior, Pinto has a staff of fifty-four assistants including three men who help guests get telephone numbers at the lobby phones, and two who are permanently assigned to duty in the railroad station. In order to be able to obtain unobtainable tickets at a moment's notice he must maintain a more or less continuous, well-timed flow of presents to railroad agents, ticket brokers, and the box office men at the opera. He must invite them out to the country on warm Sundays, take them to lunch periodically, and send flowers on the birthday of their wives.

At a hearty sixty-three, Pinto has worked in hotels for fifty-one years, has been a concierge for thirty-five of them. He perfected his German at the Victoria in Badenburg, French at the Regina in Nice and the Hotel de l'Univers in Tours, English at the Carlton in London. To take over the desk at the Excelsior he presented a record which listed his employment as concierge at the Continental in Paris, the Hotel des Palmes in Palermo, the Royal Danieli in Venice, and at the Excelsior Lido at Lido, Venice where he worked for twenty years. He can remember Duke Cirillo, the Czar's cousin whose door was always guarded by a six-foot Cossack who slept on the threshold. And King Leopold I of Belgium who had a lavatory in his automobile. And a sentimental Duke of Windsor who asked for a map with all the places marked on it where he had served as a World War I officer.

Once Pinto had to contract for a whole sleeping car from Trieste to Venice, and later from Venice to Paris. If his memory serves him it was for Lady Astor. There have been a few requests from guests which, in spite of Pinto's best efforts, went unfilled. The one that still bothers him sometimes came from a woman who insisted that he get her space from Hamburg to the United States aboard the Graf Zeppelin. He tried, hard too, as he recalls, and the lady was damn sore when he had to tell her it was impossible.

If you have a problem which proves unsolvable to the nearly infallible concierge, you might take it to At Your Service on Via Bissolati 42, an organization that guarantees to do all your dirty work at a fee. Organized in April 1942 by a pair of American wives who decided they would rather have money on their hands instead of time, At Your Service obtains translators, governesses,

baby sitters, manuscript typists, and vacant apartments. They
also provide tourists with shopping guides who know values,
prices, and fair-dealing shops. At Your Service has provided
apartments for everyone from Greta Garbo to Mischa Auer, a
long gamut for anyone to run. Once, on order, they located a
man who knew the nomenclature of all the parts of a Douglas
aircraft. It took them an hour. Their most frequent requests are
for double sockets to fit both American and Italian light fixtures,
and for American egg beaters both of which are now obtainable by the agents of At Your Service. They still haven't been
able to locate pancake-turners in Rome, which is their current
stumper.

When they first opened for business they got a lot of calls
from pranksters who asked them where they could buy items like
fur-lined bathtubs. Now the ladies feel they have proved their
salt. At least the phony calls have stopped coming in. They take
it in stride when a member of a United Nations delegation serving in Greece pops in, hands them a wad of money and says,
"Here, buy me a straw hat with blue lining and an orchid ribbon
and a gray leather bag, I'll be back for them this afternoon." In
the particular instance, which happened to have been an actual
case history, they put together the hat order, as bilious as it
sounded, with some last-minute stitching of their own. They had
a little trouble with the gray leather bag, a tough item in Rome,
but they finally turned one up in an obscure store. They hope
the lady in Greece likes it even though it is made out of walrus
hide.

One of the tourist's biggest problems abroad, if he is not
basking at a resort and taking his meals on the American or *pension* plan, is finding a place to eat every noon and night. Since
there are no lunch wagons, corner coffee pots, diners or drug
stores with soda fountains in Rome, you will doubtless be better

off ordering breakfast in your hotel room. One corner of the down-stairs dining room will be open, but most Europeans do not descend for breakfast.

The top hotels do serve a table d'hote lunch at about $2 and a table d'hote dinner at $2. By and large hotel fare is not as lovingly prepared as what you will find at dozens of Roman restaurants large and small. On the other hand, if your stomach is not as happy as it was at home you'll have an easier time getting simple foods cooked to your specifications in the hotel dining rooms.

Presuming that you are both healthy and indestructible here are some specialties of the Roman kitchen:

Fettuccine alla Matrisciana: Thin noodles made of flour and eggs, but smothered with a sauce of diced bacon, onions and fresh tomatoes, and garnished with grated goat cheese.

Gnocchi alla Romana: Round forms of farina, butter, milk and cheese, browned in the oven.

Abbacchio Arrosto: Baby lamb roasted with rosemary (a Mediterrannean fragrant essential oil) and Frascati wine.

Carciofi alla Giudia: Pickled Roman artichokes, fried in oil.

Pisellini al Prosciutto: Garden green peas stewed in butter with diced raw ham.

The following restaurants, all tried and tested, should hold you for at least a week of eating out in Rome. Don't be afraid to walk into any clean-looking place that strikes your fancy. The chances are that the food will be good, and certainly the price will not be out of line by stateside standards. The only expensive place I found in Rome was Giorgo's, behind the Excelsior, where a simple lunch or dinner without wine costs about four dollars. The surroundings are plain but durable, and the service is excellent. On the other hand, at Mario's across the street, which has tables out on the sidewalk, you can get away for less than a dollar and a half. The most expensive entree on the menu is half a roast chicken which costs seventy-five cents. Mario's gets a big play from the nearby American Embassy, serves hamburger steak and ham and eggs every day from noon on. The rest of the menu is pure, beautiful Italian.

Don't confuse the ham-and-egg Mario's with the new Bar and Restaurant Mario, on the opposite side of the Via Veneto, a block and a half from the Porta Pinciana along the Via di Porta Pinciana. Besides lunch and dinner, there is also dancing.

In the same neighborhood is Capriccio, which has a sheltered summer garden upstairs that looks a little like New York, good food, (especially *canelloni*) and a bar that is popular with Rome's foreign colony. Restaurant prices are moderate.

If you trade restaurants with Americans, a popular custom abroad, the place you will most often be recommended to is Alfredo's. Since there are at least four known Alfredo's in Rome, the one in reference is Alfredo all' Scrofa, at Via della Scrofa, 104. The specialty of the house is *Maestose Fettuccine al triplo burro,* or majestic *fettuccine* with a triple serving of butter. It is served— a mountain of it—with enough fanfare to welcome the birth of a royal heir. Cost per portion: about thirty-five cents. The desserts are famous. Besides tourists, Alfredo's gets actors and artists whose portraits line the walls. Large, noisy and gay.

A little less plush, and a little more native is Alfredo-Santa Maria Trastevere where the food is excellent, inexpensive, and you eat in the open on a cobblestone square. Along the same order, and in the same location, is La Cisterna. Trastevere is in the old town, on the left side of the Tiber. In August there is a festival in the square in front of the restaurants that livens things up considerably.

For original cooking don't miss the Ristorante Tre Scalini (The Three Steps) in the open on the Piazza Navona. The wisest move you can make is order *Bauletto Tre Scalini*. It's veal and ham sealed together with cheese, and "rolled" into what the management insists is a *bauletto* or box. If you can take it, they make a production out of *Pollo con Pepperoni*, which is chicken and peppers. The desserts are monumental, particularly *gelato Tartufo*.

While dining at the Tre Scalini, you might like to contemplate the fact that the Piazza Navona, an immense public square, was once the stadium of Domitian which seated 30,000 spectators. The fountains in the square by Bernini, and the church of St. Agnes in Agone, opposite, by Borromini, became the subject of a controversy between the two designers. The peculiar construction of the church which looks as if it was about to topple into the square caused Bernini to give one of his statues an upraised hand, as if it were fending off an imminent blow. When Borromini discovered the sculpted slur, he added an incongruous statue to the front of the church. The hands of the figure seem to say, "Tut, tut, I'm not going to fall at all."

At Passetto's you can get anything including fancy game for about three dollars a person. Artists, politicians and the Italian press go to Re degli Amici for *Medaglione degli Amici* which is concocted of ham, beefsteak, mozzarella cheese, egg and wine sauce. Suora Cecilia is headquarters for the Italian movie set, Da Tito, on the Via della Vite, ditto for the American newspapermen.

For dinner-dancing one of the most romantic spots in town is the Hostaria dell'Orso, The Inn of the Bear, which occupies a building down by the Tiber in which Dante supposedly lived during the first Holy Year in 1300. Some improvements have been made since Dante's day. It has a bar lined with hundreds of green bottles illuminated by hidden lights, a covered upstairs terrace, and candlelight. Aside from the orchestra there is also a tenor in attendance who sings romantic numbers at the tables between

PALAZZO DI GIUSTIZIA
somnolent in the summer sun

sets. Dinner will run about $2.50, and the added tariff for the music certainly won't jar you.

If you want to spend your evening at a place where Tyrone Power courted Linda Christians, as who wouldn't, let me direct you to the Monte Mario high on a hill overlooking Rome. Said Ty in an interview with Tex McCrary and Jinx Falkenburg in New York: "That's the dream spot of the world."

There is a definite dearth of Hamburger Heavens and all-night beaneries in Rome, but you can get a late snack at the Pizzeria St. Ignazio on the Piazza St. Ignazio. Once a cab drivers' hangout, it now favors the after-theater set, attracting both the artists and the audiences.

ROME

At teatime Rome has places for the romantic, for those of social conscience and for the literati. It is traditional, but romantic all the same, to have tea and watch the sun set at the Casino delle Rose in the Villa Borghese. For that tearoom touch try the Sala da Tè Babington next door to the Spanish Stairs which advertises such un-Roman delicacies as waffles, scones, muffins, tea cakes and toast, not to mention tea and coffee. One of the most interesting places around is the Caffè Greco which first opened in 1760, and has been attracting artists and writers almost since then. It has that old, ice-cream-parlor flavor, a decor which includes a statue of Mark Twain (who was a patron), a photo of Buffalo Bill (also a customer) and an account in English of the "Ninth Cavalry in the Last Battle of the Indian Wars." You'll find it near the American Express on the Via Condotti.

Since 1760, when the Caffè Greco moved in, the Via Condotti has changed its character. Today it is, end to end, the toniest shopping street in Rome. Although Rome itself is not particularly distinguished for handicraft, it does gather a broad selection of goods from the rest of Italy—glasses and lace from Venice, shoes and silverware from Florence, silk from Como, all beautifully displayed. These goods will be less expensive if you buy them in their own hometown, but at any rate, in all except the most fashionable shops or the department stores you can usually get a discount merely by asking for it. Don't be bashful, they expect it.

On the Via Condotti try Cucci for men's wear, silk shirts, ties and robes. Gucci, nearby, is well known for leather. Handbags run from $8 to about $60, about a third less than U. S. prices not counting the extra twenty percent excise tax you pay at home. Fantasia (they call it fan-ta-ZEE-ya) has an unusual collection of fashions and accessories—blouses, skirts, slacks, fanciful umbrellas, imaginative footwear and trick rainwear. It also car-

THE WEDDING CAKE
an immense white conglomeration

ries the Hermes line from Paris. Vogue carries accessories and also
ashtrays and brassware. Bulgari is the Cartier of Rome. And
Bellini has blouses for $60 and tablecloths at astronomical fig-
ures. Rossati, around the corner at Piazza di Spagna, 52, carries
linens, laces and lingerie at prices that are a good deal more
earthy.

The simplest way to sightsee Rome, if you don't mind company, is to enlist in one of the organized tours operated by such
reputable travel agencies as American Express, CIT, or Pier
Busetti. Through these agencies, or through the concierge of your
hotel, you can also hire a private car and chauffeur (at about $17
a day). Private guides are also available at rates that are stand-

ard and inexpensive. With a guide in tow you can do the sights in your own car, via public bus, taxi, horse and carriage, or on foot.

Rome's main street is the Corso, or more formally, the Via del Corso. If you follow it north it runs straight as a die along the general direction of the Tiber to the Piazza del Popolo (the People's Square) where it becomes the Via Flaminia and continues in the same straight line to the edge of the city. Should you follow it south, the other end of the Corso is anchored by the Piazza Venezia, the center of Rome. The Piazza gets its name from the Palazzo Venezia which used to be famous because it was an early example of a fine Renaissance palace; its renown now stems from the fact that its balcony was the one used by Mussolini for his jaw-jutting speeches, and the square below was the one always filled with stiff-armed Fascisti.

The Piazza Venezia and the Corso are anchored by a mammoth extravaganza in marble known as the Monument to Victor Emmanuel II. To Americans it is "The Wedding Cake." The whole edifice is one block wide and several stories high, an immense white conglomeration of stairways, colonnades, statues and bas reliefs.

The monument, sometimes called the Vittoriale, was begun in 1885, finished in 1911 and dedicated to the first king of united Italy. The tomb of Italy's unknown soldier was added after the First World War.

As you stand in the Piazza Venezia, facing the Victor Emmanuel monument the thoroughfare that veers off obliquely to the left is called the Via dell' Impero. The broad avenue which was built by the Fascist regime, runs through the early Roman forums, many of them uncovered as recently as 1932, and ends triumphantly with the Colosseum. The first forum on the left-hand side, diagonally across the street from the Vittoriano was built by Trajan, and dates from 114 A.D. Aside from the Roman Forum itself, Trajan's Forum, built by the Syrian architect Apollodorus, represents the height of Roman culture during the greatest period of the empire. The triumph of Trajan's life was his conquest of Dacia, a kingdom which corresponds roughly to the present Romania. Trajan built his forum to celebrate his victory, and it contained when completed a triumphal arch, a basilica, a memorial column, two libraries and two semicircular buildings known as Trajan's markets carved into the side of the surrounding hills. The markets and the column, decorated with a frieze commemorating the Dacian victory, still stand. The column, end to end, is 108 feet high, and the frieze that winds around it is 650 feet long and carved with over two thousand figures. A spiral staircase is cut inside its twelve-foot diameter. Originally the column was topped by a statue of Trajan, and a golden urn containing his ashes rested at the pedestal. The urn was stolen during medieval times, and the figure of Trajan destroyed. Pope Sixtus V refitted the column with a new statue of St. Peter which is still in place.

Adjoining Trajan's Forum is the Forum of Augustus, Rome's first emperor, during whose reign Christ was born. The forum began with a temple built to Mars which was dedicated on the first of August, 2 B.C., in commemoration of the defeat and death of Brutus and Cassius, the principle conspirators in the assassination of Julius Caesar.

Next door is the Forum of Nerva 96-98 A.D. A statue of Minerva still remains in the forum but the Temple of Minerva was used as a marble quarry and destroyed.

Across the street (the Via dell' Impero) is the Roman Forum, and the Forum of Julius Caesar. Tour buses stop on the terrace of the Capitoline Hill looking the length of the ruins toward the Colosseum.

FROM THE CAPITOLINE
the Roman Forums

Smallest of the city's seven hills, the Capitoline is crowned today by the Senator's Palace which has a grand staircase designed by Michelangelo for the arrival in Rome of Charles V. The artist also placed the statue of Marcus Aurelius in the court, and designed the wings of the palace which were added after his death.

More events that shaped the world's history took place among the scattered stones on the opposite side of the Capitoline than any like piece of real estate anywhere on earth. In the left foreground is the Arch of Septimus Severus who was born in Africa, reigned as emperor from 193-211 and died prosaically of old age in England. The arch also carried the names of Caracalla and Geta, the two sons of Septimus, but when Geta died Caracalla had his name erased. The cornice supported by three columns in the immediate foreground is a remnant of the Temple of Vespasian which was built in 94 by his son Domitian and later rebuilt during the reign of Septimus. The eight columns that seem to form the end of a building are the ruins of the Temple of Saturn. Although the temple originally dates from 498 B.C., it was rebuilt in 42 B.C. and again by the Christians in the fourth century A.D. Always a treasury even in its last days, the temple was once broken open by Julius Caeser to reclaim a gold ransom that was being kept in the vault under threat of a superstitious hex. The cobbled road which begins almost at the edge of the temple and runs across the forum is the Via Sacra, or Sacred Way. Actually a continuation of the Appian Way, it was the route of triumphal processions. In the foreground, between the Sacred Way and the Arch of Septimus is the famed Rostra, built by Caeser in 44 B.C., the forerunner of the soap box from which politicians and public speakers harangued the Roman crowds. The solitary pillar behind the Rostra is the Column of Phoca (or Foca), a seventh-century emperor who gave permission to Pope Boniface IV to make a church of the Pantheon. Phoca's column was taken from the Pantheon and replanted in the forum as a form of reciprocation. Despite his churchly beneficence, Phoca eventually swung from the gallows at Constantinople.

Behind and to the left of the column is the tomb of Julius Caesar which is supposed to contain an urn of Caesar's ashes. Caesar's body was cremated at this spot, and it was on this ground that Mark Antony delivered the eulogy and the call to revenge that Shakespeare imagined began, "Friends, Romans, Countrymen, lend me your ears. . . ." Two years after Caesar was murdered his nephew, Augustus Caesar, Rome's first emperor,

TEMPLE OF ANTONINO AND FAUSTINA
Caesar mourned them deeply

built a memorial temple of which only vestiges of the foundations remain.

Behind and to the left of Caesar's tomb, the large building with six intact columns in front and a long staircase leading to the front door is the Temple of Antonino and Faustina whose death he mourned deeply. The temple is probably in such good condition because it was turned into a church called San Lorenzo in Miranda.

The three columns joined by a cornice which can be seen on the right of Caesar's tomb are the remains of the Temple of Castor and Pollux. The temple was originally built in the fifth century B.C. and restored either by Hadrian or Trajan. It celebrates a legend which says that on the night of a crucial battle in Rome's early history Castor and Pollux, two gods, were seen watering their horses in a fountain at the foot of the Palatine Hill. They brought the Romans good tidings of the battle, and the Romans in turn earmarked them for immortality.

Behind the Temple of Castor and Pollux is the House of the Vestal Virgins who were sacred keepers of the flame in the Temple of Vesta nearby. The Vestal Virgins numbered six, all daughters of patrician families chosen between the ages of six and ten. Although they were considered above the law, were given seats of honor at public functions, and held a certain political importance, they were severely punished if the fire in the temple was allowed to go out, and they were to be buried alive if they lost their virginity.

The Arch of Titus in the right rear of the forum is dedicated to the victory of Titus and his father, Vespasian over the Jews and the capture, in 70 A.D., of Jerusalem. The walls of the arch, which was erected after the death of Titus, depicts Jewish prisoners and Roman soldiers carrying Hebrew seven-branch ceremonial candelabrum, liberated in Jerusalem.

Astride the far end of the Via dell' Impero sits the Colosseum, the symbol of Rome, now nearly nineteen hundred years old. Imposing by day, it is magnificent by night when the rhythmic repitition of its ancient arches are splashed with new notoriety by a battery of floodlights.

Vespasian began the Colosseum in 72 A.D. using Jewish prisoners, and it was finished and dedicated by Titus in 80, after his return from the campaigns in Jerusalem. It is 616 feet long, 510 feet wide, has eighty entrances which are still numbered, 240 staircases, and it seated, most sources believe, 87,000 spectators, or seven thousand more than the Yankee Stadium. But compared to what went on in the Colosseum, baseball, football, and the grunt and groan circuit were mere potsy. Nothing appealed to the Roman sporting blood as much as blood. For over three hundred years the big stadium packed them in with human combatants. Ten thousand gladiators were kept as a continuous stable and pitted against each other or sometimes against animals. To pep up the program during the second and third centuries, Christians were often tossed into the arena to do barehanded battle with beasts.

During the 100-day inauguration celebration, a Roman holiday which has been overlooked by few historians, 5,000 animals were killed. The floor of the Colosseum could be flooded and the program was often varied with naval battles, a diversion which was begun during the inauguration ceremonies. A company of sailors from the fleet at Ravenna were based in Rome so they could make appearances in the water battles. They were also charged with erecting the canvas cover which was stretched over the top of the Colosseum in case of rain.

The Christianized Constantine and several later emperors tried to put an official end to the mayhem matinees without apparent success. However in the fifth century a monk who came out of the east with a mission ran onto the field, separated a pair of gladiators, and implored the audience to seek quainter entertainment. He was met by a barrage, not of pop-bottles, but of stones which killed him. The next day the bloody battles of the Colosseum were ended for all time.

For a long period thereafter, the Colosseum was abandoned. Then, during the Middle Ages it was used for bullfights in peacetime, and armed as a fortress during the war. Later it became, in effect, the principle stone quarry in Rome, and blocks from the structure were used for several churches and for the Palazzo Venezia. Pope Benedict XIV put a stop to that in 1747, and

INSIDE THE COLOSSEUM
mayhem matinees

erected a cross inside to the memory of the Christian martyrs who had died on the turf to amuse the Roman spectators. The cross was removed in 1872 and finally reinstated in 1926. It is still there.

In the roadway outside the Colosseum, the large circular tracing marks the site of an immense statue of Nero which once stood there. The brick pedestal was fifteen feet high, and the statue, executed in bronze, towered 135 feet above it. Some say the Colosseum was so named for the immensity of the statue, while another camp figures the size of the stadium itself was reason enough for its name. Officially the Colosseum is known as the Amphitheater Flavium—after Vespasian whose full handle was Titus Flavius Sabinus Vespasianus. It is a hundred and fifty feet high, and its circumference—one-third of a mile—encloses six acres of ground.

One of the best preserved of all the Roman monuments is

in an earlier sky . . . an apparition

the Arch of Constantine now over sixteen hundred years old. It
stands near the Colosseum, erected by the Roman Senate in commemoration of Constantine's third victory over Maxentius in 312.
It was during this battle that Constantine saw in the sky a lumin-
ous cross and the legend "By this, conquer." Since Constantine
was known thereafter to be sympathetic to Christ, a reverence
not shared by the pagan city officials, his victories were am-
biguously ascribed on the arch to "divine" guidance. Although

the Senate ordered an ornate construction they didn't bother to have the arch built of new stone. Most of the blocks were taken from the arches of Marcus Aurelius and Trajan, and in some cases the faces of those emperors were actually altered to look like Constantine and then built into the new arch.

Mussolini, the ignoblest Roman of them all, not to be outdone, built his forum, too. You can find it by following the Corso from the Vittoriale to the Via Flaminia, and continuing on the Via Flaminia to the Tiber. Cross the river by the Milvian Bridge, where Constantine beat Maxentius for the third and last time in 312 A.D., and turn to the left. Renamed the Foro Italico, Mussolini's extravaganza featured Mussolini's own obelisk with his name on it; a large indoor swimming pool; a stadium to seat 85,000 people (intended for the 1942 Olympics) which never got finished; and a gymnastic field surrounded by dozens of garish, nude, male, marble figures each representing a sport, and simultaneously honoring an Italian city. When Rome fell the whole plant became a rest center for American troops.

Romulus using a plough is said to have traced the first outline of Rome on Palatine Hill which rises to the right of the Colosseum behind the Roman Forum. The early kings and nobles built their homes there, and the emperors and the patricians who followed found it fashionable too. Cicero, Mark Antony, Claudius, Octavius and his son Augustus—all great names of the Republic —lived on the Palatine. The house of Augustus, after he became emperor, was used as the official state palace, and with the additions of the emperors who succeeded him it spread down the side of the Palatine right into the Forum. The immensity of the royal diggings were not grand enough for Nero, however, who added extensions that reached down as far as where the Colosseum now stands. Modern excavations have uncovered the Palatine of early Rome which was covered during the Middle Ages, and the

MUSSOLINI'S FORUM
the ignoblest Roman of them all

magnificent palaces of the Republic used as foundations for
fortresses during the decadent eras which followed.

On the far side of the Palatine was the Roman Circus, an
open plain now stretching from the bell tower to the obelisk in
the center of the Piazza del Circo Massimo. It could hold 250,000
people who gathered to see chariot races. You can get a good
view by turning up the Via del Circo Massimo to the Piazza
Romolo e Remo, formerly a Jewish cemetery. The ruins you see
opposite are those of the palace of Augustus Caesar.

Of all the Roman baths none was as luxurious, none catered
to self-indulgence as the Baths of Caracalla, south of the Colosseum, near the beginning of the Appian Way. Begun by Septimus

OPEN-AIR OPERA
for Aida, elephants and camels

Severus in 206 A.D. they were first put in use by Caracalla eleven years later. Caracalla's baths never had much in common with bathing for cleanliness. The place was one huge establishment where Romans could loll around the pools, take the baths, get a massage, be anointed with oils and perfumes, prattle about politics, exercise in the gymnasia, hear readings of the latest poems, dawdle over the art exhibits, shop for clothing and new perfumes, browse around the library, and select sweet meats from the buffet tables. Bathers passed from the Tepidarium, to the Sudatorium or steam room, then to the Calidarium for a hot bath, back to the Tepidarium, and finally to the Frigidarium for a cold shower. The place was large enough to accommodate 1,600 bathers at one time, but women bathed separately, often in asses' milk. The floors were inlaid with magnificent mosaics some of which, after seventeen centuries are still in place; the walls were lined with marble, the doors cast of bronze. For service the baths employed a horde of slaves who functioned swiftly and noiselessly, moving in a series of tunnels cut underneath the main floor.

Although it was this type of indolence that most historians say resulted in the ultimate decline of the Roman Empire, the baths stayed in business until the sixth century. Rome had fourteen aqueducts which totaled nearly four hundred miles, but most of them were ruined by the marauding Goths, rendering the baths waterless and useless.

In one of the most romantic settings in all Rome, the Baths of Caracalla are now used as a backdrop for open-air summer opera. The stage is spread between two ruined red-brick towers of the Calidarium. In front is an audience of 10,000. For the performances of *Mefistofele* the Caracalla opera uses red-tinted steam, shoots off fireworks on stage; for *Lohengrin* there is a cast of 700 including Mussolini's favorite white horse; for *Aida*, horses, camels and elephants. During the intermission girl candy-butchers hawk chocolates and Coca Cola. Slipping out of the exits guarded by the elegant *carabinieri*, one can find sandwiches and cakes under the grandstands. Although it often seems like a circus, and frequently looks like a de Mille spectacle, Rome's opera which uses talent like Benjamino Gigli, Maria Caniglia and Tito Schipa, is also opera. The most you can possibly spend for a ticket is less than two dollars, and tickets can usually be obtained by your hotel concierge. Don't miss it.

From the Baths of Caracalla, on the south end of the city, it's not far to the Porta San Sebastiano gateway and the Via Appia Antica, which leads to the Catacombs. A unique attraction for pilgrim and tourist, the Catacombs are underground cemeteries dug and used by the early Christians. Built as a series of tunnels, they are so long, dark, complicated and mysterious that they have become the subject of many local fanciful tales. Foremost of the legends is the one which purports that a party of tourists led by a monk as guide once wandered afield of the regular underground routings and was never found again.

In the early, tentative days of Christianity the underground tombs were dug by individual families. Planned primarily as cemeteries, they were also used as clandestine prayer houses where Christians could worship free of Roman persecution. Estimates have placed the number of Roman catacombs between thirty-seven and forty-two, the most famous of which are the Catacombs of St. Callixtus and the Catacombs of St. Sebastian. St. Callixtus was the first accredited Christian cemetery in Rome. A deacon of the Church named Callixtus was head of the Church from 199 to 217 in which year he was chosen Pope.

The Catacombs of St. Sebastian are the most important in Rome. The excavations, begun in 1915, have so far revealed over eight tunneled miles. You can descend through the darkened depths with a taper-bearing Franciscan monk who will point out the oft-repeated symbol of the fish, secret sign of the early Christians, the invocations scratched in clay bearing the names of Peter and Paul both of whom are belived to have been first buried here. Still in existence are jars for lamp oil and for perfume which was used in burial preparations.

A basilica built over the catacombs in the fourth century contains the tomb of San Sebastian, a set of footprints said to be those of Christ, and an arrow said to be the one which killed St. Sebastian.

Near the San Sebastian Catacombs is the Fosse Ardeatine, a monument to modern martyrs and, too, a testimonial to the depravity of some men at a time when the Christian world was

THE CATACOMBS
lamp oil and perfume

already nineteen hundred and forty-four years old. The story, which has a grotesque ending, and a curious epilogue, begins toward the end of the Italian campaign of World War II. With Italy officially knocked out of the war, her intentions split between the contestants fighting on her soil, the advance of the Allies on the road to Rome infused the partisans with new boldness. A baby carriage loaded with dynamite abandoned in a nest of German soldiers, a few machine-gunnings, and the Nazis counted thirty-one fatalities among their troops. Counting ten Italians for every dead German, the Nazis quickly rounded up 310 hostages. It soon developed that another three Germans had been killed which meant another thirty hostages had to be

rounded up. An SS colonel named Dollman, who was in charge
of the retaliation proceedings called upon one Pietro Caruso head
of the *Regina Coeli* prison—or the Jail of the Queen of Heaven.
Instead of complying with the German demand for thirty prisoners, Caruso gave them a bonus of fifty. The entire group of hostages now included five generals, fifty other military men, seventy-
two Jews, and an assortment of other prisoners. They were
whisked away, and never heard from again. Men who had been
plucked from their homes or merely rounded up hit-or-miss on
the street were presumed by their families to be in prison, or
perhaps in a German labor camp somewhere in the Reich.

When Rome fell on June 4 that year a priest of the Catacombs of St. Callixtus plucked one of the first olive-drab sleeves
he saw in the city. It belonged to Mike Stern, the correspondent
then covering for the North American Newspaper Alliance. Would
the eminent journalist like to hear the story of the slaughter of
several hundred Italians by the lately departed Germans? Mike
didn't believe him. Would the journalist like to see the caves in
which these Italians had been killed in cold blood?

The priest took Stern to the face of a cliff which had been
formed by the excavations of a gravel company. Three caves had
once opened on the face of the cliff. Two, it was clear to see,
had been closed by explosions. The third was still partly open,
and from it came a terrible stench. Mike and the priest walked
through minefields to the top of the cliff. Here they could see
that the roof of the caves had collapsed. Peering down through
a swarm of flies they could see parts of bodies, all that was left
of the hostages that had been rounded up in March.

From the priest Mike drew the story. First the Germans had
cordoned off the surrounding streets for miles around. They
brought the hostages in by truck, stood them up inside the cave,

and by the light of the truck headlights, machine-gunned them to death. Then with bombs they collapsed the caves on the bodies.

When the war ended Pietro Caruso, the head of the Queen of Heaven prison tried to escape the country, but the partisans threw up a roadblock and Caruso broke his leg trying to ram his car through. He was brought to trial in Rome along with his assistant. Mistaking Caruso's assistant for Caruso the crowd grabbed the hapless underling from the *carabinieri* and beat him unmercifully. Then they threw him in the Tiber where they drowned him, and pulled his body out and hung it by the heels over a bridge. Caruso was later executed.

As for Colonel Dollman, the SS officer who had engineered the massacre, he fared better. Dollman had come to Rome in 1933 as the head of an innocuous little German tourist office. Later he became cultural attaché of the German Embassy, and took up residence in a place which is now a boardinghouse for respectable English ladies. Because Dollman was shrewd enough to dicker with Allen Dulles, head of the American OSS detachment in Switzerland for the capitulation of the remaining German forces in Italy, he was freed for his part in the Ardeatine atrocity.

When the bodies were exhumed, all but fifteen were identified. Germans had tied bombs around the necks of the fifteen, and they were unrecognizable. A magnificent memorial has been erected at the scene. The tombs are covered by a mammoth granite roof, twelve feet thick, weighing 45,000 tons. The gray stone graves, softly lighted, are always covered with flowers. Sorrow-filled women in black still spend hours in prayer and meditation over the headstones. On the cliff outside a cross and a Star of David are silhouetted against the evening sky. Dollman is living quietly in Rome where his memoirs are appearing serially in a local paper.

THE SPANISH STAIRS
for the Italians, by the French

Should you get homesick in Rome the one square where you would be sure to find Americans is the Piazza di Spagna. In the first place there is the American Express at number thirty-three, which is patrolled outside by a newsie who only sells the Continental edition of the *New York Times*. Secondly, it is near the Via Condotti, the city's elegant shopping street. And thirdly, there is the 137-step monumental staircase built in 1725 by the French ambassador to Rome. They are known as the Spanish Stairs after the square which got its name from the nearby residence of the Spanish ambassador to the Pope. The few flower-stands at the foot of the stairs are the diehards of a once flourishing flower market. The boat-shaped fountain in the square in

TREVI FOUNTAIN
that night throw a coin

front of the steps is known as the Barcaccia (meaning barge) and was done by Bernini. The first building to the right of the stairs is the memorial museum house of Keats and Shelley in which both English poets spent some time. The two poets were driven to voluntary exile in the warmer climates of Italy because both suffered from lung impairments, and probably too, because both were carrying on florid love affairs that might not have gone well at home. Both died in Italy, Keats at 26 in Rome, and Shelley at 30 somewhere in the sea between Leghorn and La Spezia. His small boat was swamped in a storm, and the body washed up at Viareggio in July of 1822. (Keats had died first seventeen months before.) Edward Trelawny, Shelley's schoolboy chum, with the help of Lord Byron, burned Shelley's body on the Viareggio beach, Trelawny taking Shelley's heart from the flames at the last moment. The ashes and the heart of Shelley lie under his tablet. Rome's Protestant cemetery holds the graves of both young poets.

Says the Shelley inscription:

> Nothing of him that doth fade
> But doth suffer a sea change
> Into something rich and strange

Beside Shelley is the grave of Trelawny. He died in England in 1881 at the age of 88, some fifty-nine years after Shelley, but his body was sent across the continent in keeping with his behest, to lie beside the poet's heart. The inscription reads:

> These are two friends whose lives were undivided
> So let their memory be now they have glided
> Under the grave let not their bones be parted
> For their two hearts in life were single hearted

Keats's grave in an adjoining section of the cemetery says simply and sadly:

> This grave
> contains all that was mortal
> of a
> Young English Poet
> who
> on his death bed
> in the bitterness of his heart
> at the malicious power of his enemies
> Desired
> these words to be engraven on his Tomb Stone
> Here lies one
> Whose name was written in water
> Feb. 24th 1821

ROME

Beside Keats is the body of the British Consul, John Severn, who was his friend. All four graves, and those of other Protestants buried in Rome, lie in the shadow of the Roman Pyramid of Cestus which dates from 1 B.C., and a Roman wall built by Aurelius in 272 A.D.

One of Rome's most formidable structures, and no ruin indeed, is the Pantheon which sits unimpaired by virtually two thousand years of existence, between the Corso and the river. Built by Agrippa in 27 B.C., and restored first by Hadrian and then by Septimus Severus and Caracalla, and finally by ensuing generations of Christians when it was converted into a church, the Pantheon is in almost perfect repair. A copy of the Pantheon of Greece, it has sixteen columns of marble brought from Egypt upholding the triangular portico. The original square interior was destroyed by fire, and rebuilt in its present circular design by Hadrian. The 143-foot diameter exactly equals the interior height. The dome is open to permit free interchange between Heaven and earth. The bronze which once covered the interior of the dome was peeled off in 1630 to gild the canopy of St. Peter's.

When the Pantheon became a church in 609, the remains of many Christian martyrs were taken from the Catacombs and reinterred there. The Pantheon also holds the tombs of Victor Emmanuel II, grandfather of the recent "Little King," and father of Umberto I, who was assassinated on July 29, 1900. Umberto's wife, Queen Margherita, is buried with him. To the right is the tomb of the incomparable Raphael who died of consumption on his thirty-seventh birthday, April 6, 1520. On his tomb is a simple sentence:

> Living, great Nature feared he might out vie Her works; and, dying, fears herself to die.

In a tomb near Raphael is Maria Antoinetta Bibiens, who loved him, and was promised to him, and died three months before him. But she is near him in death as she never was in life. Raphael loved and lived with the Fornarina, a little baker girl whose face appears in his pictures, but whose remains lie elsewhere.

Behind the Pantheon are the Baths of Agrippa, the first public baths in Rome which set a style back in 19 B.C. when they were first opened. According to the oft-embroidered tale, Agrippa and his soldiers were looking for a water source to supply the baths when a young maiden showed them a spring they had overlooked. Agrippa brought the water into town on an aqueduct, and the spring still feeds the lower sections of the city and the famous Trevi Fountain. The spring is called Virgin Water, and is considered the best of Rome, free of lime and good for the kidneys.

In a city renowned for fountains, the Trevi Fountain is the biggest, fanciest and most renowned. If the agelessness, and the beauty and the immortality of Rome has seeped into your blood as it did to Caesar and Mark Antony, to St. Peter and St. Paul, to Constantine and the early Christians, to Raphael and Michelangelo, to Browning and Shelley and Keats, and the Brazilians, the Poles, the Moroccans, and the Americans of the Fifth Army who came in the days of war, and the people of many lands who have come in the days of peace which have followed, then on the eve of your departure hurry to the Trevi Fountain. The old legend says that if that night you throw a coin in the fountain it will be your destiny someday to return.

THE VATICAN

ST. PETER'S BASILICA
the world's largest

3. THE VATICAN AND THE CHURCHES OF ROME

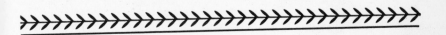

The world capital of the Roman Catholic Church is a tiny, independent state on the left bank of the Tiber totaling a hundred acres of real estate and a thousand citizens. It operates its own radio station, publishes its own newspaper (*L'Osservatore Romano*) and issues its own stamps. It has no custom duties and imposes no taxes. In its curious, confined world it has a railroad and a depot, but no trains ever leave the walls of the Vatican and none ever comes in. For its size it is surrounded by one of the most colorful, best trained, highly disciplined, most complicated cordon of police and military units in the world. Its mandates, decisions, orders and rules affect more of the globe's population than any other headquarters — national, fraternal, religious or organizational. Vatican City is probably the most powerfully concentrated capsule on earth.

The most majestic approach to the Vatican from the center of Rome is via the Bridge of Sant'Angelo. The king-sized pillbox ensconced on the opposite side of the bridge is the Castel Sant'

CASTEL SANT'ANGELO
king-sized pillbox

Angelo, built by Hadrian as a family mausoleum in 136 A.D. It was from the Castel that Puccini's heroine, Tosca, committed suicide. Once entirely covered in marble, in the fifth century it was converted into a fortress, and in one of its earliest engagements its statues were used as makeshift bombs. Two Popes were murdered by suffocation here in the tenth century. In the fifteenth a covered passage from the Vatican was completed so the Popes could use the fortress as a place of refuge. One of the first Popes to take advantage of the arrangement was Clement VII who fled down the narrow *passetto* while the Swiss guards tried to hold off the attacking forces of Charles the Bourbon.

A left-turn in front of the castle will lead into the Via della

ST. PETER'S SQUARE
under the obelisk, a crucifixion

Conciliazone, the broad approach to St. Peter's Square. The immense *piazza* 215 yards wide, is contained on either side by the half-shells of the Bernini colonnades. The columns are four deep, 296 in all. One hundred and forty-six statues of saints look down on the square from the roof that covers the columns. The Egyptian obelisk in the center of the square, brought from Nero's circus in 1586, took 900 men five months to erect. It stands on the spot where St. Peter was crucified, head down by Nero in 67 A.D. (St. Paul, a Roman, was beheaded the same day.)

Facing the entrance to the square is the facade of the Basilica of St. Peter, crowned by the great dome designed by Michelangelo. In its immensity St. Peter's defies the adjectives of the

Hollywood ad writers. It is 615 feet long, the largest church in the world. It can take, standing up, all the people who can fit into the Yankee Stadium. It can seat well over twice as many people as Madison Square Garden. Comparative sizes of other churches of the world are inlaid in the floor. Second largest is St. Paul's of London. Largely through the efforts of Cardinal Spellman the measurements of St. Patrick's in New York City is about to be added. It will be the smallest measurement on the floor.

The dominating fixture is the huge bronze canopy designed by Bernini to cover the altar. Ninety-five feet high, supported by four spiral bronze columns, it has definite Oriental overtones. The bronze was taken from the roof of the Pantheon and gilded at a cost of nearly $39,000.

Under the canopy is the High Altar where only the Pope himself or a cardinal of his special designation may say Mass. The altar was built over an early first century oratory which in turn was built on the grave of St. Peter. It is the current excavations in these depths that are said to cast new light on the true remains of St. Peter.

Elsewhere in the church is the fifth century bronze statue of St. Peter seated, his outward-thrust right foot worn thin by the pious who make it a custom to kiss it upon entering the basilica. Also Michelangelo's beautiful marble statue "Pity," depicting the Madonna holding the collapsed body of Christ. Finished when the sculptor was twenty-four, it is one of Michelangelo's few signed works. His name appears on a band across the Madonna's breast.

There are a number of copies of great paintings done in mosaics by the Vatican School of Mosaics decorating various panels.

The balconies contain relics of the church including the head of St. Andrew, the veil which Veronica used to wipe the face of

Jesus when he was carrying the Cross, a part of the true Cross which Constantine's mother is said to have discovered at Mount Calvary, a sword which a soldier ran through Christ's body sent from St. Sophia in Istanbul in the fifteenth century.

One hundred and forty-six Popes and some members of European royalty are buried in St. Peter's. Among the regal remains are those of Queen Christina Alexander of Sweden who gave up her crown to become Catholic and died in Rome in 1679, and Maria Clementina, wife of James Stuart (the Old Pretender). James is buried in the crypt, but a monument honors him and his two sons, Charles Edward (an earlier Bonnie Prince Charlie) and Henry, who was Cardinal York.

Under the tomb of Maria Clementina is the elevator which takes visitors to the roof. It's another four hundred steps to the ball on top of the dome which can hold sixteen puffing people. From floor to dome is 448 feet.

The Gate of the Bells on the left side of St. Peter's, and the Bronze Door on the right are patrolled by the Swiss Guards, the Pope's personal troops. In all, the detachment numbers one hundred plus twenty recruits. For formal dress they wear a uniform of orange, blue and red straps, bloomered trousers, and striped stockings to match a black beret and a white collar. The outfit was designed by Michelangelo who used the colors of the Medicis, since a member of that famous family was Pontiff at the time. The Swiss Guards sign up for a three-year enlistment. They get no leave during that period, but at the end of their tour they are awarded a three months furlough. All the members are actually Swiss, and they are paid in Swiss francs.

The Pope is also guarded by the Papal Gendarmes, a police organization which handles the traffic and keeps the peace. Its members are Italian, all five-foot nine or taller. They dress variously in a copy of the uniform of Napoleon's grenadiers complete

SWISS GUARD
orange, blue, and red

to the bearskin helmet, sometimes in ordinary dark work uniform, and, when an assignment necessitates it, in civilian clothes.

Other organizations more honorary than protective, include the Noble Guard, a detachment of social sons of the best Italian families; and its democratic counterpart, the Palatine Guard, whose members are drawn from the broad middle class.

To gain a papal audience visitors to Rome may present themselves at the office of Maestro di Camera in the Vatican Palace, entering the city by the Bronze Door. You will need your passport to "cross the border" into Vatican City. In any case your request will be more sympathetically received if you are equipped with a recommendation from some ecclesiastical authority at home. Americans should present themselves, with or without church credentials, at the American Embassy for instruction.

Your application will take several days, but a letter granting audience will be delivered by a Vatican messenger directly to your hotel room. The Pope will receive persons of all nationalities, and no question of religion is ever asked from the time of application to the conclusion of the audience.

If the Pope is in Rome you appear at the Bronze Door in St. Peter's Square. During the summer the Pope frequently spends several weeks at the papal villa at Castel Gandolfo outside Rome. You can get there by private car in a half an hour for about $10, or in the regular tramway in an hour and ten minutes for about twenty-eight cents. Sometimes enterprising Italian automobile owners hang around the trolley station and offer cut-rate trips to Castel Gandolfo at a variety of prices, neither as expensive as ten dollars nor as cheap as twenty-eight cents.

Although it was formerly court etiquette to appear for an audience in formal clothes — long dress for ladies, tails for men — such ceremony has been dropped for ordinary citizens appearing at the Holy See. Now it is merely requested that Vatican visitors be modestly dressed. Black is commendable, but not necessary. Ladies, of course, may not wear low-cut or short-sleeved dresses. In audience they must cover their heads and remove their gloves. Men are expected to wear coats, dark ties and, preferably, white shirts.

Your papal invitation will get you past the Swiss guards, past bustling monsignori in flowing robes of purple, past ushers in red satin breeches, red jackets, red socks and white formal shirts worn with white tie. If you are of world importance your interview will be private. If you are a citizen with a letter from your parish or a recommendation from your embassy, your interview will be semi-private. You will share your audience with thirty or forty others, all arranged by name around the room. After the ushers have rearranged you half a dozen times, a monsignor who has been keeping a watchful eye through the crack of the door announces the arrival of the Pope. There is a bustle at the door His Holiness sweeps in. He is clad in a white skull cap, white robes and red velvet shoes. It strikes you suddenly that he is tall. His face is iron gray, he wears spectacles, his hair is closely cropped. His movements are quick and alert. He moves rapidly around the line, speaking Italian, German, French, English or even Hebrew as the occasion may demand. If you are a Catholic you kneel and kiss the papal ring. "Where are you from?" he is likely to say to you. And when you tell him he may answer, "I thank you for coming." Then from over his shoulder he takes a medallion from an attendant, hands it to you and moves on. When the end of the line is reached the monsignori signal and those who wish may kneel. For those who are dictated neither by religion nor instinct, it is not necessary to kneel. The Pope offers a prayer, blesses the assemblage, and wheels to go. As he passes through the portal the ushers drape his shoulders in an ermine cape.

CASTEL GANDOLFO
a column of nuns, three by three

Outside in the square hawkers sell religious articles, post
cards and Vatican folders. Cars from all countries line the colonnades. Out at Castel Gandolfo the tiny village square in front of
the Pope's palace is jammed with cars, people and sidewalk cafes.
In the center a fountain spouts water from four sides for village
folk who fill Chianti bottles, wash grapes, and for waiters from

the cafes who wash their glasses there. A column of nuns marches by three-by-three. A diplomat in tails and his wife in a black lace mantilla get in their long limousine completely ignored by the village women who trundle past carrying basket-loads aloft on their heads.

In 1870 when Italy was united as a kingdom, Victor Emmanuel II ordered Italian troops into Rome, then a papal territory. Pope Pius IX quit the Quirinal Palace in the center of the city, retired to the Vatican Palace, and excommunicated the king. The argument between State and Church smoldered until the Lateran Pact was signed on February 11, 1929. Effected by Pius XI and Mussolini, the pact created the "City of the Vatican" as an independent territory under control of the Holy See. For its inconvenience, loss of property and revenue from 1870 to 1929, the church was indemnified 750,000,000 lire in cash, and 1,000,-000,000 lire in five percent Italian bonds. When Pius XI left St. Peter's Square to join a Eucharistic procession in July of 1929, he ended a voluntary papal imprisonment that had extended for fifty-nine years through the reign of four Popes.

With all its rambling additions the Vatican Palace is probably the largest palace in the world. The only part of it open to visitors without a passport is the Vatican Museum which was opened in 1932. A unique double spiral staircase — one way up, one way down — leads to the galleries. There is a Vatican post office on the top floor which sells post cards and Vatican stamps. The treasure-filled galleries are so long it would take an hour and ten minutes to walk them at a normal pace without taking time to look at the pictures. Among the vast collections of the picture galleries are primitives by Giotto and his school, Bellini's "Descent from the Cross," one Van Dyck, several Rubens; tapestries designed by Raphael, and the young artist's famous "Transfiguration" which was left unfinished when he died. The picture was carried after his coffin in Raphael's funeral procession. Later it was taken to Paris by Napoleon, and finally returned after the emperor's decline. Everywhere in the picture galleries you can see copyists at work, reproducing the great works. Many make miniature copies which sell for about ten dollars.

In the Sculpture Gallery, where all statues have been covered by fig leaves (by decree of the Vatican authorities), there is the famous gilded statue of Hercules found in the nineteenth century, a sphinx that dates from Nero's time, and the tomb of Constantine's mother fashioned of porphyry.

The celebrated Sistine Chapel was built in 1473 and is called "Sistine" because it was commissioned under the reign of Pope Sixtus IV. Virtually every square inch of the long chamber is decorated with great art — the floor in mosaic tile, the side walls by several Florentine masters, Botticelli, Rosselli, Signorelli, and others. Michelangelo was asked to do the ceiling, but the suggestion incurred the criticism of other masters who insisted that Michelangelo was a sculptor not a painter. The great artist who had never painted before left for Florence but later at the Pope's insistence he returned. After an intricate scaffold had been built, Michelangelo, with several assistants, painted the ceiling while lying on his back. It took over four years to finish. Twenty years later, at the age of sixty, Michelangelo began work on the "Last Judgment" which covers the altar wall. It took seven years to complete, during most of which time Michelangelo was continually annoyed by a cardinal who insisted that the figures should not be nude. In the finished painting one lost soul in hell, caught by the coils of a snake, is depicted with the ears of a jackass and the unmistakable other features of the bickering cardinal. The cracks on the wall came from the explosion of a nearby powder magazine which blew up the day the Sistine Chapel was opened, December 25, 1541.

After the death of a Pontiff, the Sistine Chapel is the traditional meeting place of cardinals who gather from all over the world to elect a new Pope. When a deadlocked vote is taken the ballots are burned with straw, the resulting black smoke which billows out of the chimney announcing the news to the crowds outside. When a majority vote is reached the ballots are burned without straw, the white smoke giving the news of a new Pope.

❦ *Holy Years*

The greatest celebrations of the Catholic Church are the Holy Years which now fall every twenty-five years, or at any time between which may be designated by the Pope to commemorate a special anniversary. The last Holy Year before 1950 was held in 1933 to commemorate the nineteenth centenary of the Redemption.

For the Holy Year of 1950 the Church laid down these four objectives:

1. Sanctification of souls through prayer, penance, and loyalty to Christ and to the Church.

2. Action for peace and for the protection of holy places.

3. Defense of the Church against renewed attacks of their enemies, penetration by true faith of erring souls, of infidels and the godless.

4. Actuation of social justice, works of assistance in favor of the humble and needy.

During the jubilee year which extends from Christmas Eve to Christmas Eve, Catholics fulfilling the prescribed conditions may acquire plenary—or full indulgences not otherwise obtainable. The conditions set forth for 1950 are considerably simpler to fulfill than the requirements asked of pilgrims during the first

Holy Years. Where it was necessary in ancient times for Romans to visit the basilicas for a thirty-day period, and foreigners for a fifteen-day period, modern pilgrims need only spend three days in Rome. During the three days they must visit St. Peter's, and the Roman basilicas of St. John Lateran, St. Paul without-the-walls, and St. Mary Major, entering each by its holy door. In each basilica they must recite the Creed, and three times the "Our Father," the "Hail Mary," and "Glory Be To The Father," and also one "Our Father," "Hail Mary," and "Glory Be To The Father" for the Intentions of the Pope.

In turn every pilgrim coming to Rome is received in general audience by the Pope. Each is given a pilgrim's kit containing a prayer and hymnbook, a guidebook of Rome and an identification card entitling the bearer to reductions on virtually all transportation.

In the traditional opening day ceremony of Holy Year, the Pontiff, using an ivory-handled hammer strikes the sealed Holy Door of St. Peter's saying, "Open the doors of justice for me." Then, striking the wall a second time, he adds, "I shall enter Thy House, O Lord." With the third hammer blow, and the words "Open the doors, for God is with us," the wall, previously cut from the inside, crumbles onto a board and is drawn away. In the meantime, cardinals designated by the Pope conduct similar ceremonies before the Holy Doors of the other three basilicas.

During the twelve months following, the Pope says Mass in St. Peter's at least once a month, and canonizations and beatifications are held periodically. There are expositions of Catholic world activity, the work of Catholic charities, sacred art, sacred music and native missionary art. On Christmas Eve of the following year the Pope ends the jubilee by laying the first bricks on the threshold of the Holy Door of St. Peter's. The cardinals follow suit at the other three basilicas. Then the doors are completely sealed with mortar and remain that way until the Christmas Eve ceremony of the next Holy Year which follows.

Although it is known that special indulgences were granted to the Crusaders, the first official Holy Year took place in 1300. Romans living then seemed to recall having heard about pilgrims coming to Rome to receive special pardons a hundred years before, but there is no written substantiation of such an event in history. During the Holy Year of 1450 one chronicler wrote "There was so great a concourse in Rome that no one could remember having seen a greater. From wherever you looked you could see the crowd, and there were more people who did not see the Pope than those who did. The jam of people going back and forth to St. Peter's by way of the Sant'Angelo Bridge never thinned until three in the morning. People slept on porches, in the streets, many families became separated in the crush and so they went about lost, calling one another, a thing that was a pity to see." Overtaxed by the tremendous weight of the unprecedented crowds, the Bridge of Sant'Angelo gave way, collapsing into the river, and killing one hundred and seventy-two people. In 1575, without benefit of railroad, motor car, or airplane (and in spite of a plague raging elsewhere in Italy) there were 300,000 foreigners in Rome for the opening day ceremony of the Holy Doors.

Originally, Holy Years were held every one hundred years, but it was soon decided to cut the interval to fifty years so that each man in his lifetime would have an opportunity to gain the jubilee indulgence. Later the period was reduced to thirty-three years, the time Christ spent on earth, and finally to the present interval of twenty-five years.

The Holy Year of 1950, the first jubilee year when pilgrims could come to Rome on transoceanic aircraft, added a new note to the ancient fourteenth century words of Maestro Bonsiuto:

All ye from near and far, and ye whom the
sea divides from our shores, tear masts from
the woods, unfurl your sails, and ply your
oars so that you may come and touch the
Holy Doors of Rome.

Although Rome once had a thousand churches, it is still, with
several hundred places of worship, probably the greatest "city
of churches" in the world. The three most important after St.
Peter's are the basilicas of St. Mary Maggiore, near the railroad
station; St. John Lateran, about ten blocks south of it along the
Via Merulana; and St. Paul without-the-walls, on the south end
of town, near the Tiber, along the road to the seashore at Ostia.

The Church of St. John Lateran, of which the Pope himself
is archbishop, is considered the cathedral of Rome and the mother
church of the world. The first church on the site was built by
Constantine who had given the Lateran Palace, next door to the
Popes for use as an official residence. The Popes used both the
church and the palace until the seat of the papacy was moved
to Avignon in 1305. What an earthquake didn't destroy of the
church in 1347, the Barbarians who invaded Rome the next year,
finished. When the Popes returned to the city the church was
rebuilt and dedicated to St. John the Baptist and St. John the
Evangelist. It now contains the skulls of both St. Peter and St.
Paul brought to the original church by Constantine, and the table
on which the Last Supper is believed to have been served. The
four bronze columns around the altar come from the Temple of
Jupiter and date from the fifth century B.C. The doors of St.
John's are Rome's oldest. They were taken from the Roman senate and are believed to date from 300 B.C.

Most any time during a pleasant day the square in front of
St. John Lateran is jammed with hundreds of mothers and children. Across the square in the Church of San Salvadore is the

famous Scala Santa—the Holy Stairs, twenty-eight steps of marble which can only be mounted on one's knees. For such an ascent Catholics may gain a thousand-year indulgence. Originally brought to Rome by Constantine's mother, they are said to have been used by Christ. During the reign of Pope Clement XII in the eighteenth century so many people were using the stairs, he had all the steps covered with planking. The wood has been worn out and replaced three times since.

St. Mary Major, largest church dedicated to the Virgin, was born of a fanciful legend. On the fourth of August, 352, the Virgin Mary is said to have appeared in a dream both to the Pope, and to a devout lay citizen of Rome, commanding them to build a church where snow would fall the next morning. A snowpile on the fifth of August is, to say the least, unseasonable in Rome, but find snow they did, and so the church was built on the spot. Among the most important relics of the basilica are five boards said to come from the original manger. The bones of St. Mark the Evangelist are in a sarcophagus here, and the church contains, among others, the tomb of the Borghese Pope, Paul V, and his predecessor, Clement VIII. One of the most celebrated treasures of the city is the painting of the Madonna and Child which hangs over the altar. Believed to have been painted by St. Luke, the picture was carried through the streets by St. Gregory in an effort to stop the plague of 590.

St. Paul without-the-walls was first built by Constantine over Paul's tomb. The church was rebuilt into a beautiful basilica in the fifth century. In 1823 it was completely destroyed by fire. The magnificent new basilica was rebuilt from funds that flowed in from all over the world. Six alabaster columns came from the Viceroy of Egypt, and the side altars of green malachite from the Czar of Russia. Among the relics of the church are the bones, with the exception of the head, of St. Paul. Among its decorations are the portraits of sixty-three Popes finished in mosaics. The cloisters, like the front of the basilica have been planted with great palm trees. In the monastery above the cloisters, where the Benedictine monks indeed make Benedictine, the brothers tried to hide Jews and high-ranking Italian officers sought by the Germans. Although the property of St. Paul's belongs to the Vatican, and is therefore extraterritorial, the Nazis forced an entrance and removed the refugees. The Pope registered a protest which the German forces refused to honor.

Even the most pious can tire of churches and Rome is a logical place for the ennui to set in. Probably, however, you will want to have a look at San Pietro in Vincoli, St. Peter in chains, which houses Michelangelo's masterpiece of scupture, "Moses." The church was originally built by the Empress Eudoxia in 442 to hold the chains which were used to bind St. Peter both in Jerusalem and while he was held captive in Rome. The church has been remodeled several times, but the chains have been preserved and are kept in the altar.

The "Moses" by Michaelangelo is part of a mausoleum dedicated to Pope Julius II. It was Julius' original idea to have Michelangelo create for him a magnificent memorial which would perpetuate his memory. Michelangelo drew up gigantic plans calling for some forty statues, and forthwith left for Carrara to choose the marble. When he got back several months later the Pope had changed his mind. Julius proved so fickle to his own ideas that he died before an agreement with Michelangelo was reached. The "Moses" and its companion figures of Leah and Rachel are by Michelangelo, the others having been finished by other artists. The remains of Julius, as a matter of fact, are not even inside the memorial, but repose instead, in a tomb in St. Peter's.

In case you were thinking about getting married in Rome,

the most fashionable place to do it is at the church called Santa Maria degli Angeli which Michelangelo adapted from the Baths of Diocletian. Built in 300, the Baths of Diocletian were the largest in all Rome, and it was the old *tepidarium* that has become the elegant church. Social Romans tie the wedding knot today where, sixteen centuries ago, gouty Romans worked out the kinks.

Under the current democracy in Italy, the great palaces for which Rome was noted have largely changed hands. The Quirinale Palace, once the royal residence, is now the home of the President of the republic. Palazzo Torlonia, where Mussolini lived, is now a museum. The American Embassy, next to the Excelsior, occupies the old Palazzo Margherita where lived Margherita, widow of the assassinated Umberto I.

ENVIRONS OF ROME

HADRIAN'S VILLA
many a bacchanalian beer bust

4. IN THE ENVIRONS OF ROME

Villa d'Este

No kin to the Como Hotel, the Villa d'Este, in nearby Tivoli, was once one of the most elegant villas of the elegant Renaissance. Built by Cardinal Ippolito d'Este, the son of Lucrezia Borgia in 1550, it was once a Benedictine monastery, and before the First World War passed into the ownership of the Crown Prince of Austria who was killed at Sarajevo. It served as a home for a short while for Franz Liszt and before the Second World War it was a music school for American girls. The rooms of the villa have slipped into disrepair, but the feature of the grounds in the old days were its 2,000 fountains all gravity powered, which were landscaped and terraced in the park below. The gardens were bombed by mistake during the Second World War, bursting pipes and turning the park into a lake. The lake has since been drained, some of the landscaping restored, and at least 600 fountains are again spouting water at the rate of 250 gallons every second. The travel agencies conduct organized tours.

❧ *Villa Adriana*

The Emperor Hadrian built not a villa, but a royal retreat, a small city where he and an army of friends could rest or revel. There were facilities for both. Every building which struck Hadrian's fancy in his travels about the world was reproduced at his Tivoli residence. He had built, for example, an open-air Greek theater with a double tunnel where spectators could take refuge in case of a shower. There are ruins of a Latin theater which was covered, a hall of bedrooms in which the mosaic floors are still visible, and a walled walk so constructed that strollers could choose to walk in the sun or the shade depending upon the season. When the emperor wanted to be alone he retired to his private den, a one-story house surrounded by a moat. Well, it's a system G. Garbo might like to look into. The ruins, which are in remarkably good condition, set in a park of lovely trees, seem to suggest that Hadrian was a fast man with a bacchanalian beer bust. The most recent excavations were made fifteen years ago by the American Academy in Rome.

Most organized tours cover Villa d'Este and Hadrian's Villa in one day, stopping for lunch in Tivoli. The town was a resort of the wealthy Romans of the early days many of whom built summer villas and temples there. Two temples, Vesta and Sybil, remain. There is legend, too, that the origins of Tivoli predate the foundation of Rome by some four hundred years. There is a stop to see the cascades of Tivoli, which, though reduced by the demands of nearby industry, are still worth a look.

❧ *Sulphur Baths*

En route between Rome and Tivoli are the Acque Albule,

a source of natural sulphur water. You really won't have to *look* for the baths inasmuch as they smell to high heaven. If you can stand the quaint scent you'll probably come out of the baths feeling better than when you went in. There are several pools of sulphur water, even a sulphur waterfall. Mud packs, massages and such forms of primitive torture are available on the premises.

❧ *Ostia*

Should you hear the call of the surf while in Rome, it is twelve miles along an excellent highway to Ostia, the Lido di Roma. There is a good beach facing on the Tyrrhenian Sea. A number of public beach clubs serve lunch and rent bathhouses. They are more adequate than elegant, catering to Italian families of moderate means rather than tourists.

❧ *The Country Club*

Rome's country club probably is the only golf course in the world that uses old Roman ruins as hazards. A nine-hole course is in use, and the second nine is in the making. There is an excellent open-air swimming pool, and lunch is served in summer on the outdoor terrace. The members are mostly Italians and Americans from the large colony that has taken up residence in Rome since the war. You can probably get guest privileges through your hotel or the embassy. Nonmembers, incidentally, are restricted from taking photographs. Some say it is because the whole place was built by Count Ciano as a comfortable coruer from which to run Italy's foreign affairs. Others insist the ruling derives from the incident of a strange guest who appeared one

ANZIO'S HARBOR
it's such a short, pleasant ride

day and had himself photographed in dozens of poses all over
the club. All he wanted, it was revealed later, was to be shown
in good company. Turned out the guy was Lucky Luciano.

🌿 *Anzio*

It's such a short, pleasant ride from Rome down to Anzio,
it seems hardly possible that the American forces on the beach
took five miserable months to slug their way out. Anzio was just
a plain middle-class Italian seaside resort on January 22, 1944
when the United States VI Corps landed there, behind the German lines. The idea was to disrupt communications in the rear of

the German troops holding up the Cassino front. In the landing force was the United States 3rd Division, a British Infantry division, and American Ranger and Parachute units. The Germans got the idea in a hurry. Before January was out the Allied units were contained in a band of infantry and steel which included the Hermann Goering Panzer Division. From the surrounding hills the German artillery whacked away all winter at the beachhead positions and the ships that came in to reinforce them. The spring came and the Allies were still contained, but on May 23, the VI Corps, reinforced now by the 34th and 45th Infantry Divisions, the 1st Armored Division, the 100th Infantry Battalion composed of Americans of Japanese descent, and an additional British division broke out of the beachhead, joined troops coming up from the south, and headed for Rome which fell on June 4, two days before the Normandy invasion

Anzio is back in business now being a middle-class Italian seaside resort. When the residents who had been evacuated by the Germans came back to town, they found it a wreck. They still don't quite know whether to blame the Americans or the Germans. Most everything has been cleaned up now, and everyone agrees the place looks better than it did before the war. You can get a good seafood lunch at the open-air restaurants that line the port, and you can hire a boat for a lazy sail around the bay. There aren't any memorials in evidence, or any guided tours of the battlefields. One wall in town still bears the painted sign *Off Limits by order of the Port Commander*. There is a new hotel, too, remodeled from a villa, and named Hotel Clark, after Mark.

Walking through the forests of umbrella pines at Santa Anastasio you can see the outlines of foxholes and artillery emplacements all covered with a quilt of brown pine needles, bedded down for posterity. There are a few shell containers around, and bits of tin ration cans. On one the letters are still clear. "Army

Anzio's Beach
out on the sands it's deathly quiet

Field Ration C," it says, "B unit—Biscuit, Confection, and Beverage." Out on the sands it's deathly quiet. There isn't even any wreckage. And the only memorial is a post with a strand of rusted barbed wire. That, and the sea, the sand, and the dark forest of umbrella pines beyond.

Nettuno

From Rome you take a train to Anzio and hop the local bus to Nettuno. It runs every twenty minutes. There is also regular bus service from Rome to Nettuno with a stop at Anzio. Take your choice.

AMERICANS AT NETTUNO
"Mister, they're all famous"

Nettuno holds the results of Anzio, the last resting place of the brave. It is the site of one of the two American military cemeteries left in Italy. The other is in Florence. The Nettuno cemetery opened one day after the invasion started, and it has since taken in the dead from twenty-three other smaller cemeteries. It will be a permanent installation with a chapel and a war museum. The 7,831 crosses and Stars of David have to be repainted at the rate of 350 a day, but marble memorials have been ordered and are being made at Merano.

There is a book which visitors may sign, and one Anzio veteran who returned wrote, "Glad to be visiting instead of being visited."

American civilian personnel operate the cemetery aided by white-gloved Italian attendants. "Anybody famous buried here?" somebody once asked the American in charge. "Mister," he answered, "as far as I'm concerned they're all famous."

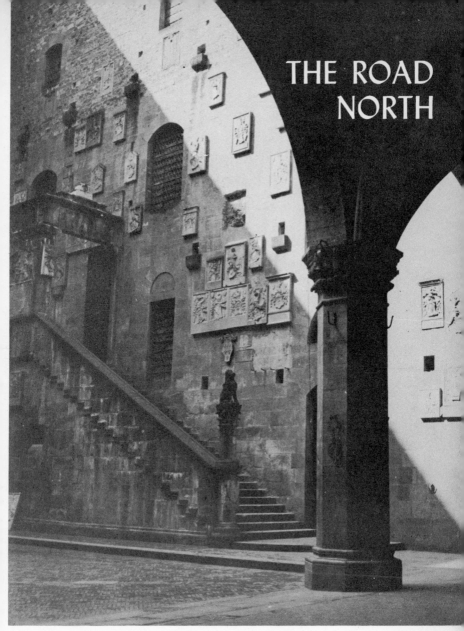

THE ROAD
NORTH

...is the road to culture

5. THE ROAD NORTH

ASSISI — SIENA — FLORENCE
PISA — BOLOGNA — SAN MARINO

The road north from Rome is the road through the Umbrian hill towns, through Tuscany, through miles of countryside covered with olive trees glinting silver-gray in the sun, and dwarfed elms that support the vines of grapes strung between them. As the road winds north along the narrow peninsula that is Italy it can veer left toward Genoa and France, or right toward Venice and Yugoslavia. In either case it will seek the sea, finding the Mediterranean on the left and the Adriatic on the right.

You can cover the road in your own car, by train, or most practically, by CIAT buses. Should you enter Italy from the north, it is quite simple to cover the same sights working toward the toe. From Rome, CIAT's Pink Ribbon Tour heads for Florence through Siena, and returns from Florence to the capital via Perugia and Assisi. The Blue Ribbon Tour reverses, coming southbound by way of Siena and northbound by way of Assisi and Perugia. Both tours operate between April and October. During the rest of the year the Silver Ribbon Tour runs over the same route, daily in both directions.

The northbound run by way of Assisi, which leaves Rome about 8:30, stops in the ancient town for lunch and a visit. The most famous citizen of Assisi was St. Francis, founder of the Franciscan order, in whose memory an elaborate church was built. Born in 1182, son of a wealthy Assisian merchant, Francis became a gay young blade about town, a dissolute, twelfth century playboy known for his sharp talk and rakish dress. During a battle between nearby Perugia and Assisi, nineteen-year-old Francis was captured and imprisoned. When he was finally released by the Perugians some months later and returned to Assisi he developed a critical illness. Recovering, Francis forsook the flamboyant ways of his former life, and turned to God. In 1210 he organized the Franciscan Order of Mendicant Friars whose tenets were self-denial and poverty. Francis gained many followers, and as Capuchins, Minorites, and other names his order developed adherents all over the continent. Visions of the Virgin and of Christ are said to have appeared to Francis while he prayed. Once in 1224 he underwent the stigmata, which according to Roman Catholic belief are wounds supernaturally inflicted upon mortals in the form and shape of the wounds inflicted on Christ when he was crucified.

Two years later, on October 4, 1226, at the age of forty-five, Francis died. Two years after that he was made a saint. Meanwhile, Brother Elias, Vicar of the Franciscan Order undertook the building of a church to commemorate his memory. As a mark of especial humility St. Francis had asked to be buried on Assisi's Infernal Hill, where criminals were always executed. He had chosen the place because it was considered the least desirable location in town. It was decided to build the church there, and by order of the Pope, the name was changed to Hill of Paradise.

ASSISI
Francis forsook his flamboyant ways

Money flowed in from all over the world, and many men of the region who had known the saint, came to work on his church without pay. The Lower Church was finished in two months short of two years, a record for those days. To protect the body from those who might steal parts of it as relics, Brother Elias secreted it in a vault. After a continual search through the years by ecclesiastical geologists, it was finally discovered in 1818.

LUNCHEON AT THE SUBASIO
beyond, the flat Umbrian plain

From the place where the bus stops in Assisi it is a long walk up the Hill of Paradise to the churches of St. Francis on top. The Lower Church is cryptlike, heavily decorated on the walls and ceilings with frescoes, mostly by Giotto. The original resting place for Francis's bones, carved out of solid rock, can be seen by descending two flights. The Upper Church was completed nine years later, in 1239. It is pure Gothic, its ceiling and walls covered with Frescoes, mosaics, and stained glass windows which have been installed again since the war. The floors are inlaid marble.

Brothers from the monastery on the grounds act as guides for the tourists. One who speaks English is Brother Angelo Cal-

miere who looks eighteen, is actually thirty-one. He was formerly
the bartender of the Officer's Club at Foggia where he spent the
war setting up drinks for the American 304th Bombardment
Wing. That's where he learned English.

Since your luncheon trade is big business in Assisi you will
doubtless be plagued during your visit by solicitors from each of
the town's restaurants. The best bet is the Hotel Subasio, near
the top of the hill, which serves a table d'hote luncheon for 800
lire on gingham-covered tables set on a vine-covered terrace looking out on miles of flat, grape-covered Umbrian plains. The shops
along the main street have a fair selection of needlework blouses
and pottery locally made.

From Assisi it's fifteen miles to Perugia, an old Etruscan
town on the highway to Florence. Perugia has two ambassadors,
Perugian Chocolate, the Hershey of Italy; and the artist Pietro
Vannucci, nicknamed Perugino, who was Raphael's employer and
teacher. Founder of the Perugian School, Perugino has left to his
adopted city some of his greatest works many of which are in
the Collegio del Cambio.

The Italian University for Foreigners in Perugia offers
courses from April through December in Italian literature, history of art, Italian geography, Italian history and Italian thought
through the centuries. There is also a special biennial course on
Etruscology, which I take to be a study of the ways of old Etruria,
an ancient land whose geographical confines were largely those
of the present day province of Tuscany. Anyway, there are concerts and excursions all through the year, and students are en-
titled to free entrance to all the picture galleries, museums and
monuments. Some 13,000 students have matriculated at the university since it opened in 1928, the largest numbers having come
from Germany, Italy (Italians resident abroad), Switzerland and
the United States, in that order. Some sixty-eight countries have

SIENA'S PIAZZA DEL CAMPO
a brawl on horseback

been represented through the years including sixteen men and
women without any country to claim at all.

One of the loveliest towns in all Italy is Siena, on the main
Rome-Florence highway to the east. On CIAT buses it's a southbound stop on the Blue Ribbon Tour, and a northbound stop
on the Pink Ribbon Tour. No other town seems to have retained
its medieval atmosphere as successfully as Siena with its narrow
alleys, its colonnaded windows, old palazzos, with rooftop battlements, and wrought-iron decorations on the doorways. Siena is
built on three hills and as you puff up the crowded streets past
the Gothic, stone-faced buildings that forbid passage to broad
buses and even hem in pedestrians, you will burst suddenly onto

the Piazza del Campo, the city square. An immense area it is, inlaid with brick pavement and faced almost all around with curving buildings, mostly Gothic in character. Forbidden to traffic, the fan-shaped square slopes downward toward a great bell tower known as the Torre del Mangia, part of the Palazzo Pubblico. The palazzo was begun in 1289, and the bell tower, 334 feet high, was added in 1338. A plague which is said to have taken some 30,000 lives in 1348 put a general damper on things in Siena, and the chapel at the base of the bell tower commemorates the ultimate deliverance of the city from the epidemic.

In the thirteenth century, even before the awakening of Florence, not far up the road, a distinctive Sienese school of painting developed. During the two centuries in which it flourished before spluttering to virtual extinction, the Sienese School produced Guido da Siena, Duccio Buoninsegna, Simone Martini, the two Lorenzettis—Pietro and Ambrogio, and Il Sodoma (real name: Giovanni Bazzi), a Lombardese who came to Siena under patronage. Many of their works are on the walls of the Palazzo Pubblico.

Siena is at its medieval best, however, for The Palio, the traditional horse race in the square which takes place every July 2 and August 16. Siena's horse race resembles nothing that ever happened at Churchill Downs or Belmont Park, being more akin to a Pier Six brawl on horseback. It began, innocently enough, back in the thirteenth century when the magistrates of the city decided that the popular sports of Elmora, which involved stone-throwing, and Gioco delle Pugna, which called for jousting with blunted instruments, were too rough for growing young gentlemen. A type of football called Giuco delle Pugna, in which the ball was put into play in the piazza by throwing it from the bell tower, came into vogue. Eventually it was suppressed, too, and the citizens turned to bullfights.

Siena was divided at the time into a number of wards, called contrade, and in all sports the contrade competed against each other for the city title. Each contrada entered a bull in the competition and marched it into the piazza on bullfight days, accompanied by floats built in the shape of animals. Aside from being decorative the floats provided protection for the bullfighters if the bulls got too rambunctious. The bullfights were finally prohibited in favor of buffalo races, but the animal-shaped floats which the entrants used became lasting nicknames for the various contrade. In 1650 the buffaloes were replaced by horses, but the various wards were already well-known by such names as Eagle, Snail, Panther, Owl, Unicorn, He-goat, Porcupine, and many others. The names have stuck right up to the present day.

Horses competing in the Palio may resemble the brewery wagon species more than Seabiscuit, heft being considerably more worthy an attribute in this competition than grace. Ten such animals are chosen in time trials and are awarded by lot to the contrade chosen to compete. A sand track is laid out around the great piazza, and wooden benches are set up in front of all the buildings. Although it is considered bad taste to bet on the outcome because the race has religious overtones, it is standard practice to bribe a jockey, or push, kick, run down, head off, or otherwise tactfully impede the progress of the opposition.

The afternoon of the race each contrada escorts its horse and jockey to its own chapel where both are blessed with holy water. The horse is marched right inside the church, and should he forget himself therein, that is an omen of good luck. In the square, most everyone is dressed in medieval costume. During the procession the famous flag-wavers of Siena twirl their standards like bandleaders at college football games, throwing them thirty feet in the air, and, most of the time, catching them.

The explosion of a firecracker, a most fitting symbol, signals the start of the race, a grueling, thundering affair with at least one curve, called the San Marino corner, where all but the expert stand an odds-on chance of coming a cropper. So many entries have whizzed right off the tanbark and out of the square at at San Marino corner, that in Siena a man who has *gone to San Marino*, is a man who has lost his way. It is a rare Palio indeed, in which horses do not break legs, and riders are not thrown. The technical fact that a horse crosses the finish line without a rider, however, in no way disqualifies the entry from victory. The excitement does not die at the end of the race, it begins. The winning contrada gets a flag for its efforts, reason enough to celebrate far, far into the night.

Siena's highest ground is crowned with its fourteenth century cathedral, an ornate affair, both Romanesque and Gothic. The campanile, and the columns inside are zebra stripes in alternate bands of black and white marble, the colors of Siena. Atop the arches runs a continuous line of terra-cotta busts of the Popes. Some seventy pictures portrayed with inlaid marble makes its floor probably the most famous in Italy. The duomo also contains a famous pulpit carved out of marble by the Pisanos, father and son, in 1268. The stairway was added in 1543.

By the early fourteenth century the Sienese began to feel that their cathedral was too small for the likes of Siena, and even though the first church was not yet completed, work was begun on a larger one. The plague of 1348 depopulated Siena, and the plan was given up. The unfinished grand nave still stands near the old cathedral, after 600 years still abandoned, and all but forgotten.

The School for Foreign Students of the University of Siena offers three summer courses beginning the first of July and finishing at the end of September. A Language and Literature Course is designed for those with elementary knowledge of

Italian which they wish to improve. An advanced Language and Literature course is designed for those with a good knowledge of Italian who wish to make a deeper study of Italian culture. There is also a course of lectures on the History of Italian Civilization which is given in English. The university runs a hotel, and there are planned excursions in the Tuscan vicinity.

For three hundred years of the Renaissance, Florence, a city astride the Arno about the same size as greater Toledo or Denver, or Springfield, Massachusetts, was the wellspring of art, architecture, literature and science. From the thirteenth through the sixteenth centuries, while Florence was variously a republic, a virtual empire under the Medicis, and finally a duchy, the city produced Dante, Petrarch, Giotto, Boccaccio, Cellini, Leonardo da Vinci, and the incomparable Michelangelo. Poetry, paintings, sculpture and intellectuality sprang from its cultivated citizens like automobiles out of Detroit.

Now, three hundred years after the decline of the period, Florence, indoors and out, is undoubtedly the greatest museum in the world. But even aside from the gift of art passed down from the Renaissance Florentines, the modern city has inherited the craftsmanship of the artisan. It is world famed for leather goods, silver, ceramics, linens and laces, and high-fashion shoes, all hand-worked with exquisite precision, imaginative artistry and patience. As a culture center and a shopping center, Florence is an all-year-around attraction for tourists, students, scholars and buyers. While it draws the art student who seeks to probe the works of Giotto as a pioneer realist who first departed from the stilted style of the Byzantines, Florence also rents permanent space to Gimbels and Macy's who maintain permanent purchasing commissions there. Florence in the spring of 1847 attracted the newlyweds, Robert and Elizabeth Barrett Browning, who were escaping the London weather and Mrs. Browning's autocratic

FLORENCE

. . . the greatest museum in the world

father. They took an apartment in the Casa Guidi near the Pitti Palace, where they lived and wrote for fifteen years. Although the Uffizi Galleries in Florence, probably the most complete in the world, echo the cultured appreciative murmurs of art connoisseurs from all corners of the globe, the city's hundreds of shops simultaneously resound with the conversation of the bargaining tourists who come to Florence because it is the best shopping city in Italy.

One hundred and eighty-five miles north of Rome, Florence is four hours from the capital by fast train, or a full day by the sightseeing tourist buses either via Siena or Perugia and Assisi. The city has a fair selection of hotels, outstanding among which is the Excelsior, one of the finest hotels in the country. It overlooks the Arno on the Piazza Ognissanti, a small quiet square away from the downtown district. Neat, compact, and expertly run by a staff of multilingual employees, the Excelsior's cuisine is particularly noteworthy. With the lire averaging 675 to the dollar it was charging 1,200 lire for lunch and 1,200 lire for dinner for meals that would cost twice that in New York. Rooms with bath and balcony with view of the Arno cost 2,500 lire single, 4,500 lire double. Facing the Excelsior across the square is the Grand. Both hotels are under Swiss management, run by the sons of Geraldo Kraft who started in the hotel business in Florence in 1892. Spotless as a clean sheet, both hotels are run in typical precise Swiss fashion. Although both are officially classified as de luxe, the Grand is somewhat less expensive than the Excelsior. Also de luxe is the Savoy, on the bustling Piazza della Repubblica. There are four first-class establishments from which to choose, the Anglo-American, Baglioni, Minerva and Roma. If you are ladling out your lire with care you can get by in the second-class Croce di Malta — the Maltese Cross — for about a dollar a night.

The Baglioni is perhaps best known for its Terrazza Giardino, or Roof Garden, a pleasant, romantic place which, except for the lack of man-made skyline, could just as well be in Brooklyn Heights. There is drinking and dancing until two a.m., no cover, no minimum and no entertainment tax. The management manages to pay for the music by a rather novel method whereby you pay an additional fee for what is known as the "first consumption." Successive consumptions are billed at the ordinary price. If you are drinking *whisky Americani,* as an example, the first shot will set you back 750 lire, subsequent slugs, 500 lire. Having the first drink at home will fail to shake the Baglioni's steadfast policy.

The Florentine kitchen is built on a foundation of Tuscan olive oil, supported by rich, heavy Chianti wines. The oil flows like a Texas gusher. Chianti is the local wine, and the reds are as virile as Burgundy. Meats *alla Fiorentina,* are just plain grilled, without benefit of spices. In any case so you won't go foodless in Florence, here are some typical local suggestions: *Bistecca all Fiorentina,* a plain, grilled porterhouse steak. *Fagioli all'Uccelletto,* small white beans stewed in tomato sauce and sage. *Trippa all Fiorentina,* tripe stewed in tomato sauce and dusted with grated cheese. *Pollo di Valdarno Fritto,* chopped chicken dipped in the yolk of an egg and boiled in oil. *Cieche all Pisana,* tiny eels cooked in olive oil with garlic, sage, and pepper to liven things up, and topped, natch, with grated cheese.

Of Florence's restaurants, eating at the subterranean Buca Lapi, Via del Trebbio No. 1, will probably be the nicest thing that ever happened to you in a cellar. Open since 1880, and purportedly the first of the Florentine cellars, Buca Lapi has covered its otherwise murky depths with hundreds of colorful travel posters. Big, thick, charcoal-broiled steaks are the specialty and Buca Lapi is about the only place that serves them east of

Danny's Hideaway, the Press Box or Gallaghers in Manhattan's steak belt (and at half the New York price).

Buca di San Rufillo, which presumably is not the original *buca* of Florence, is a good one all the same. In summer, tables, waiters and customers come up for air to an enclosed Florentine greenery upstairs, decorated with leaves and bamboo. Some heavy-footed music is on hand, and occasionally the violins stroll over to the tables for some point-blank serenading. Piazza dell' Olio No. 7 is the address, near the cathedral.

For those days when you *have* to have something American (and you will have them), visit Doney's on Via Tornabuoni No. 75, a blood relation of the Doney's in Rome. The Florentine Doney's advertises iced tea and iced coffee, and the "original G. Washington coffee." Dinner is as low as $1.50. Strictly small and Italian, on the other hand, is Da Zi'Rosa on Via dei Fossi No. 12. There are some 150 items on the menu, and no matter what you pick, you'll have a hard time eating two-dollars worth. Across the street from the cathedral you can eat from gingham tablecloths in the street at the Ristorante Sasso di Dante. According to a much-handled rumor, Dante (who died in 1321) used to sit there and ruminate. A bust of him reposes on one of the tables to make things authentic.

La Sostanza, on the Via della Porzellana, near the Excelsior, is tiny, but eminently Florentine. Try their *crostini,* bread with anchovies, olives and liver. Just as the war was ending La Sostanza's owner saw two children playing with a hand grenade they had found. He told them to throw it away, and they obeyed him to the letter. Only they didn't throw it far enough, and the grenade exploded killing both children and the man as well. The restaurant is being run now by his two sons. One serves, the other cooks, and the old mother fans the fire.

Also characteristically Florentine is the Grotta Guelfa, Via

Pellicceria No. 5. Go on Fridays when it is loaded to the rafters with jabbering merchants in town for market day.

Most every European city has an elegant teashop near the local American Express office. In Florence it is the Leland at Via Tuornaboni No. 15 around the corner from American Express at Lungarno Corsini No. 8.

After dinner there is always something doing in the Piazza della Repubblica. Tables are spread all over the square, and at places like Pazkowski's you can sit with the students, the tourists, and the townspeople, eat ice cream or sip a Negroni, and watch the continous entertainment that is boomed out to the open-air audience.

Should you only be in town between trains Florence has a half dozen "day hotels," unique establishments where you can bathe, change your clothes, and take a nap. The Firenze at Via Sassetti No. 5, and the Stazione S. Maria Novella at the station plaza, are two such places.

Although small shops dealing in all the artisan's goods which Florence produces are scattered all over the city, there are, by and large, two main shopping districts—Via Calzaioli which has less expensive merchandise, and Via Tornabuoni, the quality center where merchandise and prices are aimed at the tourists. Shops are open from 9:30 in the morning until 12.30, and again from 3:30 until 7:30.

For men's wear try Arfango at Arte della Lana, which carries Borsalino hats, collapsible umbrellas, doeskin sport shoes, and the usual haberdashery line. Ferrucci and E. Del Soldato Bardi at Tornabuoni No. 35 have fine men's silk ties and hand-blocked squares which can be worn as handkerchief or neckerchiefs. Bardi also has departments for ladies and children's wear. Bellini at Tornabuoni No. 9 is the headquarters of the Bellini chain which operates high-priced linen shops in Rome, Milan and Monte-

FERRAGAMO OF FLORENCE
with Garbo above ...

... and workmen below

catini. Blouses run as high as 29,000 lire, *mousseline* tablecloths with Florentine lace, up to 1,000,000 lire. For leathers, of which Florentine shops have a wide selection of cigarette boxes, wallets, desk pads, photo albums, compacts and hand-stitched goatskin handbags, you'll do well either at Francesco Bruscoli at Borgognissanti No. 97, or at Silvio Luti at Via Parione No. 28. *On parle English* at both places. Alinari Brothers is one of the best places for prints in Italy.

In searching for addresses in Florence, red numbers are for shops and black numbers are for private apartments. The numbers flow in the same direction as flows the Arno. All you have to do is go over to the shore and see which way the river is flowing.

One of Florence's most successful artisans is Ferragamo, who designs and manufactures one of the most artistic, imaginative, and successful shoe collections in Italy. Ferragamo sells to Saks Fifth Avenue, Lord and Taylor, Nieman Marcus, Woodward and Lathrop, and Adrian in Beverly Hills, among many others. He has several retail stores scattered throughout Italy, but his flossy customers like the Duchess of Windsor and Garbo, who may buy twenty pairs at a time, always consult the master himself at his Florence headquarters.

Ferragamo, a sturdy, youngish Italian, with a formidable shock of hair, learned his trade from an old cobbler in Bonito, near Naples. After an apprentice period Ferragamo opened his own shop. It was small, he recalls, but he was only thirteen at the time. Two years later he shut up shop and went to America, where he soon discovered that machine-made shoes didn't agree with his temperament. He wandered out to California, where in the course of a visit to a film studio, his eye caught an assortment of cowboy boots which decorated the feet of some of the itinerant hoss opera extras. Ferragamo was shortly in Santa Barbara making cowboy boots for Westerns. Graduating to the luxury trade, he moved to Hollywood where for a time he occupied himself turning out custom-made shoes for the stars. Thirteen years after he had left, Ferragamo returned to Italy and started his own factory. When his first eighteen samples were finished he took them to America, wrote orders, and then whisked back home again to start work. To insure himself a supply of labor skilled in his own methods he opened a shoemaking school for young boys.

In spite of the inroads made by machinery in all industries, there is not one machine in Ferragamo's factory. "We don't even have a perforating machine," he says proudly in excellent English, "every shoe is caressed by hand from beginning to end." In Florence, Ferragamo works in the Florentine tradition.

If you want to entrust yourself to the merchants of the open market you might pick up a bargain or get a fleecing at the Mercato Nuovo, the "new" market which was built in the sixteenth century. Although it was once devoted exclusively to the sale of quaint articles of straw it now offers leather souvenirs, and such items of the advanced scientific world as Pond's cold cream, and Conti's shampoo. In the center of the market is a slab of marble known as the Scandal Stone. Merchants whom the public considered unfair were stripped of their trousers and bounced, *derrière* down, on the marble. Nowadays when a man assumes an unabashed air he is referred to as one who has had his rear-end bounced on the scandal stone. The Mercato Nuovo is also decorated with a bronze statue of a wild boar done by Tacca, which is a copy of the Greek or Roman original which reposes in the Uffizi Gallery. Here Florentine women used to fill their water jugs and stop to hatch a little gossip about such popular feminine subjects of the day as men, money and the Medicis. The boar has a shiny nose because the legend has been spread (pre-

THE PONTE VECCHIO
no oversight

sumably by the local chamber of commerce) that if you rub it before you leave you will return to Florence some day.

The greatest concentration of jewelry stores is located over the Arno River—on the ancient Ponte Vecchio. Built in the fourteenth century, the bridge not only carries regular traffic, it also supports the shops which hang over the water on both sides, and a top-story corridor which once connected the Uffizi and Pitti galleries. Of Florence's six former bridges the Ponte Vecchio was the oldest. It was the only one left standing by the Germans when they retreated from Florence after a two-week battle in the summer of 1944. No oversight, the Ponte Vecchio stands as a memorial to one of the few sentimental moments in the history

RUINED RUINS
Florence was a two-week battle

of the German at war. To make the bridge unusable by the pur-
suing Allies, Nazi forces blew up whole city blocks on both sides
of the span. The net result of the maneuver was that American
bulldozers quickly cleared the debris around the entrance to the
bridge, and Allied forces were shortly pouring across it in full
pursuit. The people of Florence weren't very happy either because several ancient buildings had been demolished to block the
bridge, and a number of people in town weren't altogether sure
that the Ponte Vecchio was the most important bridge to save
anyhow. Most Florentines considered the Ponte Santa Trinita the
most beautiful, and they intend to rebuild it. They have all the
pieces except the head of one statue.

THE ROAD NORTH

To get around in Florence you have your choice of taxi or horse carriage. Should you be stout of limb and thick of sole you might have a happier time making your way on foot since the regulations for paying cabs in Florence is the most complicated public declamation since Einstein's autobiography. What is more, Florentine carriage drivers have a habit of beating their horses, a practice to which American tourists object strongly. Anyway, an official bulletin of the local tourist bureau has this to say about taxis:

> *The second tariff of the taximeter will operate both during daytime and night within the boundaries of the Florence municipal area. The driver is entitled to receive FIVE times the amount indicated on the taxi meter, plus a fixed charge of 150 lire, whatever the length of the drive.*

The capitals and the bold face type is theirs, not mine, but it shows they must have been just as startled as I was. I shall not bore you by going through the entire document, but just for the hell of it you might like to know that you will incur extra charges when: there are more than three passengers; it is nighttime; the cab returns empty from the Piazzale Michelangelo, Cascine Park, or the city boundaries; it returns empty on race day afternoons from the race track or the trotting track; or if it returns empty on football afternoons from Communal Stadium. Furthermore, you will rack up an extra tariff if your suitcase is larger than one foot by one foot, eight inches, or if you have in custody either a trunk or large box (measurements unspecified).

About the same schedule of extra fares is applicable on horse carriage trips excepting the question of sending back an empty carriage. The penalty for this infraction is seventy-five lire from the town tollgate on a flat road, or one hundred lire on uphill roads. Now then, if the carriage rides back to town for a distance of 300 meters on one of ten roads, the names of which I shan't bother to list, or on the adjacent lanes of those roads, the charge is one hundred lire. How a passenger dropped at the race track on race day afternoons, or at the town tollgate (on a day when he has perhaps been run out of town) is supposed to determine whether the cab or carriage goes back empty is not explained in the directive. There is no extra charge for having a sick aunt in Cheyenne, a six-room apartment in San Francisco, or for letting your membership in the Buffalo chapter of the B.P.O.E. lapse for thirty days.

Some thirty-five guides are licensed by the city, and charge 2,000 lire a day to escort a party of four, 160 lira for each additional person. The charge for half a day is 1,400 lire, 120 lire extra for each person over four. There are public motorcoach tours of the city by travel bureaus every day. American Express covers the whole city in a day, visiting the Medici chapels, the cathedral, Giotto's Tower, the Basilica of San Lorenzo, the Piazza della Signoria, Piazza Vecchio and the Uffizi Gallery in the morning, and the Pitti Palace, the Piazzale Michelangelo, Church of Santa Croce, and out to suburban Fiesole in the afternoon.

Florence is as full of art as Rome is full of ruins. There is enough architecture, sculpture, oils, frescoes, and bric-a-brac, charted and uncharted, to keep an avid art addict goggle-eyed for months. Since the average tourist will be more footsore in the art galleries than footloose in Florence after two days this book will become no catalogue of the Tuscan treasures. Florentine guides have a habit of adopting a more-cultured-than-thou attitude especially when it comes to machine-made Americans. This will review the likelier sightseeing prospects, but if you cover

PALAZZO VECCHIO
a rather startling sight at first

them all or if you follow your guide blindly and obediently, you are a likely prospect for gallery-gout, Byzantine-back, or jaded eyeballs, three common tourist ills.

The most important square in the city is the Piazza della Signoria, in effect, an outdoor museum. Many of Florence's most important statues, most of them naked and unadorned, are right out on the pavement, a rather startling sight at first. The dominating building of the square is the Palazzo Vecchio, surrounded by battlements, and topped by a tower. It was built, during uncertain times, in 1298. Used first as a hall for public debate, and as an official residence for the Signori, a title given to the presiding head of the Florentine state, it later sheltered some of the ruling Medicis. When Italy was first united and Florence was capital, the palazzo was a government building. It is used today as a city hall, although some of the rooms remain a museum. The tower bell which still rings out over Florence was once a public annunciator which called the city officials to work, the public to assembly, or the men to arms, depending upon how it was rung. The piazza entrance of the Palazzo Vecchio is flanked (as you face it) by the immense statue of Michelangelo's "David" on the left, and "Hercules and Cacus" by Bandinelli on the right. The original "David," Michelangelo's first important piece of sculpture, finished when he was twenty-eight, is in the Academy of Fine Arts. The busy group off the left of the Palazzo Vecchio is the Fountain of Neptune by Ammanati, 1875. The semisheltered museum on the right of the door of the palazzo is known as the Loggi dei Lanzi. First built as a place where politicians and citizens could blow off steam during inclement weather, it now houses some important pieces of sculpture, among them—Cellini's famous "Perseus" in bronze which was unveiled on the spot in 1554, the "Rape of the Sabines," "Hercules Slaying Nessus" and others.

Now a pleasant piazza thronged with tourists, the Piazza della Signoria as the virtual forum of Florence, was the scene in other days of the most important events of the city's turbulent history. It saw the long struggle between the Guelphs who backed the papacy and the Ghibellines who supported an imperial government. Civil war flared throughout the thirteenth century. In the early fourteenth century, with Dante taking sides, the factions feuded again, this time under the names of the Bianchi *vs.* the Neri, the Blacks against the Whites. The Black, or church cause, which embraced the old ideas of the Guelphs drew the outside support of Charles of Valois and the Whites were overwhelmed and massacred. The few survivors, Dante among them, were exiled from the city.

In 1348, Florence underwent a second catastrophe. The Black Death swept the city taking 100,000 people, more than one-third of the entire population.

The next century Florence came under the rule of the Medici family which was to govern the state on and off during the next three hundred years. But in 1498, just after the Medici reign had begun, the Piazza della Signoria beheld a dramatic episode.

It started quietly enough in 1490 when a Dominican monk named Girolamo Savonarola became prior to the monastery of San Marco. With magnificent oratory Savonarola raged against the corruption of the papal elections, and the profligate ways of the citizenry. As more and more Florentines came under the almost hypnotizing effects of his speech, he moved to the cathedral itself where he held forth against both the Pope Alexander VI, the head of the Church, and Lorenzo de Medici, head of the state. The Pope excommunicated him, and soon he was incarcerated in the Palazzo Vecchio where he was tortured. In May of 1498, when he was forty-six he was hanged in the Piazza della Signoria, and his body burned publicly in a pyre. A bronze plaque in the Square marks the spot.

A considerably more happy event takes place in the Piazza della Signoria the first Sunday in May and again on June 24 when all Florence turns out for the celebrated football game, *calcio*. A parade of citizens done up in Renaissance costumes marches through the streets to the Square. The contestants, also dressed up, represent opposite sides of the Arno. Unlike American football, there seems to be not as much interest in the actual play of the game as there is in the spectacle before and afterward. In the evening after the *calcio* there is a large dinner for the players, and music and dancing all over town.

SANTA MARIA DEL FIORE
three-color cathedral

The Cathedral of Florence, the Santa Maria del Fiore, is the
third largest church in Europe, and probably the most colorful.
The exterior is designed in red, green and white marble, cut in
an ornate pattern of boxes, arches and triangles. The church was
begun in 1296 by Arnolfo. Giotto succeeded him in 1334, building the matching bell tower which stands alongside. Brunelleschi

added the dome, a work of fourteen years, and Santa Maria del Fiore, St. Mary of the Flower, was consecrated in 1436. Michelangelo copied Brunelleschi's dome for St. Peter's. The interior of the cathedral has two fifteenth century della Robbias, the "Resurrection" and the "Ascension," in terra-cotta relief, and Michelangelo's last and uncompleted work, the "Descent from the Cross." The artist was over eighty when he stopped work on it because he found a flaw in the marble. Over forty stained glass windows from the early fifteenth century representing the best collection in Florence, which were removed during the war, are being installed again.

The Baptistry, across the street from the cathedral, which dates from the eleventh century, is probably the oldest building in Florence. Every Catholic baby, including Dante, born in Florence is baptized within its still sturdy walls. But the Baptistry is most famous for its sculptured doors, the work of Lorenzo Ghiberti. They occupied Ghiberti for some twenty-eight years, and were finally completed in 1452. Michelangelo once said they were "worthy of Paradise," and ever since they have been known as "The Gates of Paradise," an attraction that draws tourists, oglers and street hawkers. The doors were removed during the war, thoroughly cleaned and polished, and discovered to be made not of bronze as had been supposed, but of gold.

The Church of San Lorenzo, which is near the Baptistry, dates from the fourth century, but it was rebuilt in the fifteenth century largely with the help of the famous Medicis. Worked on by Brunelleschi and Michelangelo, the church was virtually adopted by the Medicis. In great pageantry Lorenzo the Magnificent was married here, and in great sadness the body of Michelangelo lay in state in 1564. The Medici Chapel adjoining the church, begun as a Medici mausoleum in 1604, is one of the most fabulous interiors on the Continent. Its walls and floors are inlaid with granite from Egypt, green serpentine and jasper, and intricate mosaics, marble from Siena and Carrara and Corsica, even petrified wood and precious stones. The decorations to hallow the memory of the Medicis cost the family one millon pounds in gold before the dynasty died out in 1737. Every succeeding government, including conquering powers, have felt the necessity of adding to the unfinished elegance. The ceiling was painted during the Austrian occupation, and Napoleon once had plans to build a grand altar. The present Italian government has finished the floor, and plans eventually to replace the altar which is now a camouflaged wood model.

A passageway leads from the chapel to the new Sacristy, entirely designed by Michelangelo in 1520 for the tombs of the Medicis. Working for ten years, Michelangelo created two magnificent sculpture groups, one for the tomb of Giuliano, Duke of Nemours, who was the son of Lorenzo the Magnificent, and the other for Lorenzo, Duke of Urbino, who was the father of Catherine de Medici. Lorenzo the Magnificent, under whose reign the Florentine Renaissance flourished, lies in the Sacristy all but unmarked. The monument honoring him was planned by Michelangelo, but never begun.

Another church in Florence worth a visit is Santa Croce, on the opposite end of town, near the river. Because it contains the tombs of many great Italians, particularly Florentines, it has been called the Westminster Abbey of Italy. Buried here are Michelangelo, and Machiavelli whose life was a constant struggle with the Medicis. Galileo who rests here too, was born in nearby Pisa which fell under the domination of Florence. There is a cenotaph honoring Dante, but his remains are in Ravenna where he died in political exile. The church contains the celebrated pulpit by da Maiano which Ruskin called the "swallow's nest of Santa Croce" because it has no visible means of entrance. The stairs

THE GATES OF PARADISE
...are gold

are hidden inside a pillar. Among its other treasures is Donatello's "Annunciation," carved out of gray sandstone, one of the wonders of the Renaissance; frescoes by Giotto; and a late della Robbia, by Giovanni, the third of the della Robbias. One of the oldest churches of the Mendicants, (it was begun in 1294), Santa Croce nonetheless has the most modern organ in Italy. It was installed

in 1926 to commemorate the 700th anniversary of the death of
St. Francis.

Florence's two main art gallaries are the Uffizi, off the Piazza
della Signoria, and the Pitti Palace, on the opposite side of the
Arno, near the Ponte Vecchio. Uffizi means offices, a name which
was given to the building because it was built to house the government bureaus. The private collections of the Medicis formed
the nucleus of the art treasures which the Uffizi now holds. The
picture gallery has the most complete collection of the Florentine
School in the world. Among the contributors: Cimabue, Giotto,
Fra' Angelico, Filippo Lippi, Botticelli, Filippino Lippi, Ghirlan-
daio, Leonardo da Vinci, Fra' Bartholomeo, Andrea del Sarto and
Michelangelo. Among the work of the outlanders are paintings
by Perugino, Raphael, Corregio, and the two Venetians, Titian
and Giorgione. In the Tribuna, an octagonal room, there are five
original Greek statues brought to Florence in the sixteenth century. Most famous of the pieces is the "Medici Venus" recovered
from Hadrian's Villa, and "The Wrestlers," which dates from the
third century B.C. During the war a bomb dropped on the Uffizi.
The windows were closed and the concussion tore the whole
grotesque ceiling from its moorings and sent it crashing to the
floor. By the summer of 1948 the entire ceiling, piece by piece,
had been set back in place. The reconstruction was only possible
because years before a group of German researchers had photographed the design inch-by-inch in color. The Uffizi is open from
ten to four on weekdays, ten to one on Sundays.

Across the water the Pitti Palace, begun by Luca Pitti, a
wealthy Florentine banker in the fourteenth century, has been
receiving new twentieth century notoriety at the hands of Cole
Porter. During the long run of *Kiss Me Kate*, a tenor sings wist-
fully every night and twice on Wednesdays and Saturdays of Alice

of Firenze in her "pretty, itty, bitty, Pitti Palace." Luca and his family lost their fortune before the palace was completed, and it wasn't finished until the sixteenth century when the wife of Grand Duke Cosimo I bought it. It became the official residence of the grand dukes until the end of the Medicis. The Austrian archdukes lived there when they came to Florence, and later, when Italy was finally unified in 1865 and Florence became the capital, the Pitti was the official residence of the kings. When the capital was moved to Rome in 1871, the royal apartments of the Pitti were kept available for crown visits.

The most important part of the palace now is the gallery which has some of the best-known masterpieces of the world. All the pictures are hung in profusion, as they were displayed centuries ago, but the better-known works are hung to the left and the right of the doors so they may be easily seen. Among the masters represented are Raphael, Perugino, Andrea del Sarto, Fra' Bartholomeo, Giorgione, Bellini, Titian, Velàsquez, Rubens and Van Dyck. Among the eight Raphaels on display in one room are the "Madonna of the Grand Duke," so-called because Grand Duke Ferdinand III carried the painting with him wherever he traveled; and the "Madonna of the Chair," which Florentine art critics insist is probably the most famous painting in the world. The two Madonnas are estimated to be insured at between five and ten million dollars in gold each. In an adjoining room is the portrait of the Fornarina who did double-duty as Raphael's mistress and model. The "Sistine Madonna," for which she posed, is reported to have been taken from the Dresden Gallery by the Russians.

Random points of interest in the private royal apartments are the Throne Room where Victor Emmanuel II was crowned first king of Italy; the Banquet Hall, in which the last man to have lunch was Hitler; and the fragile Ballroom, hung with crystal chandeliers, used only recently as a recreational hall by American GI's.

The Boboli Gardens on the palace estate were used during court days as an amphitheater. From time to time some of the grounds are still used for out-door theatrics, a popular European endeavor.

The Pitti keeps the same hours as the Uffizi, ten to four weekdays, and ten to one on Sunday.

As an optional place to visit mark down the Bargello, formerly the Justice Palace, now the National Museum of Florence. It is famous for sculpture. Giambologna's "Winged Mercury," the symbol of a hundred messenger services in the United States is in the Bargello. It was originally used as a fountainhead in a Medici villa in Rome. The other works include Donatello's "St. George" in marble, his "David" in bronze, and his bust of Nicolo' da Uzzano in terra cotta. Architects and art students will also find interest in Florentine palaces such as the Palazzo Medici or Riccardi, the extravagant home of Lorenzo the Magnificent. One of its frescoes, the Journey of the Magi was once photographed by *Life* for a Christmas issue.

❧ In the Environs of Florence

FIESOLE. In Etruscan times, Fiesole was a thriving town, and Florence was its suburb. Fiesole once even overshadowed Rome. Nine hundred feet above sea level and twenty-five minutes from town on the bus, Fiesole is now little more than a place to go for dinner or for a view of Florence, and the valley of the Arno. It has a Roman theater discovered in 1809, and a number of villas most famous of which is the Villa Palmieri where Boccaccio is supposed to have done the research for his *Decameron,* and a medieval monastery built on the hill above town.

AMERICAN CEMETERY. A permanent American cemetery is located on Highway 2, the Via Cassia, six miles south of Florence near Scopeti. It contains the graves of more than 4,000 soldiers many of whom fell in the battle for Florence, and many others who have been moved from temporary cemeteries elsewhere in Italy.

The grounds are open from eight until noon, and from one until half-past four. SITA buses, which make the trip in about twenty minutes, stopping at the cemetery gate, have five trips daily from the Central Station and two from Maso Finiguerra. Street-car #37, from the Via dei Serragli in Florence runs out to Tavarnuzze, about two kilometers from the grounds. There are no suitable lodgings or restaurants in the vicinity, and visitors had better plan on using Florence as a base.

MONTECATINI. Thirty miles from both Florence and Pisa along the route of the Autostrada, the express highway, Montecatini is a spa after the old European fashion. It came into prominence after the social decline of Karlsbad, and now plays host every year to some 30,000 to 50,000 visitors, of every nationality. The season runs from April through the end of November, and the spa is particularly jammed with Italians during the warm month of August. Foreigners are advised to go in the spring and fall.

Montecatini's waters are loaded with sodium chlorate and chloro-sulphate-sodium, and they sure taste like it. In these days when a man is liable to be radioactive before he knows it, Montecatini can boast radioactive waters. Drink some and a Bikini goat has nothing on you. Anyway, Tamerici and Torretta, which are the names for the strong waters of the spa, are "gently purgative." Regina and Tettuccio, the medium waters, are a little

MONTECATINI
a Bikini goat has nothing on you

more medium. Rinfresco increases the urine. One way or another, that is, taken internally, or bathed in, or mixed with dirt and made into a mud pack, the waters of Montecatini are good for: gastric difficulties; liver ailments; such intestinal unpleasantries as diarrhea, constipation and colitis; such metabolism defects as diabetes, uricemia, and gout; not to mention obesity and dermatosis.

While you are partaking of the cure daily in the marble halls of Montecatini, you may also amuse yourself by taking in the night horse races, listening to the afternoon concerts while-you-sip-the-waters, or by playing tennis. Among the town's better restaurants are the Centrale, the Gran Bretagna and the Gastone.

Of its 257 hotels and pensions La Pace, which only recently was blessed with a sojourn of the Duke and Duchess of Windsor, is the best. Even so the rate will be less than ten dollars a day American plan. If you pronounce it as if the name were La Potcheese, everyone will know what you are talking about. Other first-class establishments are the Locanda Maggiore and the Bella Vista.

When the Allied armies had moved the line far enough north along the boot in 1944, Montecatini, lock, stock and baths, became a Fifth Army rest center. More than a million troops came through the town on leave. The hall where tourists get a fashionable mud bath today is the exact same place where the GI's dumped their battle-filthy clothes, took a bath, and received a whole new uniform. Besides creating one million ambassadors for Montecatini, the Fifth Army also repaired the aqueduct, and sprayed so much DDT around that flies and mosquitoes have steered a wide berth of the town ever since.

Although Montecatini's waters come to the surface at natural temperature there are natural steam baths nearby at the Giusti Grotto in the town of Monsummano Terme. It was a favorite haunt of the Fascists who used to travel up to the baths to sweat things out.

An architect named Bonanno who wanted to build a bell tower for his city and failed, brought the city undying fame which his success would never have achieved. Bonanno, now known as Bonanno Pisano, lived in Pisa. In 1174 he began to build a tower as an adjunct to the church, similar to the tower in Siena and Giotto's tower in Florence. Using only white marble, Bonanno got sixty feet high before the tower began to list. He stopped construction, and for sixty years the tower remained unfinished. Bonanno died in the meantime, but some work was done in 1260, and finally by 1350 the present tower was finished.

It is almost 170 feet high, has 294 steps, holds eight bronze bells weighing 22,000 pounds, and leans twelve feet over the green Tuscan turf. Pisa's leaning tower is the most celebrated tilt in history. For 100 lire you can climb the 294 stairs all the way to the top. It's a dizzy off-center walk, like the Fun House in Coney Island, with nothing to entertain you en route in the narrow stairway except a sign which reads as follows:

> Keep the Tower clean please!
> A W.C. does not exist on the Tower;
> it is outside at your disposal
> (Torelli St.)

There are no railings on some of the upper stories, and if you want to make it all the way up to the bells, unless you're a steeplejack you'll find the sledding a little scary. There is a guide at the top, and, as I say, eight bells, one of which was knocked out of tune by a bomb fragment in the recent war. Seven or eight people have committed suicide by diving from the tower, one in July 1948. Galileo made some of his first tests in the law of gravity by dropping objects from the tower's top.

Adjoining the Leaning Tower is a Baptistry and the Cathedral of Pisa, both done, like the tower, in ornate white decor. On the same grounds is the Campo Santo, an old church burialground. The earth was imported in 1203—fifty-three shiploads of it — all taken from Mount Calvary in the Holy Land.

Fifty miles from Florence, Pisa is a regular stop on the CIAT bus route between Florence and Genoa. It is the seat of a famous university, has 75,000 citizens, and like Florence, is split by the Arno River. Older than Rome, Pisa was once a power. It had a strong navy, which turned back the Saracens in a decisive battle off Palermo in 1063. Pisan troops spearheaded the attack on Jerusalem during the First Crusade just before the turn of the eleventh century. The city was weakened finally by the constant

PISA'S TOWER
Tilt!

civil strife between the Ghibellines and the Guelphs. The Genoese navy broke the back of the Pisan fleet in 1284, and from then on Pisa fell under the influence of Florence, her burly brother on the west.

Fourteen miles north of Pisa (and fifty-six miles from Florence mostly on the autostrada) is the seaside resort of Viareggio where the sea gave up Shelley's body after the poet was drowned. One of the best beaches in all Italy, Viareggio has twelve uninterrupted miles of surf and sand. The town, which consists chiefly of some 150 hotels and pensions, is laid in square city blocks, divided by broad streets, a novel arrangement in Italy. Although Viareggio's location approaches the Riviera, the winter temperature averages below fifty. The season runs from May through October, but things are hopping hardest during July and August. Mostly a substantial, middle-class resort for Italians, Viareggio has only one de luxe hotel, the Principe di Piemonte, on the Piazza Puccini, and two first-class hotels, the Astor and the Grande Albergo e Reale, both on the Viale Carducci.

Aside from its natural endowment of sand, which grain for grain might outweigh Sahara, Viareggio is blessed with a magnificent forest of umbrella pines, nearly nine million square yards of them, fronting along the sea. It is a four and a half mile drive, mostly through the pines, to Torre del Lago on Lake Massaciuccoli, which was the home of Giacomo Puccini. The house of Puccini, the composer who gave the world *La Tosca, Madama Butterfly* and *La Boheme,* has been preserved almost as he left it when he died in 1924. It is open to the public. Left scattered on his piano are some of his letters, his glasses, and the blotting paper that dried the last letters he wrote. Immediately behind the wall is a family chapel, and inside the walls are the actual tombs of Puccini, his son and his wife, buried one above the other. Elsewhere in the house are his boots and shoes, his shotguns, his hunting clothes, stuffed birds, autographed photographs of opera stars, a screen made of mother of pearl and ivory sent to him by the Japanese government after *Madama Butterfly* was performed, also the pillow on which he laid his head to die, and his death mask.

There are excursions from Viareggio to the quarries of Carrara where Michelangelo went to choose his own blocks of marble four centuries ago, to La Spezia, the Italian naval base which was plastered by our air forces. In Lerici, just outside La Spezia, there is a modernistic new restaurant, clean, bright and decorative, sitting right beside the sea. Splitting the billing between history and nature, it calls itself the Shelley e delle Palme.

BOLOGNA
not one leaning tower, but two

The straight route north from Florence will land you in
Bologna, sixty-three miles away, in plenty of time for lunch. In
ancient, individualistic Bologna, the people live the good life.
The first thought is of one's stomach. Bologna is famous for
Bologna sausage, Bolognese cooking, arcaded streets, and old
Bologna U. The unofficial capital of cuisine for all Italy, Bologna
drapes most dishes in heavy meat sauces, and suggests you wash
them down with sweet *Moscato*, red or white muscatel, the grape
of the neighborhood. The combination is not recommended for
pregame luncheons of football players.

Bologna has at least two excellent restaurants, one of which
is world-famed, and the other should be. The better known, and

BOLOGNA'S ANCIENT ARCADES
ladies lectured behind curtains

more expensive of the two is Al Pappagallo—The Parrot, at Piazza Mercanzia No. 3. In its dismal, dark-paneled room Pappagallo has played host to Tyrone Power, Orson Welles, Princess Margaret Rose, Ernest Bevin, Duff Cooper and dozens of others since it first swung open its doors in 1916. Most famous dish in the house, strictly for the gourmet, is *Tacchino alla Cardinale*, a breast of turkey cooked with truffles and *pecorino* cheese (smelly), all enclosed in a *vol-au-vent*, or pastry form. If you eat the works your check will run about $3.50 per person not including wine.

The Sampieri Restaurant at Via Sampieri No. 3 has a pleasant brick garden, and lively inside rooms with red velure on the walls and hung with paintings. You can gorge yourself to the strains of street musicians who come in to play *O Sole Mio* on an archaic *mandolina Napolitano*. Eat, if you're brave, *lasagne al forno* — layers of *pasta* weighted down with meat sauce and cheese, or *cotolette alla bolognese* — a slice of veal wrapped in melted cheese.

In either place, or at most any other restaurant in Bologna, here are some items you are bound to find on the menu:

Tortellini: Envelopes of pasta stuffed with pork, breast of turkey, ham, eggs, Parmesan cheese.

Tagliatelle alla Bolognese: Fine noodles with meat sauce and cheese.

Lasagne Verdi alla Bolognese: The 'Verdi' refers to the green color of the *lasagne*, not to the composer. The *lasagne*, large noodles really, are turned green by boiling them with spinach. Naturally you eat them with meat sauce and cheese.

Petti di Tacchino alla Bolognese: Breast of turkey again, sliced in cutlet form, dipped in the yolk of an egg, breaded and fried in butter.

Costolette di Vitello alla Bolognese. Veal cutlet dipped in egg yoke, breaded and covered with a slice of ham, crumbs of Parmesan cheese and truffles.

In Bologna the rolls come shaped like an H, and are called *crocetta*, meaning, small cross. And the best place to get a cup of coffee, since it is fashionably epicurean to have your coffee elsewhere than at a restaurant, is Viscardi. The best hotel in town is the Majestic Grand Albergo, formerly known as the Baglioni, located on the Via Independenza. Comfortable, sedate and substantial, it is officially classified as de luxe.

Bologna has not one leaning tower, but two. Constructed of brick in the twelfth century, they lean toward each other like a pair of friendly drunks. One tower is 317 feet high, the other, 163

RIMINI
on the Adriatic, square umbrellas

feet high, and they got that way from an earthquake. Almost every street in town is covered with arcades, which permit a shaded walk in summer, and a protected walk in winter. The arcades in the Merchant's Square are from the twelfth century. The Fountain of Neptune done by Giambologna in 1566, which portrays the King of the Sea, naked and muscular, flanked by children playing harmlessly with dolphins, is considered a work of some importance by those whose interest it is to consider such things.

The University of Bologna was founded in the eleventh century, making it the oldest college in Europe. By 1262, when both Dante and Petrarch were undergraduates, the enrollment was nearly 10,000. There are 18,000 students in the schools today, including 500 Americans and English. Human anatomy was first taught here in the fourteenth century. There have been many women professors, but during the same epoch a lady professor named Novella d'Andrea, whose charms were apparently obvious and irresistible, was required to lecture behind a curtain. The school thought it would be less distracting for the boys that way. Bologna has always had a curiosity about bodies, experiments with humans having been made for the first time in the Archigymnasium of the Piazza Maggiore. The university is particularly noted for medicine and surgery.

The regular schedule of the CIAT buses which depart from Florence in the morning and arrive in Bologna for lunch, allows time in the city afterward for a sightseeing tour conducted by a city guide in the same bus. If you wish you can push on to Venice the same afternoon. However, CIAT has an overnight excursion from Bologna to the seaside resort of Rimini, the independent republic of San Marino. and Ravenna, city filled with Byzantine mosaics. Transportation, hotel room in Ravenna, dinner, breakfast and guide and entrance fees are all included in the fare which comes to about $10. The excursion service meets buses going to and from Venice and Florence. For anyone with an extra day to spare, it's a worthwhile junket.

The road from Bologna to Rimini is straight and true, right to the sea, splitting the Romagna country down the middle. The Romagnese people delight in art, which has a distinct Oriental flavor, in choral music, and in Romagnese cooking which differs somewhat from the weighty concoctions of nearby Bologna. There is in the first place, the *piada*, a thin cake made without yeast; *pappardelle*, a macaroni pie with giblets; *brodetti*, a fish soup; and as a main course, large *Comacchio* eels cooked either with tomatoes or sage and laurel. The wines of Romagna, Sangiovese, Albana and Trebbiano are light and merry.

Should you be on the CIAT excursion, the stop in Rimini will be short, but long enough all the same to see the broad stretch of sand, colored for miles with the rectangular pieces of canvas hung on poles which Adriatic sunbathers use for beach umbrellas. The sailboats that cut the waters of the Riviera Romagnola have an Oriental cut, and are patched bright-colored cloth designs. A virtual blockhouse on the Gothic Line which was defended by the Germans, Rimini fell finally to British troops of the Eighth Army on September 21, 1944. Bologna was never captured until the following spring.

Some fifteen miles of sand fringes the Adriatic at Rimini. Much of the town has been rebuilt, and has that flat, scrubbed, pastel seaside look. Of the dozens of hotels and pensions in greater Rimini about the best you can do are hotels officially classified as second class. Among them are the Amati, the Astoria, the Corallo Nadina, the Excelsior, Savoia, Quisisana, Stelle Polare, Villa Rosa and Tonini. Rates for a single room with bath are less than $2 a day, less than $4 with full board. But a room with private bath is a hard item to find. The season runs from May through September and there is a colorful water carnival in August.

From Rimini it is fifteen miles to San Marino, an independent republic of some twenty-five square miles, and 20,000 citizens, 6,000 of whom live abroad. San Marino, without taxes, customs, or border guards, has always been a haven for refugees. Among the most famous was Garibaldi who disbanded the Roman Legion there in 1848. Among the most numerous were the 100,000 exiles who flocked to the republic during the Second World War. For some unexplained reason, San Marino which has existed as a republic since the ninth century was bombed on June 26, 1944 with a loss of sixty-three lives. It was also invaded.

All of San Marino's real estate is composed of three mountain peaks. Most of the town sits atop the most westerly of the three peaks, necessitating a long, winding drive to the top. When you leave your car on a terrace on the mountainside, enter the town on foot through a gate. From there it is an uphill walk

SAN MARINO
no taxes, no customs

to the Piazza della Liberta, a miniature Italian square with cafes, and a Lilliputian capitol with typical battlements, known as the Palazzo Pubblico. There are sixty members in the legislature who twice a year, on April 1 and October 1 elect, amid much pomp and fuss, two captains regent who operate the country by dual control. The legislature is elected by the male population. San Marinese women are not given a vote. Among the honorary citizens of San Marino who are commemorated on the walls of the Palazzo Pubblico are Garibaldi, Verdi and Abraham Lincoln. Many of the honorary citizens would view the present government of traditionally freedom-loving San Marino with a quizzical eyebrow. The republic has recently elected a Communist slate.

GATES OF THE REPUBLIC
Communism and gambling

Lately, too, San Marino has installed a government-sponsored gambling house which is now operating under rather crowded conditions, in a former theater. The crowd which comes to gamble is undoubtedly a good deal less elegant than the set which frequents Monte Carlo. On the other hand the enterprise is one of the few Communist-run gambling houses in the world.

San Marino is noted for its *Pan del Santo,* a special kind of chocolate wafer that is eaten with Biancale di San Marino, a muscatel. The shops put up one-portion packages for curious tourists. One of the quaintest inns in the neighborhood is La Taverna, on the government square, which is done up after the Tyrolean motif, with Tyrolean paintings, antlers, brick-colored

PIAZZA DELLA LIBERTA
Garibaldi, Verdi and Lincoln

tile, and chandeliers that are glass grapes. Ninety cents will get you a full dinner. The Hotel Titano which has a pleasant mountainside terrace and a good restaurant is open all year around. San Marino was used as a background for some of the scenes of *Prince of Foxes* with Tyrone Power and Orson Welles.

Ravenna, once capital of the Western Roman Empire, seat of the Viceroy of Byzantium, has never achieved its ancient prominence. But it is a museum of the early Byzantine art, and it stirs memories of Dante, Boccaccio and Byron who came later. Ravenna is built inland, but a narrow canal which winds part of the way through the city's once celebrated umbrella-pine forest, connects with Marina di Ravenna, the port on the Adriatic. In the days of Augustus, when the topography was different, the Roman emperor kept his fleet of over 250 galleys in the ancient town of Classis, three miles outside Ravenna. The old harbor is approximately marked by the Church of Sant' Appollinare in Classe which during the recent war stood in the middle of a no-man's land. For four months the German line was on the River Unité and the Allied line was on the Savio, twelve kilometers away. Tanks patrolled the roads, and the church was severely wrecked. It was restored in April 1949 in time for the 1,400th anniversary of the church which was consecrated in 549 A.D. The church has the most recent Ravenna mosaics, dating from the fifteenth century. The Ravenna mosaic technique makes use of glass bits for all colors except white, for which marble is used. To give an effect of third dimension, broken pieces are formed and turned. The church also has some eighty-five sarcophagi from the fifth century, many of which now contain the bones of local bishops.

The Church of Sant' Appollinare Nuovo, built by Theodoric the Great in 500 A.D., became a Christian church sixty years later. The walls are literally covered with magnificent mosaics.

LA TAVERNA
antlers and muscatel

One side depicts a procession of twenty-two virgins, the other side, a line of twenty-six saints, and there is a mosaic of the city of Classis, and another of the Palace of Theodoric. All told the church has some 500 square yards of mosaics, of which 350 are original and the rest restored. The processions on the sides are in Byzantine style, while the mosaics above the windows and between them are in Roman style. You don't have to be a connoisseur to distinguish them. The Roman technique is naturalistic, the figures are active, and the faces are expressive. They usually worked on dark backgrounds. The Byzantine style is impressionistic, symbolic and stiff. They worked on gold backgrounds.

Theodoric's tomb is a round, formidable two-story pillbox,

capped by a roof of Istrian stone one yard thick, eleven yards across, weighing 300 tons. When Theodoric died in 546 he was buried in his bathtub, an immense fixture of maroon marble nearly four feet high. The tomb had already been built when he died, but no staircase leading to the entrance was ever found.

Some of the most beautiful of Ravenna's mosaics are in the Church of San Vitale, built in the sixth century in pure busy Byzantine style. The pillars are carved, the walls covered with semiprecious marble, even the floors are paved with mosaics. The altar is Oriental alabaster, four inches thick, but it shows the light of a match held on the opposite side.

The oldest mosaics in town gild the interior of the tomb of Galla Placidia, the beautiful and adventurous empress. Daughter of Theodosius, emperor of the Eastern Roman Empire, she was taken prisoner in Rome by a barbarian conqueror and carted off to Gaul where she married her captor's successor. When her husband died she went to Ravenna to live with her brother. She later became empress of the Western Empire. The center sarcophagus is Galla Placidia's, the other two those of Constantius and Valentinian III, her son. Through an opening in the tomb of the empress it was possible to see a wrapped mummy. But in 1877 a boy lit a match in the aperture and the mummy burned. Brilliant mosaics cover the inside walls of the cryptlike tomb. The one over the entrance can best be seen by holding a card in front of the eyes to shut out the exterior light.

Dante's remains, by a chain of curious circumstances, rest in a tomb in Ravenna, a city in which he spent the last three years of his life in peaceful exile. Because of Dante's part in the civil strife, Florence several times promised him death if he returned, later offered to let him come back if he would pay a fine and walk in the dress of humiliation through the city. He declined, preferring to enter Florence only without shame. In Ravenna he

GALLA PLACIDIA'S TOMB
a boy lit a match

went to Venice on a diplomatic mission and while there caught a fever. He died in Ravenna on September 14, 1321. Buried in a church, Dante was later vindicated by the Florentines who requested the return of his remains to his native city. Michelangelo offered to build a suitable tomb for him in Florence, but the people of Ravenna still demurred. An appeal by the Florentines to Pope Leo X, a Medici of Florence anyway, finally worked, and the Pontiff intervened. A delegation from Florence went to Ravenna to investigate the tomb, and found it empty. Franciscan monks had bored a hole through the wall and the urn, and removed the bones to save them for Ravenna. They lay hidden in a box, sealed in a wall until 1865 when they were rediscovered.

Now Dante at last lies quiet by the light of a lamp which was a gift from Trieste. Florence sends down a bottle of oil every year to keep the lamp burning. On the 600th anniversary of the death of Dante in 1921, a bell, voted by popular subscription was added to his tomb. It is tolled every night thirteen times. Across the courtyard is the restored house of Byron. The memory of both poets is kept as a tranquil shrine. The area has been ordained a silent zone by civil authorities.

The best hotel in Ravenna is the Nuovo San Marco, completely reconditioned and reopened in June 1949. It has thirty-two rooms decorated in inexpensive modern furniture. Probably it is the only hotel in traditional Italy in which goldfish swim in a tank recessed into a dining-room wall. Two dollars is top price for room and bath.

For all its mosaics and monuments, one of the greatest sights in Ravenna is the town square at night. From the front door of the hotel turn right and walk one block. On soft summer evenings hundreds of tables are spread all over the cobblestone piazza. Each group of tables belongs to one of the half a dozen *caffès* under the surrounding arcades, but where the tables of one end and the other begins is hard to tell. Street singers play under a pair of fifteenth century statues. A policeman in white cap, white coat and black trousers, a cigarette holder clamped between his teeth, rides through on his bicycle. The illuminated clock in the tower strikes ten, and back in the U.S.A. a mother, out for the evening, might begin to wonder about getting home to the baby-sitter. There are no baby-sitter problems here. When the women go out they take their babies with them, carrying them in their arms, wheeling them in carriages till all hours of the night. For the table-sitters, the standers, the leaners, the strollers who fill the square, automobiles are not much of a hazard. Every fifteen minutes or so one rattles through. But the bicycle traffic is heavy, particularly with young men pedaling young ladies on the handle bars. Now and then a motor bike or a motor scooter might splutter past. And the only other voice from the frenzied world outside is an occasional Coca Cola bottle on the tables among the cups of *espresso*. That, and a neon sign which showers an unnatural light on the front of the sixteenth century building from which it hangs.

VENICE

"Madam, this bus doesn't float."

6. VENICE

Whether you've come to wive it wealthily, or whether you are just on your way to Venice, you'll find Padua an ornamental city, worth a stop en route. Coming to Venice from the south or from the west, it is almost inevitable that you pass through Padua first, which is quite like submitting a deep sea diver to intermediate pressures before you bring him all the way to the surface. Like Venice, Padua is an ornamental city, and like Venice it reflects an Oriental caste. Its huge Church of St. Anthony, which overwhelms the tiny square, is capped with mosques and towers like a Persian temple. Supposedly it was designed by Niccola Pisano, and it contains the bones of St. Anthony, known locally as Il Santo. It is a short walk from the square through the arcaded streets, to the park of Padua, a unique enclosure entirely surrounded by a canal. The canal is bordered on both banks with rows of statues, and spanned by ornamental bridges of stone and marble.

Padua is claimed by its most partisan historians, to be the

PADUA
for a diver, intermediate pressures

oldest city in Northern Italy. At any rate some of its citizens
became the first Venetians in a way that we shall shortly see.
In its earliest days Padua developed a talent for breeding horses
and wool-bearing sheep, a pair of skills which made it rich, and
in the due course of natural progress, powerful. At one time it
was allegedly able to mobilize 200,000 troops. But twenty-five
miles to the east, Venice, through curious circumstance, grew even
more powerful, and Padua eventually passed under its control.

The University of Padua, which was founded in 1238, has
become one of the most famous universities in the world. On its
faculty at one time or another were Galileo, Sobieski and Scali-
ger. The intellectual air of the city attracted Giotto, Lippo Lippi

and Donatello. Giotto left the interior of the Church of Madonna dell' Arena, called the Chiesa di Giotto, covered with his frescoes. It's a tiny chapel, but some consider the interior to be the most important example of Giotto's work, and one of the most memorable pieces of art in Italy. Donatello left the bronze statue of the Venetian general Gattamelata.

From Padua the road to Venice lies straight and flat across the Venetian plain. A small canal, like an overflowing rivulet, appears along the side of the road. The canal was once the water road from Venice, and many rich Venetians built country villas here in sight of soil and trees. Most famous is the Villa Pisani owned originally by a grand family of Venice. Casanova wrote some of his memoirs in the villa, and Napoleon and Josephine visited it by gondola. Hitler and Mussolini met there in 1939.

Mestre is the nearest mainland point to Venice, but an aqueduct known as the Liberta Bridge now permits cars to drive as far as the Piazzale Roma, near the railroad station on Venice proper. The road ends there, and if you've come by auto you will find a thousand-car garage where you can store your vehicle until you leave Venice.

It is the custom of the CIAT system upon arriving at a terminal point to deposit passengers in turn at their respective hotels, so perhaps the question of the American lady wasn't so silly. When the huge motorcoach pulled into the Piazzale Roma from Padua one recent summer afternoon, and began unloading passengers and baggage, the lady turned to the hostess. "Aren't you going to take us to our hotels?" she demanded. The hostess, who was busy answering questions in three languages turned to her, and with some restraint explained, "Madam, this bus doesn't float."

Although Venice has been where it is for a good many years, and is exactly as it appears in its pictures, practical-minded

no cars, no horses, no dust

North Americans still find it difficult to comprehend the existence of a city which, by choice, has waterways for streets.

Venice is incredible.

It has over a quarter of a million inhabitants who live on 118 islands which are huddled together two and a half miles off the mainland, and a mile and a quarter from the open sea. The islands are divided by 160 canals and connected by some 400 bridges. No one seems to have taken the bridge census exactly.

Except perhaps for tiny gardens hidden in the courtyards of villas, Venice has no trees, no grass, no flowers. It has no cars, no carriages, no horses, no bicycles and no dust. One moves on foot—crossing the canals by bridge or ferry or by public steamboat which makes all the local stops, by motorboat, or by gon-

for a busy canal ... a traffic light

dola. One hour you are on a train or riding a country road on a bus, and the next you are in a gondola, baggage and all, pulling away from the Piazzale Roma for your hotel. Steamboats and barges fill the canals. Gondolas that are ambulances, gondolas that are hearses, gondolas that are yellow and red and deliver Coca Cola, gondolas that are privately-owned and are propelled by gondoliers in immaculate white uniforms with bright-colored sash around the waist and bright band around the hat. There is so much traffic on the ancient canals the city government has lately installed a traffic light at a particularly dangerous intersection.

The chain of events that made Venice the most celebrated waterworks in the world began in the fifth century with the invasions of Attila the Hun. Advancing from the north, the Barbarians drove before them many citizens of the northern Italian cities. Many of the refugees fled out to Venetian islands, settling first on Torcello, which was sparsely inhabited then by fishermen and boatmen. The first homes were built of mud and reeds, and protected by ditches from the rising tides. But the Venetians, who had formed their city as a sanctuary, soon learned how to improve their living conditions. Each century of life by the water made them keener in the ways of the sea. In their first excursion, in 1000, they crossed the Adriatic to clear the Dalmatian (Yugoslavian) coast of pirates. Then they put their maritime training to profitable use by contracting to outfit the fleets of the Crusades. They strung a network of refitting ports along the Adriatic, the Aegean and the Mediterranean seas. The lifeline reached as far as the Holy Land.

The bustling commerce of Venice created wealth, and soon the wealth sought power. Led by the Doge, or ruler, and spurred by certain influential families, Venice was able to alter the clear-cut religious intent of the Fourth Crusade into a personal assault on Constantinople. That *coup* of derring-do and diplomacy only invited the jealousy of the Genoese, who were mariners, too, and the two cities went to war. It was a long and bloody struggle that finally ended more than a hundred years later when the Venetians bottled up the entire Genoese fleet in a harbor. Venice now turned her interests into the establishment of territorial interests on the mainland. In the meantime, in the East, she became involved in an unsuccessful war with the invading Turks. The European nations, anxious for their own security, formed the League of Cambrai, and stripped Venice of all her Continental territory, right up to the lagoons. It remained for Napoleon in 1797, to force the abdication of the Doge, and end the republic of Venice forever.

VENICE

But during her palmier days, which lasted right up to the end, and in some small ways still continue, Venice lived giddily on the tremendous wealth she had amassed. She was the center of rich life and elegant trappings. She developed a splendid school of art, among whose mainstays were Giorgone, Titian, Tintoretto, Paolo Veronese and Palladio. Great palaces lined the canals, and many houses were decorated from roof to waterline with brilliant frescoes. The city developed a sense of the theatrical and an aptitude for festivals which it has never lost. When I arrived in Venice on a fairly typical Sunday evening recently, the great square of St. Mark's was packed. Blue lights were playing on the ancient mosaics over the doors of the cathedral, giving the whole building, with its Byzantine mosques silhouetted against the sky, the semblance of an unbelievable vision in an Oriental dream.

St. Mark's Square is the heart of the city. The guidebook assures me that it is 192 yards long, and (since it is not exactly square) from 61 to 90 feet wide. It is bordered on the long sides, by a pair of wedding-cake structures, and on the ends by St. Mark's Cathedral, and a palace built by Napoleon's order in 1799. In front of each of the hundreds of arched second-floor windows all around the Square, this night, was a three-foot electric candle, burning with an amber light. Out of the windows of the Royal Danieli Hotel, a block away, it was perhaps two hundred yards to the Italian light cruiser *Raimondo Montecuccoli* anchored in the lagoon. Her decks were strung with white light bulbs from bow to stern.

The reason for all the fuss was the annual lottery which was about to take place in the Square. Venice loves a party, no matter what the reason. On the eve of the third Sunday in July everything stops in Venice for the Redentore. Gondolas and barges are fitted up with lanterns, with musicians, sometimes with entire

ST. MARK'S SQUARE
in every window a candle

orchestras, and sometimes with whole picnic tables. Fireworks split the black sky as the whole procession glides down the Giudecca Canal (so-called because it divides the Giudecca, an island where Jews were once confined, from Metropolitan Venice). Carried by the tide, the music, the wine, and the gentle poling of the gondoliers, the fleet winds up on the beach of the Lido to watch the sun come up out of the sea.

In September the bunting and the crowds come out again for the annual gondoliers' regatta. Motorboat traffic is stopped for the race which features light racing gondolas. The race is really secondary to the pageantry. St. Mark's fills up, too, in summer when the excellent orchestra of Venice, framed in the

Square, plays for the local burghers and whatever tourists want to sit in. Red, green and yellow tables of the sidewalk cafes stretch out in formation across St. Mark's, and on concert nights a cafe chair in the Square is a premium location. But whether it is a special evening, or just another night in history, no one really cares how long you take to sip a Vermouth or an iced coffee—a concoction which involves two inches of whipped cream on top of the glass, and a ball of ice cream inside. Should you linger late at Florian's, the most famous of St. Mark's cafes, the waiter will come to collect the bill, and to tell you please not to disturb yourself, to stay as late as you like, and not to worry about finishing your drinks in a hurry. It is a pleasant night, and he will tell the night man to take in the glasses.

The pigeons of St. Mark's, which for international renown dip no wings to Capistrano's swallows, bathe all day in their own fountain alongside the cathedral. They rise and flap their wings, and scatter excitedly when the noon gun explodes. And sharply at two each afternoon the city's entire pigeon population winging in from kilometers around, swoops down on the far corner of the Square where the municipal feeder appears with a sack of municipal corn.

At other times of the day the pigeons work hand-in-hand with the corn peddlers and the photographers. When the tourists come, the corn peddlers shake a cone filled with corn. That brings the pigeons down. The tourist poses with them while the photographer snaps the picture. You can notice a camaraderie among the corn hustlers and the pigeons, for sometimes the birds swoop down when there are no tourists, but the corn men always dole out a few kernels just the same.

Venice, which has so much culture and quaintness, is almost as heavily endowed with international glitter. Its Lido, an upholstered sandbar fifteen minutes away by motorboat, is one of

AMONG PIGEONS AND PHOTOGRAPHERS
an understanding

the most popular royal seaside relaxing stations on the Continent. Both Venice and Lido-Venice are well stocked with hotels. The point is, when coming to the city, whether to live the lacquered life of the Lido and take your culture as a side-order, or whether to live along the ancient canals in the shadow of St. Mark's and just go out to the Lido for a ration of refinement.

The hotels of Venice are along the Grand Canal near the Square, or on the Riva degli Schiavoni, the main waterfront street. Traditionally the place where ships from overseas landed, the Riva degli Schiavoni is a welter of bustle at almost any hour. At five in the afternoon during the tourist season, it is jammed with an ever-changing horde of people. If you picked out a random handful they might prove to be a boatman who has just moved a bargeload of Venetian glass to a warehouse, a sailor from Milan on the way to his ship, an urchin without shoes on his way to his begging station in front of the Theatre de Fenice, a middle-aged automobile dealer from Dallas in full dress on his way to a dinner dance at Lido, two schoolteachers from Marseilles coming from the art galleries, a university professor who speaks French, English, German and his native Italian on his way from being the guide on an afternoon guided tour, and a pair of Princeton juniors in from an afternoon on the beach on their way to a pair of Martinis.

One of the most famous of the Riva degli Schiavoni hotels is the Royal Danieli. It fronts right on the lagoon, the horde passes beneath its windows, and the whistle of the steam ferry bleats against its luxurious sides. Originally, which is to say, back in the fourteenth century, the building was a palace which belonged to a Venetian VIP. During the 1800's the palace passed into the hands of one Miss Niel, a Greek, who operated it as an inn. An Italian on his way to Miss Niel's would say he was going da Niel, which originally got corrupted to Daniel, and finally Italianized to Danieli. A gondola from the railroad station or the Piazzale Roma will glide right up to the door of the Danieli in about twenty minutes, where bellboys in immaculate whites lift you out. The Danieli's lobby is an ornate, marble-covered arrangement, decked out with trick arches, balconies, columns and a magnificent fourteenth century staircase. Recently the Danieli built a new wing also fronting on the Riva degli Schiavoni. The outside is plain, but the rooms are immense and modern, and there is a new roof garden on top. Open all year around, the hotel has radiant panel heating.

Venice never saw much of the war, but as the chase for the German remnants turned north, both the British and the New

Zealand forces raced for the Danieli. General Fryberg, who led the New Zealanders, was very happy his troops won because he had spent his honeymoon at the hotel twenty-five years before. A less successful race, namely Dewey's for the presidency, ended up at the Danieli too. The governor came to the hotel early in 1949 for a rest. Nello, the bartender, fresh from a success making a special cocktail for the Christian Democratic Party (a Bianca Fiore: gin, kirsch and lemon) whipped up a concoction for Dewey too. Ingredients of the Dewey cocktail: vermouth, gin, kirsch and an olive. You can still get one. Just ask for a Dewey.

Among the other de luxe category hotels of Venice proper are the Grand and the Gritti Palace which, like the first-class Europa and Luna, are above the Square and directly on the canal away from the bustle. The Europa is the only hotel on the canal with a terrace garden, an oasis of green in a courtyard. The Gritti, small and elegant, is probably the best of Venice's hotels. It is named for Andrea Gritti, a fifteenth century doge, whose family later lived in this ancient palace. Done up in silks, and marble, and period furniture, the petit Gritti always has a houseful of celebrities. On a recent summer's evening waiters serving on its flower-decked waterside dining terrace were flitting between Sir Duff Cooper and Lady Diana, Douglas Fairbanks, Jr. and his wife, Joan Fontaine with Joseph Cotten and Slim Aarons, *Life*'s Italy-based photographer. The management was breathlessly awaiting the arrival of Toscanini.

Sinclair Lewis wrote most of a new book in a second-floor Gritti suite overlooking the canal, and Lewis and Hemingway later met for the first time at the Gritti bar.

Princess Margaret Rose came to the Gritti and was greeted at the hotel's dock with a deep bow by Raffaele Masprone, the charming, courtly, monocle-wearing manager. The Princess occupied Suite 110-111, went to the Taverna La Fenice for dinner,

AT THE ROYAL DANIELI
Dewey descending a staircase

and for laughs she and her maid took pictures of each other leaning out of a Gritti window. When she went out for a ride on the canal she hopelessly snarled gondola traffic. She had a very good time. According to the story, her entire trip was originally cooked up by Ward Price of the *London Daily Mail*, who launched the idea of having the Princess come to Venice. Eventually the plan was broadened to include much of Italy, the Pope and Capri included.

Should you stay at the Gritti or even visit it, ask Signor Masprone, whose family has been in the hotel business for decades, to produce his guest book. It starts with U. S. Grant who came to Milan in 1878 and contains signatures of Verdi, Von Molke,

MARGARET ROSE AT THE GRITTI
for laughs, a picture

Marconi, Bleriot, Mussolini, Toscanini, Otto Kahn, Benes, Goering, Rommel, Ley, Himmel, Kesselring, Wallis Windsor and Edward, Sinclair Lewis (who signed "with great happiness") and Ernest Hemingway ("to our home in Venice 1948-1949") and most recently, "Margaret, Princess of Great Britain and Northern Ireland, 24 May 1949." Masprone also has an atlas in which Eisenhower signed across the face of France and Germany, and Mark Clark across Italy. A busboy under Oscar at the old Waldorf in 1906, Masprone later worked at the Fairmont in San Francisco. From 1927 until 1943 when the Germans burned it, he was manager of the Excelsior in Naples. In the fire he lost a priceless collection of 500 photographs of famous guests, all autographed.

VENICE

Neither the fire, nor the years have dimmed Masprone's recollections of famous people. When Kipling was in the house one year, Mrs. Kipling was ferocious in her effort to keep her husband from being photographed. She smashed cameras right and left, on sight. Determined to add the British author to his picture collection, Masprone called on an old friend who for years had been a trusted agent of the Italian secret service. The investigator rigged up a special camera, and took Kipling's picture through the buttonhole of his shirt. The print burned with the rest of the collection.

Masprone's one-time guest was Barbara Hutton's uncle who was in the hotel recuperating from an operation. One day he called Masprone upstairs. "How much do you think the municipality would want for that fountain?" Hutton asked the rather startled manager. Masprone looked out the window at the fountain, a rather large, and not extraordinarily attractive fixture. "You want to buy it?" he asked uncertainly. "I don't want to buy it," Hutton explained, "I just want it removed, the noise is driving me crazy." Masprone dissuaded the magnate from buying the fountain and insisted he could solve the problem with dispatch. He did, merely by having the thing shut off.

Each evening at six the international colony, vacationing in Venice, almost with the punctuality of the pigeons, reports for cocktails at Harry's Bar, a tiny edition of New York's "21," near the entrance of the Luna Hotel. Harry's has hot canapes and a posh clientele, and no one seems to know which attracted which. A whopping slug of Scotch goes for $1.20, and a third of a tumbler of American whiskey for 90 cents. A dinner of filet of sole Casanova cooked with mushrooms, white wine, curry and rice is $2.50. Pure Italian restaurants, which cater to the Italian as well as the tourist are about a third less, but Harry's gets everybody. Richard Halliburton once pushed his way out through its swinging saloon doors, jumped into the canal, and, on a bet, tried swimming to the railroad station. He was arrested and fined. And one morning in 1937, quite by coincidence, four kings were imbibing in Harry's at the same time.

Harry, or Giuseppe Ciprani, as he is officially carried on his identity card, was a barman at the Europa Hotel in 1929 when he became familiar with three American habitués who always ordered Bacardis. In due course the Americans, whose names he didn't know, returned to America. Three years later, the same three Americans walked into the Europa bar, whereupon Harry ushered them to their favorite seat, and without further ado mixed three Bacardis. The trio was noticeably touched.

One day two of the threesome departed leaving the third member, whose name was Harry Pickering, not only solitary but sad. It became clear to Ciprani that Mr. Pickering, a man of some wealth, was being kept from his money by a rather stringent allowance. The barman lent him 15,000 lire. Four months later Pickering came back to repay Ciprani and to suggest a partnership. Ciprani and Pickering started Harry's Bar in 1931, specializing in American dishes and good liquor. After fifteen days, so the story goes, passengers arriving from New York were asking not for the Doge's Palace, but for Harry's Bar. Ciprani bought out Pickering in 1936, including the unofficial use of "Harry" as a first name. Everyone is just wild about calling Giuseppe, Harry. And when his son was born, what do you think he christened him?

Harry's bar has opened a country inn on Turcello, a romantic little isle not far from Venice. A motor launch runs from the bar to the inn. Hemingway went out for lunch in the fall of 1948, and came back forty days later. But more about Torcello anon.

It was Marco Polo of Venice, one of the first travel-book writers, who is supposed to have introduced spaghetti, an old Chinese dish, to the Italians. In spite of the heritage, Venice, like

HARRY, NEE GIUSEPPE
three Bacardis

most northern cities eats more rice and *polenta* than it does spaghetti. Polenta is a ballast made of corn flour, served on a wooden board, and eaten with fish. On Fridays in Venice try *Baccala Mantecato*, which is dried codfish soaked for twenty-four hours, boiled, and mixed with oil and garlic. Most any day you will find *Risibisi*, rice cooked in broth with green peas; *Risotto con Pecci*, rice in broth with mussels. Everywhere you'll see *scampi*, large shrimp-type seafood with a scalloped back, and, to my mind, not as flavorful as shrimp. In any case you ought to try them broiled on a skewer, fried in oil, or boiled with oil and lemon. If you're even more pioneering, look for *Granceole*, Venetian crabs, boiled and seasoned with oil and lemon, and *Moleche*, small soft crabs, berled in erl. One of the best Italian wines is white *Soave*, a local product from nearby Verona. And from the Venice-Trieste area comes *Mostadura* an unfermented wine which leaves you both happy and glib until you try to get up. *Valpolicella* is a dry and local red. One of the best places to come by all this is the Taverna la Fenice, a big, pleasant restaurant with tables and chairs spread in the open. It is near La Fenice, the opera house of Venice and considered one of the most beautiful theaters in Europe. Also the Quadri, opposite the Florian in the Square, but go up to the second floor. The ground floor is just a coffeehouse. Somewhat less expensive, but good all the same, is the Trattoria Al Colombo, S. Luca 4619, not to be confused with Al Columba, another restaurant totally unrelated.

Venice is such an involved system of alleys, bridges and canals, for sightseeing you will probably do better to enroll in a conducted tour operated by a travel agency. CIT, American Express, and most of the other agencies have a morning tour beginning at 9:30 which travels by foot, and an afternoon tour, departing at 3, by gondola. There are also morning and afternoon trips leaving from the wharfs on the Riva degli Schiavoni for the nearby islands of Murano, Burano and Torcello. You can go to the Lido on your own virtually at any hour of the day or night. Embarking for a tour of the town on foot, you ought to know that Venice has only one piazza, and that is St. Mark's, or as they say, San Marco. It also has one piazzetta, and that is the one in front of the Doge's Palace, leading from the lagoon to St. Mark's Square. To Venetians all other squares are *campi*, or *campielli*. Narrow streets are called *calli*, except the first ones to have been paved which are called *salizzade*. A street between rows of shops is called a *ruga*, and streets which were formerly canals are known as *rio terra*, and short streets are called *rami*. In Des Moines life is simple.

BASILICA OF ST. MARK'S
entrance to the East

The Basilica of St. Mark's capped with its Byzantine
mosques, fills the east end of the piazza, almost as if it were the
symbolical entrance to the eastern world beyond. Its foundations
were originally laid in 830 as a shrine for the body of St. Mark
which had been stolen in Egypt by two Venetian sailors. The
present Basilica was built in 1065, and contains countless treasures brought home from the corners of the earth by the wander-
ing ships of Venice's great merchant fleet. Just above the entrance
are the famous bronze horses which are believed to be Greek.
They once adorned Nero's Arch in Rome, and later were taken
by Constantine to Byzantium (Istanbul). Napoleon took them
when he finally knocked over the Venetian Republic for all time,

but they are back in place. Built, like most of the rest of the city, on teakwood piles, the floor of the church is as bumpy as a backwoods road. The ceilings are covered with typically Byzantine mosaics, 40,000 square feet of them, all done with gleaming gold backgrounds. Among the treasures is a pure gold statue of the Virgin Nicopeia, encrusted in rubies and pearls. It is exhibited only on Saturdays and Sundays. Although St. Mark is the patron saint of Venice, Venetians thank this Virgin for three miracles — 1. Deliverance of the city from a plague in the sixteenth century; 2. Deliverance from the collapsing bell tower (a few days before the old tower tumbled in 1902 it showered the populace with bits of mortar which many considered a Heaven-sent warning); and 3. Deliverance of the city from bombing.

The bell tower, or *Campanile,* as the Italians call it (from *campane* which means bells) is an exact replica of the old one which fell on 14 July 1902 at 9:55 A.M., killing one cat and three pigeons according to the official casualty list. The area around it had been roped off for days because of the loose mortar which had been falling in the Square. The new *Campanile,* begun in 1903 and finished six years later, was financed by world-wide subscription, such being the international reverence in which Venice is held in the hearts of all men. The original loggia of the old *Campanile* withstood the collapse and now decorates the new tower.

The tower rises some 325 feet, and from the observation tower, which is nearly at the top, there is a magnificent view of the city. Eastward you see the waterfront; westward the main land; south, beyond the Lido to the Adriatic; and north toward the route to Trieste. The Campanile holds office hours from 8:30 until 12 noon and again from two until seven. You can either walk to the top, or for a few cents more, take the elevator which is considerably easier.

Opposite the Campanile is the Torre dell Orologio, the famous

FROM THE CAMPANILE
south to the Adriatic

Clock Tower which was built four years after the discovery of America. The blue and gold clockface, decorated with signs of the zodiac, faces the Square. Two bronze hammer-wielding figures called The Moors, stand on the roof and beat a huge bell every hour on the hour. At Christmas and Whitsuntide, before an assemblage in the Square, the Three Wise Men emerge and bow to the Virgin while an angel plays a trumpet.

The long building with its arches and battlements alongside the Clock Tower is called the Procuratie Vecchie, which was once the residence of city magistrates. Opposite is the Procuratie Nuova, once the Royal Palace. Sealing the Square on the end opposite the Basilica is the palace built by Napoleon. All three buildings now house restaurants, travel bureaus and shops which hide from the summer sun and the winter mists under the cover of the arcades.

The Piazzetta, the small square which is an approach to St. Mark's from the water, is dominated by the Doge's (or Ducal)

Palace, a fabulously ornate structure which was home to the 120 doges of Venice from the first whose rule began in 697, to the last whose rule ended in 1797. Doges were always elected for life, and a doge's son was ineligible for election. As prime manifestation of the best in Venetian Renaissance, the Doge's Palace represents the work of nearly a hundred painters, sculptors, and architects among the most famous of whom were Titian, Tintoretto, Giorgione, Andrea Palladio and Veronese. All except Palladio were pupils of Giovanni Bellini. Paolo Caliari is the real name of Veronese who was born in Verona. Tintoretto's real name was Jacopo Robusti. He was called Tintoretto because his father was a dyer. Titian lived to be ninety-nine, Giorgione died at thirty-three.

The courtyard of the palace, unadulterated renaissance, has two fancy wellheads which are a trademark of the squares of Venice, and the monumental Giant's Staircase, flanked by statues of Mars and Neptune. Doges were traditionally crowned on the top of the staircase between the symbols of naval might. Among the most interesting rooms are the Hall of the Four Doors, designed by Palladio and decorated by Tintoretto. The wall paneling and the banquettes are original, but the floor is new terrazzo instead of the original parquet. The Diplomat's Waiting Room has four paintings by Tintoretto. On the east wall is Veronese's "Rape of Europe," distinguished by its typical bright tones. Tintoretto worked mostly with dark values. In College Hall, where the doge received the diplomats, the 500-year-old ceiling is hand-carved wood covered with 22 karat gold. Ceiling paintings are by Veronese. Of the wall paintings, Tintoretto's "Mystical Marriage of St. Catherine" is considered the most important work. The gilded single-handed clock is seventeenth century.

The gilded old Venetian Senate Hall has a famous ceiling painting by Tintoretto showing Venice, as Queen of the Sea,

THE TORRE DELL OROLOGIO
an angel plays a trumpet

receiving the gifts of the Adriatic, among them shells, coral and
pearls. The painting was stolen by Goering, turned up in Rome,
and later was recovered from Germany. The Doge's throne is
flanked by panels representing the ancient Greece of Demos-
thenes and the old Rome of the Caesars. The memory of what
happened to Greece and Rome was supposed to have a sobering
effect on the legislative action of the senators. Of the eight large
paintings in the room the most important is said to be the allegory
of the League of Cambrai by Palma il Giovane. The League was
a bloc formed against Venice by France, Spain and the Holy See
in 1508 to deprive the republic of much of its Continental territory. The doge depicted is Leonardo Lauridant who gets his his-

BRIDGE OF SIGHS
for Fornaretto, two lamps

tory's credit for building the Rialto Bridge. All the senate seats are the same ones in which the Venetian senators dozed and debated.

In the Hall of the Council of Ten a secret panel connects with the jail by the famous Bridge of Sighs which can best be seen from the Riva degli Schiavoni. Of the sighs emitted by prisoners trudging between the jail and the Council Room, where their cases were tried, observers estimate that ninety-five percent were the unhappy ones of the convicted, and five the happy sighs of the exonerated. Two lamps burn eternally on the Bridge of Sighs, they say for the memory of Fornaretto, a baker who was falsely sent to death. One night on the way home from work Fornaretto discovered the body of a Venetian noble. By a peculiar twist of clues, fate and circumstance the crime was hung on the baker. The public petitioned for his freedom, but Fornaretto was condemned to death. Finally one of the highest ranking nobles of the city confessed the crime, but Fornaretto was hung before his pardon arrived.

All political offenses and misdemeanors alike were judged in the council hall under a ceiling painted by Veronese. The painting was later taken by Napoleon.

Many of the cases which came before the Council of Ten originated in a foyer in the Palace which was decorated with a lion's head. In the lion's mouth was a slit where informers could slip unsigned letters which conceivably would raise doubts about the indicated citizen's loyalty. The informers' letters were read by three judges who constituted a sort of Un-Venetian Affairs Committee. Suspects were placed under surveillance, and if found guilty, hanged.

Elsewhere in the Palace is a trophy room which contains two-handed swords, lances, captured Turkish trophies decorated with the half-moon, and the original armor of Henry IV of France. Henry was short, but clever. Although there are those who find interest in the helmets worn by the Doge's personal guard, the biggest drawing card in the Trophy Room is the chastity belt with which military men, off for the wars, insured the fidelity of their wives. The one which was in Venetian vogue is a belt of iron fitted with sharpened metal prongs to keep adulterers at a distance. Also in the collection is a machine gun with twenty revolving barrels, a bevy of Turkish flags and an early cannon.

The world's largest painting, "Paradise" by Tintoretto stretches across the top of the throne in the Great Council Hall. Over 600 figures are in the painting, and the heads of most of them are portraits of the artist's personal friends. Tintoretto did best by himself, giving to the central figure of Christ, his own face. Tintoretto's wife is the Virgin. History agrees that Tintoretto wasn't very modest, but in those days nobody questioned a great artist, and Tintoretto qualified as that. Around the top of the wall are portraits of doges, two to a panel. Seventy-eight are in this room, the rest in an adjoining chamber. There was room for thirteen more doges when the line was ended in 1797. A black veil covers the portrait of one Marino Faliero, an autocratic doge who was beheaded in the courtyard of the Palace in 1355 when a plot to make himself dictator of the Republic was uncovered in the nick of time. The Great Council Hall was used for the combined assembly of nobles and magistrates, and sometimes for state receptions. It measures 90 feet wide, 180 feet long, and is 45 feet high.

Of contemplative interest to all married men is the "Last Judgment" by Palma the Younger which hangs in the Voting Room off the Great Council Hall. In the massive work the artist depicts his wife in three circumstances. With long blonde hair, bare chest, and a green robe she is beautiful in Paradise. Lying on her side with her right hand elevated, she offers mixed emotions in purgatory. In hell she lies on her left side, covers her chest and wears a look of definite apprehension. At the exit, the kneeling lady in the lower picture on the left wall is Catherine Cornaro, Queen of Cyprus. Afraid of the power of Venice, she offered the Republic her crown and her country. Venice accepted, gave her sanctuary in a splendid palace on the Grand Canal. It is now a pawnshop.

In the depths of the Palace are the cells and torture chambers where the Republic confined the enemies of state and of society. Nobility got a wood floor and a hard bed, but commoners just got soft Istrian stone of which the entire Palace is constructed. Some cells were called wells, because during high tide prisoners found themselves knee-deep in water, rats and foul debris of the sea. Tides have risen so high in Venice that on occasion gondolas have skimmed along St. Mark's Square. Prisoners lucky enough to get out of the dungeon, were also lucky if they had not gone mad, or in the darkness, blind.

Lord Byron once spent three days and three nights in a cell to get an impression of the life.

Before leaving the Doge's Palace, walk along the beautiful loggia of the Foscari Gallery, a terrace overlooking the *piazzetta*. Two of the columns are of red stone, and between these were read the public proclamations. Often the proclamations included announced the names of those who would be hung. Traditionally the gallows were slung between the two columns in the *piazzetta*. Atop the left column is a lion with the wings of an eagle, the symbol of Venice, for 400 years one of the richest, most powerful states in the world. On the other column is St. Theodore, before 1521, the patron Saint of Venice. Both columns were brought from Constantinople and have stood on the *piazzetta* since the twelfth century. Before the guilty were hanged they always prayed to the soul of the unjustly accused baker, Fornaretto. And after they were hung, though it was a horrible sight, the Venetians said to each other that at least they had died in a beautiful frame.

In the postwar craze to shoot moving pictures on actual location, historic Venice has been a stage setting for many films. Orson Welles and a whole company took over the Doge's Palace one day, filling it with spotlights, cameras and costumed actors. Wire was spread all over the ancient floors like black spaghetti. Orson wearing a white shirt unbuttoned to his navel, and a long floppy silk ascot was standing on the Foscari Gallery overlooking the Square. He was talking to the press. "Why use natural backgrounds?" he thundered in answer to a question. "Look out there!" he commanded, sweeping his arm over the view. "That's the Piazza San

THE RIALTO BRIDGE
"What news?"

Marco! That's the Piazza San Marco!" he shouted with uncommon fervor, wrapping up his entire argument in one exclamation.

Some scenes from the *Prince of Foxes* were also shot in Venice. For a gondola scene the city, out of hospitality, stopped traffic on certain canals where the company was working. That burned up a Venetian who demanded to be let through. "You cannot go through," a policeman explained, "they are making a picture." "Raphael made a lot of them," the art-minded Venetian shot back, "but he never stopped traffic on the canals."

Striking out on foot, you can walk from the Square to the great Rialto Bridge, which has twenty-four stores along its span. Once a drawbridge that could be raised to let warships pass, the

IT'S A BRIDGE
but it has twenty-four shops

Rialto collapsed in 1444 from the crowd which had congregated for the wedding of the Marquis of Ferrara. Although Michelangelo and Andrea Palladio both submitted designs in competition for the new bridge, the accepted design was the work of Antonio da Ponte. As a link between the markets and the St. Mark's quarter, the bridge has always been one of the busiest in Venice. From Venice to Broadway, via Shakespeare's "The Merchant of Venice," came the expression, "What news on the Rialto?"

In the fantastic bustle of the markets on the other side of the Rialto you'll see a conglomeration of foods that is assembled nowhere else in the world. In the fish market you'll see dogfish, swordfish, eels from one inch to one foot long, *scampi* and purple lobsters. And since Venice has a great cat population because it has a rat population, one merchant sells nothing but fish for cats. A portion sells for 1/67th of a cent.

Gondola tours glide down the Grand Canal like an invading fleet, with four or five tourists in each craft. The guide stands up in his boat and shouts the commentary. A floating rubberneck tour is almost as interesting a sight as the sights themselves. Gondolas are long, sleek black boats made of oak, high in the front and even higher in the back. The bow is fitted with a brass plate shaped like a silhouette of the doge's hat with six teeth added underneath. The gondolier stands on the back, one foot slightly behind the other, propelling the gondola by a forward, pushing motion of a long oar, as you would backwater a rowboat. Gondoliers wear white middies, and sometimes basque shirts underneath, and straw hats with colorful bands. Sometimes they just wear old clothes. Few of them, the travelogues be damned, ever sing. They are members of a tough union, they haggle over prices, and usually it is best to ask the price first, then let the hotel concierge at your destination be your bargaining agent. Going around a blind corner a gondolier shouts in Venetian dialect, either *apre mi!* (keep to the left), or *sciastai!* (keep to the right). Once gondolas were painted bright colors according to the rank of nobility of the owner. As an added bit of decoration, they trailed a bit of colored damask. During a plague they were painted black, which has become the traditional color. The gondoliers are locked in a mortal struggle currently with the *scofisti,* the motorboats which zip along the canals creating waves that smack against the boat bottoms, and generally making gondoliering a good deal more difficult. The waves of the *scofisti* also expose the teakwood pilings to the air, which increases the rate of rot. Theoretically motorboats are not supposed to travel faster than seven kilometers an hour. Speed cops travel in oar-propelled gondolas.

GONDOLAS AND SCOFISTI
apre mi!

Anyway, slipping down the Grand Canal, past the gaily colored barber-pole pilings, and the great Renaissance *palazzos*, here is what you might look for: The Church of Santa Maria della Salute opposite the Europa Hotel which was erected by the state in appreciation of the sudden cessation of the plague of 1631, which came to an end as if by divine intervention. A pontoon bridge is stretched across the canal during the annual church festival. Inside are paintings by Titian and Tintoretto. Across the canal next to the Grand Hotel is the house of Othello and Desdemona of Shakespeare's tragedy. Farther down the canal, on the same side as the church, is the Palazzetto Dario, a crumbling building decorated with colored marble, once the home of Gabriele

D'Annunzio. The first bridge under which you will pass is the Ponte dell Accademia, which though 200 years old, is still called the "temporary bridge." Still standing on the right side is the ivy-covered home of the Doge Marino Faliero who was beheaded in disgrace in 1355. Beyond is the Palazzo Rezzonico where Browning died, marked by a plaque, and farther on the Vendramin Calergi Palace, surrounded by brightly-painted poles, where Richard Wagner wrote part of the *Walküre* and later died. And on a side canal past the firehouse is the place where the crippled Byron lived and from which he swam the entire distance to the Lido.

One of the best trips in Venice is the half-day motorboat tour that covers Burano, Murano and Torcello, three suburban isles of Venice. Burano, five miles from Venice, is an island of some 7,000 people mostly fishermen, many of whom have never seen an automobile. Burano is the lace island of Venice. While the men sail out to catch eel, sole and *scampi*, the women — young girls and aging matrons — crowd into the lace school to spend their days making Burano and Venise, two types of lace. Schoolgirls work seven to eight hours a day, study from eight to ten at night, get about seventy cents a day. Each lace worker operates as part of a team, working only one part of the pattern, some stitching by hand, others sewing on Singer machines. A handworker can finish eight or ten inches a day, but if the nuns who supervise the girls don't pass on the lace, the work is unraveled and begun again. An eleven-piece luncheon set of ten place mats and a runner might sell for 415,000 lire, tiny lace butterflies which take six days to make, 4,000 lire. A lace collar of Venise which is about three months work, costs 30,000 lire.

Murano, nearby, is the center of Venetian glass manufacture. Travelers on tours are always given a glass-blowing exhibition, usually in the studio of Antonio Nason, before being ushered

MURANO
glass and roasted eel

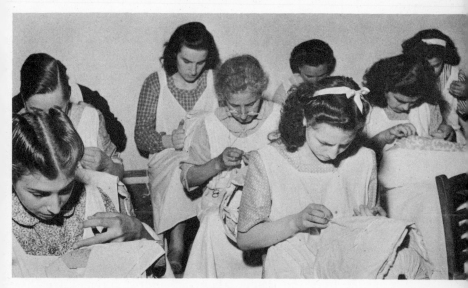

BURANO
while the men fish

through the showrooms. Most Venetian glass reflects the charac-
teristic Oriental caste of the Byzantines. Often it is ruby, blue
and green, dripping with gold decoration. Nason's is almost 200
years old, but the glass industry on Murano has been going since
the ninth century. Luigi Sordillo, a Nason partner who speaks
perfect English, says the company sells such American firms as
Wanamaker's and Marshall Field's, but tourists coming to the
plant on Murano are given wholesale prices. A 64-piece set for
example, including water, champagne, wine and liqueur glasses
will set you back 40,000 lire. A gold-decorated or engraved set
might bring a million and a half lire. All prices were quoted with
the lire at 675 to the dollar.

Should you stay on Murano after the tour sails back to
Venice, you might look up the Mazzega, a restaurant where they
cook the fish in the same oven in which glass is baked. The favorite
dish is *Bisato sull Ara,* which is roasted eel, cooked in the oven,
and turned forty-seven times. Sinclair Lewis's hangout when he
was on the island was the Romano, where the fishermen come to
eat *Rissotto di Seppioline,* black rice and octopus.

The musky quietude of Torcello, the third island, seems to
pervade one's soul, like an exquisite, long-sought peace. An aged
woman lolls in the sun only moving to lift a jug of water to her
lips to drink. A solitary barge glides down the canal among the
reeds. Torcello, founded in 280 A.D. was the first Venice. It once
had a population of 50,000. But Torcello was difficult to defend,
and surrounded by sweet water, its marshes were a breeding
ground for malaria. A Bubonic plague which struck in 1439, drove
the people from the island. About a hundred farmers live there
today—they and the ancient eleventh century Church of St. Fosca
with its marble shutters, and the seventh century Duomo with the
favorite chair of Attila, King of the Huns, and its eighth century
mosaic of the Last Judgment. Next door is the country branch

TORCELLO
once there were 50,000

of Harry's Bar, a quiet inn which hardly alters the peaceful land-scape. Yet in this remote hideaway is a guest book proving the presence, at one time or another, of Duff Cooper, Merle Oberon, Cass Canfield the publisher, John Gunther, Constantin Alajálov the artist, and Winston's girl Sarah, among many others.

Of all the places in Italy, travelers can feel least self-conscious about bargaining for better prices when shopping in Venice. The city deals in tourists, and the merchants of Venice through cen-turies of Oriental trading, have got into the habit of establish-ing an asking and a selling price. I personally watched one trades-man drop fifty dollars on a lace banquet cloth on the opening haggle. Of course the elite shops have a standard, usually unwavering price. One of these is Asta, on St. Mark's Square, which has tablecloths from $50 to $1,000. You'll have to spend $200 to get one with lace. Bridal veils run from $60 to $1,500. Asta's did the trousseau for the Princess of Egypt, counts among its customers Mary Pickford, the Selznicks, the Fairbankses and Barbara Hutton. Probably its highest priced item is a reproduction of a ceiling in the Doge's Palace done completely in Burano lace. Price: about $10,000.

Giovanni Seno, on the Calle Larga San Marco, has laces, embroideries, blouses, and a selection of leathers as well. Twelve mats, twelve napkins and a runner cost about 55,000 lire; Burano lace on an Irish linen tablecloth with twelve napkins is about 180,000 lire.

❧ *The Lido*

A stylish, sandy shoal fifteen minutes by fast motorboat from the heart of Venice, the Lido protects the city from the open sea. On its warm sands, in its elegant hotel rooms and gay ballrooms and immaculate streets which hum with the tread of underslung, convertible Fiats and pastel Cadillacs, the Lido likewise protects its cultured flock from the hard world of the mainland to the near northwest. Nearly a half of the seven-mile island is flat beach from over a hundred to nearly three hundred yards wide. Here in summer, separated by a moat of Adriatic sea from the humdrum and the hurly-burly, come the heiresses and movie moguls, the long-haired movie stars, the society matrons trailing their long-haired dachshunds, the citizens of two continents who have turned a fast buck, or for that matter, even a slow one.

In summer, motorboats of the Compagnia Italiana dei Grandi Alberghi leave from the Royal Danieli for the Excelsior Palace

THE LIDO
underslung Fiats, pastel Cadillacs

in Lido every half-hour. Public boats operating from the railroad
station in Venice make four stops, and reach the Lido in about
twenty minutes. A slower (and cheaper) boat stops eighteen times
and takes one hour. Although farther out in the sea, the Lido is
bereft of canals. By special arrangement you can take your car
from the Piazzale Roma to the Lido by ferry.

There are any number of hotels and pensions on the Lido,
but the flossy life centers about the Excelsior Palace, one of the
great hotels of the world. In the years before the war came Barbara Hutton. Here she met Alexis Mdivani whom she later married. Sadder and wiser, and in ill health she returned in 1949
wearing Chinese pajamas, her familiar costume. If the social

whirl was led in the old days by such a sprightly arbiter as Princess Jane San Faustino, an American who married an Italian title, the leaders today are the Pacific Coast potentates from Hollywood. An immense cigar, followed at a distance by Darryl Zanuck is a familiar sight along the Lido. During the annual International Film Festival the potentates held a sort of court in their *cabañas,* like Indian chieftains pitching tepees before the big tribal conclave.

The film festival is an outgrowth of the annual Venice art show which was first started in the Nineties. The festival idea has spread to music and the theater, and more recently in Venice, to tennis championships, rowing, cruising and fishing boat regattas, a congress of the dance, pigeon shooting competitions, air meetings and speed races for private planes, an international horse show, and ultimately to a spring philatelic meeting.

A typical day of all who come to the Lido, except perhaps the philatelists, begins at about eleven a.m. with an appearance at the cabaña. The cabañas of the Excelsior, shaded by awnings supported by blue and white poles, stretch literally as far as the eye can see. Should anyone venture near the water, they will be watched by the hotel lifeguards who dress in flaming red shirts, blue shorts and straw hats worn with turned-down brim. Lying on the beach absorbing the summer Italian sun, the vacationist can refresh himself with fruit borne by a fruitseller in immaculate whites who trudges up and down the sands carrying his canopy-covered fruit tray on his head. Or he can buy souvenirs for the children back home from a burnished hawker who makes models of the Adriatic sailboats and carries his stock, likewise, on his head. The more energetic guests, perhaps those too young to have been permitted to stay up all the previous night, will surely be playing *tamburello* on the beach. One man whose custom it was to relieve himself of hangovers by relaxing on the beach described the game this way: "You're lying on the beach taking it easy, see,

THE EXCELSIOR'S DOCK
to the sandy shoal, fifteen minutes

BARBARA WAS BACK
wearing Chinese pajamas

when two fellows start beating a ball on a goddam goatskin over your head. It goes bong, bong, bong, bong. That's *tamburello*." Actually *tamburello* is played by two people each of whom holds a round goatskin-covered racquet that resembles a tambourine. Standing perhaps a hundred yards apart they hit a tiny rubber ball back and forth to each other. Each hit sounds like a rock thrown against a snare drum.

About two or three o'clock in the afternoon the assemblage gathers for lunch in the Excelsior's Taverna, a cryptlike restaurant with a straw roof, seventy-five yards from the sea. Over the tomato-colored tablecloths one might see Anna Magnani the roughneck star of the Italian films, or Ambassador Dunn, the gentle emissary of the American State Department. At the entrance a crowd of barefoot bobby-soxers is mobbing a star in the manner perfected by the juvenile hordes who prey in front of The Stork and "21" in New York. The star turns out to be Maria Montez, in bathing suit. She turns and runs for the sanctuary of the bar.

The guests who are not stars return to the cabañas to loll until four or five when they go to the bar or the bridge rooms. They dress in time for a nine o'clock dinner. At least once or twice a week there are huge galas held outdoors and lighted by sparkling jewels and fireworks. Sometimes a dance floor is built on the beach. While the fireworks burst over the Adriatic, models from Paris parade the style of the *couturiers*. It was at such a fashion show at the Lido in 1925 that beach pajamas were first introduced.

During the film festival, which usually runs from the middle of August into September, there are nightly showings of entries in the modernistic movie theater across the street. The theater is dark all year except for the twenty days of the festival. If there are neither films nor galas, there is always the Casino de Venezia Lido, near the theater, which has gambling in public or private salons, and its own cabaret. Built at a prewar cost of a million dollars, it is decorated with Italian marble, Italian silk and Venetian glass. Its thirteen roulette wheels, eight baccarat tables, and two *trente-quarante* games have a total play of a hundred million lire a day. The casino's own ferry runs from 3 P.M. to 5 A.M. picking up the sportsmen at all the hotels from the Venice railroad station to the Lido.

A day on the Lido, for the hardiest members of the international set, ends at four in the morning. But one baggy-eyed hotel man, weary at the end of a gay postwar season thought the night really ended later in the morning. "The Lido life," he said disgruntledly, "starts at four in the afternoon and ends at six in the morning. It's an upside-down existence," he went on. "This is no man's land for a rest."

Not all Lido living is done on the hopped-up schedule of an inverted clock face. There are those who live in moderation at the Excelsior, and those who live almost primly at the Grand Hotel des Bains, down the road. Prices run about twenty percent less than the Excelsior in the less elegant Hotel des Bains. All rooms face on the sea or the private park which insures reasonable quiet for the Italian families who are the hotel's most important clientele. The beach is the continuation of the Excelsior's and there is an excellent restaurant called the Pagoda, two stories up over the sand and sea.

And for anyone who would like to relax for an hour from the world of eyewash and eyeshadow, the Lido has an inelegant little retreat a few blocks from the Excelsior known as the Alla Vida. A *trattoria* in the conventional Italian fashion, it has tables set up in an arbor of honeysuckle and wisteria vines. Full meal with wine costs about $1.40 per person.

On the far end the Lido has a number of low-priced hotels, and public bathhouses on a stretch of beach equally broad and equally sandy.

Planes for Venice land directly on the city's airport on the Lido. Hitler's plane landed there in 1934 for the first Hitler-Mussolini meeting. As the plane from Germany made a landing and taxied up, Mussolini and his entourage were waiting. Hitler stepped out of the plane, took one look at Mussolini, and reportedly said, "I don't like him." So began a beautiful friendship.

The Lido has another remembrance of the war, too. It's the great Italian liner *Conte de Savoia*, one-time pride of the Atlantic. Its 48,502 tons charred and rusted, the *Conte de Savoia* lies just off the pleasant island, a total wreck.

THE DOLOMITES

deep rose and kelly green

7. THE DOLOMITES

The Dolomites are the Italian Tyrol. South of the Brenner Pass and Innsbruck, and north of the Venetian Plain the Dolomites stretch about seventy miles wide and extend about sixty-five miles deep. Tucked in the northeast corner of the country, they take their name from the French scientist, Comte de Dolomieu. As a mountain range they are actually a continuation of the Alps, but since — as Dolomieu discovered — they are magnesian limestone, they have a tendency to chip and erode, leaving bold, jagged, perpendicular peaks stabbing into the Alpine sky. In the sun the Dolomites reflect a deep rose hue which contrasts with the kelly-green grass carpets which cover the valleys between peaks. And clustered in the center of the carpets, as if great hands had lifted the edges of the grass and shaken everything down into the folds, are the Alpine villages of white plaster and pine board in the Tyrol style.

In the Dolomites the men often wear *lederhosen*, Alpine hats, and are given to pipe-smoking and mountain climbing. On Sun-

outworn methods, ancient superstitions

days the older women wear black shawls, about all that is left of
the mountain costume which is sometimes still dusted off for wed-
dings and church festivals. For such occasions the ladies don black
high hats, red jackets with black piping, brocaded cuffs of gold
and lace collars pulled together with pink ribbon. The skirt is
black, gold fringed and flowered, and the low black shoes have
a large silver buckle. The clannish mountain people live in tiny
villages, sometimes no larger than a group of five houses. They
farm by outworn methods and live by ancient superstitions. In
September when the hay is cut they gather it into huge bundles
which are tied in aprons. The hay makes a load perhaps four feet
square which is lifted onto the head — the twelve-year-old son
and the eighty-two year-old grandmother each taking a turn —
and carried into the barn.

When anyone dies in the Dolomites the neighbors immediately
take over the arrangements, preparing for the burial, seeing that
mass is said, that the bells are rung, and that the rest of the
family has food. And it used to be that they sewed the feet of the

For a Safe Return
a cross of salt

deceased in black socks as a sign that he would never walk again. But when a child died there was always a party and a dance, because it was believed that its soul went straight to paradise.

One of the oldest forms of social government in the world exists among the mountain farmers. Most of them are still members in a cooperative grazing system, fraught with tradition, which is now over 1,000 years old. Every April the farmers gather in the village to choose a shepherd who will take their collective herds into the high grazing country and keep them there all summer. The shepherd must keep a vigilant eye over the cattle during the day, bring them back to a shed in the hills at night, and send the milk down to the owners below. When applying for the job in the spring the shepherd appears before the villagers and removes his hat which is passed from farmer to farmer. Each man can drop either a white bead or a black bead into the hat, the latter customarily signifying disapproval. When a shepherd has been picked the mayor reads the announcement. While reading he keeps one foot on the rock as a sign that his proclamation is unwavering.

In fall the shepherd brings down the cattle from the mountains, but before entering a barn he throws a cross of salt on the floor as a symbol of thanksgiving for their safe return.

The mountain people also have a ceremony for courting, one version for summer and another for winter. In summer a boy serenades a girl from the street. If she lights the window he can, if nimble enough, climb up to the window and talk to her. In winter the male is invited inside without a serenade. But he must leave the house precisely at the moment the girl's father winds the clock.

The Dolomites are tourist country in both summer and winter. Among the likeliest resorts are Cortina which is pure Alpine, Bolzano which is as Teutonic as a German band, Merano which is what they call in Europe a "climate station," and San Martino di Castrozza, one of those unbelievable little spots on the globe to which some romanticist always promises some blonde he is going to take her before they both die. All these places can be reached via a network of public buses known as the S.A.D., the Societa Automobilistica Dolomiti. The S.A.D. buses are neither as new nor as comfortable as the CIAT line, but they have glass tops and they get you there with at least a minimum of comfort. If you are driving your own car you will find the twisting, turning Dolomite roads too narrow for driving a bus or a Cadillac. But the surface is good, and the views incredible.

A part of Austria until the peace following the First World War, the Dolomites inherited many of the beer hall and sausage characteristics of the Germans. The influence is particularly strong in the western Dolomites, but the whole area was always popular with the Germans before they stopped crossing borders for pure pleasure in 1939. The mountain dialects, however, are neither German, French or Italian. Gardera or Gardena, the original language of the Alps, is incomprehensible to the Italians. A vest in Italian is *panciotto*, but in *patois* it comes out *croggioto*. A hat is a little closer. It is *capallo* in Italian, and *ciapel* in mountain talk.

Largest of the Dolomitian resorts is Cortina d'Ampezzo, which happens also to be the largest winter sports station in all Italy. Cortina was once a part of the Venetian Republic, but was ceded to Austria as an aftermath of the Austro-Venetian War in 1511. For a while the area passed under the French rule of Napoleon, but reverted to Austria until it was finally awarded to Italy for her part in the Allied cause of 1914-1918.

German elements took over for another stretch in World War II, using Cortina as a hospital until partisans liberated the section in April 1945. The resort became an Allied rest center, and the mountain village filled with English, Polish, Americans, Australians, New Zealanders and French.

Cortina d'Ampezzo, if you want to be technical, is really thirty-seven tiny villages of which Cortina, in the valley, is the main one. A summer and winter resort, Cortina is a four-hour morning drive by S.A.D. bus from Venice. Leave the canals after breakfast and you are in the mountains before lunch. You can also come by rail, changing at Calalzo to the blue and white electric mountain railway. The diesel-powered *Littorina Express* comes up from Venice five times a day, and takes three hours.

Cortina offers magnificent scenery, relief from the Italian heat, nine holes of golf, tennis and mountain climbing in the summer; hunting for deer and chamois in the fall; and winter sports

CORTINO D'AMPEZZO
leave the canals after breakfast

when the snow falls. It will be the site of the winter Olympics of
1956. The best hotel, the Miramonti, just outside town, was leased
as a rest center for United States troops in Trieste until the summer of 1950. The first-class Cristallo Palace, however, has a won-
derful location high over the town, with an open tea-terrace commanding the view, an open-air swimming pool, tennis court, and
an enclosed basement night club when things turn cool. During
the high season (July 25 to August 25 and December 20 to January 10) the single rate for room and bath with all meals runs
about 4,000 lire plus the usual 18 percent additional for tips and
taxes.

The Savoy Hotel in the village itself has a roof solarium for sun baths in both summer and winter, and a tiny five- by twelve-yard tiled pool just for cooling off. The water is heated and dunkers are protected from the Alpine breezes by a glass wall. A heated tunnel connects the main hotel with its annex across the street. A new night club in the hotel is decorated with rawhide leather fixtures and corduroy seats. The Cristallino, another night club, uses a decor of bird cages which house exotic-looking canaries. Across the street the Hotel Post, an alcove of which was once the town post office, has a salon done up with paneled walls and pewter mugs. About the best of the second-class hotels in town is the Bellevue which has a large night club, a small den with a fireplace and a large American clientele.

Aside from farming, the mountain people also turn out some handsome, often intricate handicraft which is for sale in the shops of Cortina. The Industria Ampezzana, a cooperative, has a beautiful collection of boxes and tables with inlaid mother-of-pearl and hardwood. The style, called Tarkasi, was brought to Cortina from India by an Englishman. Cigarette boxes with the inlaid work cost about 1,700 lire, inlaid checkerboard tables about 9,500 lire. There is also a selection of locally-made wrought iron. The Chedina Frajo has Alpine wall clocks carved like a chalet with an Alpine miss in a swing serving as pendulum (7,000 lire), and a selection of hand-carved bottle corks sculptured into heads of men and women who tip their hats or kiss each other.

Bredo's has a chic collection of Italian-styled sportswear at some rather fancy prices. Fashioned in original designs are Bredo's fur-lined raincoats, suede jackets and winterwear. For skiing they show black ski pants worn with black ski boots and a lamb-lined gabardine jacket with fur-lined hood. The ensemble, less the boots, costs 50,000 lire.

Summer or winter there are excursions in Cortina up the Monte Faloria cable car. In Italy a cable car is a *teleferica* or a

funivia. It swings all the way up to 2,120 meters above the village
(there are 39 inches in a meter). In winter a sleigh funicular takes
you up to 2,300 meters. At any rate there is an observation tower
on top which the Germans used as an aircraft station during the
recent war. It was their dismal duty to report the hundreds of
American bombers who flew directly over Cortina every day
coming from Foggia to bomb the Innsbruck and Munich area.

In July the mountaintop is covered with red flowers of pigmy
rhododendron plants set among the evergreen trees and the rose
Dolomitian peaks. It's the time of the year to bring a jug of wine
and a box lunch and set off down the mountain trails. Three trails
start from the observation tower and each is marked by blue, red
or yellow spots painted on the rocks.

A Viennese named Grohmann came to Cortina to go mountain climbing in 1863, and his accounts of his adventures created
the first tourist interest in the town. Mountain climbing is still a
popular sport, and participants coming to Cortina in summer can
always pick up a guide in front of the Cristallino. Like almost
everything else in the Dolomites, the guide fees are inexpensive,
ranging from 2,000 to 20,000 lire according to the climb. The most
popular of the difficult climbs is the southeast ride of Punata
Fiames. It's a two-hour hike to its base, a three-hour climb to its
summit, and a two-hour walk home. The guide fee is 12,000 lire.
Most popular of the novice climbs is the Cinque Torre, the Five
Towers. It takes three hours to get there, an hour and a half to
climb, and two hours to return. The guide fee is 2,000 lire.

A seventy-mile twisting, turning trip over the Great Dolomite Road takes you from Cortina to Bolzano. In some places
the road is a series of flat S curves and turns so sharp that the
traffic can only proceed in one direction at a time. In the S.A.D.
bus, the seventy miles of winding and turning, climbing and descending, takes a full day. But the scenery is beautiful, completely

July is the time of the year

different from the real character of Italy. There are no olive-skinned, shoeless, sad-eyed kids by the side of the road. One sees big touring cars, tops down, full of European tourists wearing, after the European manner, white leather helmets, eye goggles and sometimes dusters. For a joy ride the Continental decks himself out like a tank captain. By lunchtime the bus puffs into the Pordoi Pass where passengers can get a bite to eat and a look at the Maramalada, highest peak in the Dolomites. The mountain is 11,020 feet, the pass 7,384 feet. A number of plain inns, one about as good as the other, will serve you a moderately-priced, simple meal. After lunch you can watch the motorcyclists roar through the pass in wolf packs. They wear helmets, goggles, sometimes black SS raincoats, and black Wehrmacht boots, looking for all the world like the storm troopers some of them obviously were. They nibble picnic lunch on the grass, compare each others' motorcycles, clatter in German, stomp about in their boots, ignore the tourists, snooze on the side of the road, and finally roar away. Some of them are Austrian, some Italian, and perhaps some are Swiss. They make a very weird sight.

Not far out of the Pordoi Pass, on the road to Bolzano, is Canazei in the Passa Valley, a center where Alpinists begin mountain walks and climbing expeditions. It has an elevation of 4,808 feet, in case you keep track of such statistics, and there are a number of small hotels of which the first-class Dolomiti is the best by a couple of lengths.

By teatime the bus is on the beautiful grounds of the Grande Albergo Carezza al Lago, fifteen miles from Canazai, fifty-four miles from Cortina. The 460-room first-class summer hotel has tennis courts, the only eighteen-hole golf course in the Dolomites, and a stone terrace looking out on the pines and the peaks. It's a short walk to the lake which reflects a turquoise tint akin to the color of Lake Louise in the Canadian Rockies.

As the Great Dolomite Road winds into Bolzano it is lined on both sides with grapes and *gasthauses*. The "gasthaus" lettered in old English on the side of the inns is the German word for the Italian *trattoria,* and in this district the Dolomites are about as Italian as Vienna. Bolzano is a business town on the main road that connects with Innsbruck and Munich. In the old days it was a transit point for the German and Austrian tourists coming down for a holiday in Merano, Carezza al Lago and Cortina. The hotels are filled instead with Americans and British, and Allied personnel working with the Occupation Forces in Germany who choose the Dolomites because they are both near and different. The best establishments, should you be staying overnight, are

PORDOI PASS
wolf packs on motorcycle

the Laurino and the Grifone-Bristol which is famous for its restaurant. Both are first-class.

Fifteen miles north of Bolzano, three-quarters of the way to the German border is Merano, once the Austrian city of Meran, now all-year-around Italian resort. A climate station where Europeans seek sanctuary from bad weather in their own hometown, Merano is most popular in spring and autumn. The mornings and the evenings are air-conditioned by the cool winds off the mountains, and there is little rain. In spring the apple and pear blossoms cover the fields all the way to Bolzano. In fall the visitors come to Merano to take the grape cure, a highly publicized purgative program. If you're suffering from nosebleed or fallen arches you're a likely candidate for the cure. It involves, as one Italian explained, "eating grapes until, like *pasta*, they come out of your ears, and that is supposed to cure you." The laxative effect comes, according to one opinion, from eating wine grapes instead of table grapes. More cynical sources say the result derives from the insecticide with which the grapes are sprayed all summer. At any rate, eating as many grapes as you can cram down your throat will have the same effect on your system whether you cram in Merano or Michigan. It just happens that Merano has been built up as a pleasant place to go for it.

There are ten kinds of red grapes and ten types of white grapes in Merano. The most famous white wines are Terlano and Termeno, the best-known reds, Sandbichler, a heavy Burgundy, and Santa Justina and Santa Maddalena.

Besides absorbing, in one form or other, the Meranese grape, visitors to Merano may also purge their purses at the local racetrack. The Grand Prix of Merano, an international sweepstake, is the big racing event of the autumn season.

For less dynamic endeavor there are excursions to the sixteenth century castles built in the environs by Austrian aristocrats. Many are owned today by English, Swedish and Dutch magnates. There are trips to the original village of Tyrol which in the twelfth century gave its name to the entire mountain area. It is fifteen minutes from Merano.

With thirty hotels Merano was quickly turned into a hospital center during the war, first by the Germans, and later by the British and Americans who also used it as a leave center. The three best hotels, the Palace, the Parc and the Grand Hotel Merano never re-opened. Principally it has been a problem raising the money for new furnishings.

About the best in town is the Savoy, which by a stretch of the government's imagination, is officially listed as first-class. Its dining room is quite good, but the furnishings are a little tired too. The hotel was used by the Germans as a convalescent home for the SS, and as a rest center for Americans. It charges 3,000 lire with full pension, 4,000 lire if you want a private bath. The best

Grapes and gasthauses ... *and* herren *in lederhosen*

of the second-class inns are the **Bellevue**, the **Excelsior** and the **Continental**. Rates in any of the three run about 2,500 without bath, 3,000 with bath, all meals included.

Lately Merano has taken to capping the fall season with an international sports festival which comes to an end with a great fireworks display along the banks of the Adige River. The

Meranese and the tourists pack the shores, and jam the bandshell in front of the Kuurhaus where the local band pumps out the oompah. The musicians dress in black vests and green suspenders and wear black hats with red bands, and flowers stuck in the band. The music reminded me a good deal of the aggregation that comes over from Yorkville every Christmas to play "O Tannenbaum" in our backyard, but the *herren* in *lederhosen* and high white socks pounded their palms vociferously. The refreshment stands were packed with rich pastries and chocolate. Soldiers of a mountain regiment wearing dashing Robin Hood caps with long feathers wandered through the streets. For all the world it could have been prewar Austria, or for that matter a Victor Herbert operetta.

camellias, azaleas, peace and quiet

8. THE LAKES

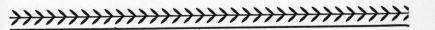

Nestling up against the Swiss Alps whose melting spring snows have for centuries been their source of water are the famed Lombard lakes, the vacation place for tycoons and Toscanini, the center of silk and sailboats. The largest of the lakes, reading from left to right, are Maggiore, Lugano and Como. A fourth, Lago di Garda, the largest lake in Italy, lies to the east, under the Dolomites, about midway between Milan and Venice. Milan, which is just south of Maggiore, Lugano and Como, and west of Garda, is the tourists' turntable for lakeshore resorts.

Lago Maggiore is a long, curling worm of a lake, running generally north and south, stretching its far-end several miles into Swiss territory. Locarno, where the pact was made in 1925, sits on its northern tip. It is a Swiss city. On the west shore is the Italian resort of Stresa which in total is one lake-front street bordered with hotels on one side, and open-air cafes and restaurants on the other. You sit by the side of the lake with a trayful of pastries, you watch the white ferries puffing back and forth,

LAKE MAGGIORE
on the north, the Swiss

the skiffs with their flat canvas canopies stretched over the top to keep out of the sun, the hills rising in the background almost straight out of the water, and you contemplate nothing. In Stresa, where everything is peace and quiet, the season opens at Easter and closes in September. In April and May the walks are colored with camellias and azaleas, and the crowd at Eastertime is heavy. High season, which means higher rates because the hotels are full, comes in July, August and — depending upon the weather — the beginning of September.

There are some seventeen hotels in Stresa, of which two, the Grand Hotel et des Iles Borromées and the Regina Palace, are de luxe establishments. The Grand Hotel et des Iles Borromées — no one ever thinks of calling a hotel simply the Statler — is a rich old house facing directly on the lake. It overlooks the Borromean Islands from which it takes most of its unwieldy name. Like the equally elegant Regina down the street, the Grand sets up its tables out of doors when the weather is good, in full view of the lake across the road. It has dancing every night, three championship tennis courts, and although there is no beach, there is swimming from the dock in front of the hotel. It's a twenty-minute drive or a ride on the *funicular* to the nine-hole golf course on the heights.

Because Stresa is on the route of the *Simplon-Orient Express* which connects Paris with Rome, Vienna, Belgrade and Istanbul, the resort gets its share of diplomatic conclaves. The most famous was the Stresa Conference of 1935 which brought together Sir John Simon and Ramsay MacDonald of England, Pierre Laval and Prime Minister Flandin of France, and the Italian delegation headed by Mussolini. The Duce tried to ring in the Germans but the other countries refused. Each delegation had a floor at the Grand Hotel excepting Mussolini who stayed on Isola Bella, one of the Borromean Islands. The hotel guest book, however, contains the prewar signature of Mussolini, an inhibited scribble written in letters a quarter of an inch high. The last guest to register before the war started was an Englishman, the late Duke of Kent. Postwar visitors have included A. J. Cronin and Ernest Hemingway who occupied Room 156 in the fall of 1948, and signed himself in the guest book as "an old guest." Hemingway mentions the Grand Hotel et des Iles Borromées in *A Farewell to Arms,* a book banned by Mussolini. The Italian version was finally published while Hemingway was in Italy on his postwar trip. The most recent royalty at the hotel was the omnipresent Princess Margaret Rose who took Suites 104 to 107.

Aside from the fact that most of the ferryboats were strafed

STRESA FROM THE GRAND HOTEL

in the dining room, a horse

and sunk by Allied aircraft, Stresa escaped from the war virtually unscathed. After the hostilities it was for a time a Fifth Army Officers' Rest Camp. At the Grand, which like other hotels in town, was pressed into immediate service to house the officers during their five-day leaves, there was a party every night. Once

FOR AN AFTERNOON EXCURSION
three islands

an officer walked a horse into the dining room and ordered two breakfasts, and occasionally in the morning the kitchen staff would find pyramids of beer cans built on the terrace in front of the lake. A Romanian singer named Dina Duca, who was brought up from Milan to entertain the officers, married an American captain by the name of Wes Ross. Such was the pattern of activities that took place in the army's rest centers after the shooting stopped.

Rates nowadays in the refurbished Grand Hotel run 4,000 to 5,000 lire for a room and bath per person, American plan. Or, if you would rather have it figured this way, a double room with a tiled bath and a balcony over the lake would cost about $6.50 for two people without food. The Regina is about the same, and the attractive, red-painted Milan Hotel (first-class) which has a pretty, flowered terrace is about ten percent less.

Little boats along the lake front will take you chugging across Maggiore for an excursion to the Borromean Islands, all three of which can be covered in a morning or an afternoon. Largest of the islands is Isola Madre — the Mother Island — which was once a rocky isle, has long since been turned into one of the finest botanical gardens in Europe. Among the many botanical "firsts" which it proudly advertises is the largest rhododendron plant in Europe (it is forty-five feet high), and the palm tree with the broadest trunk in Italy. Climatically ideal, Isola Madre, in its imported earth, grows over 1,000 international varieties of plant life, among them: Indian willow, Japanese papyrus, Chinese bamboo, Australian mimosa, Japanese white orange, Louisiana cypress, Mexican pine and Algerian cedar. Elsewhere on the grounds, to complete the romantic idyll, is a cage full of lovebirds. For visitors who come to Stresa for Easter, April brings out the red rhododendrons and camellias. By May, somewhere among the Casmirian cypresses and the tropical breadfruit trees, bloom the blue rhododendrons, and the whole island is covered with azaleas in many colors. If your peregrinations among the plants give you aching arches, you can stop in for refreshment at the Restaurant La Piratera which has an open terrace near the water.

Isola dei Pescatori — the Island of the Fisherman — is a tourist's curiosity by day, and a quiet isolated fishing village of 300 people at night when the tourist boats come no more. The few fishermen you see during the day are spreading their nets to dry or scraping their boats. But most *pescatori* sleep during the day and take their queer, round-topped little boats out at night to fish in the quiet darkness for perch and trout.

Not far away is the main island of Isola Bella, which Count Charles Borromeo named after his wife Isabella. Its total population is seventy, mostly fishermen and fishwives, and the people are said to look alike and think alike. There are a few small inns on the island for those who seek isolation even from the quiet shore resorts of Maggiore. The most important single attraction of Isola Bella is the Palazzo Borromeo where through

ISOLA DEI PESCATORI
in the darkness, perch and trout

the years the Borromeos played host to visiting European royalty. It was built by Count Vitaliano Borromeo in 1650, is Baroque in design, and still is full of expensive *objects d'art*. Most of the chandeliers are Murano glass, the tapestries Flemish, the porcelain Viennese. Napoleon slept in the palace during the Italian campaign, in a bed with a white satin cover and a canopy fourteen feet high. His room also contains an eighteenth century washstand, and it is highly likely that Napoleon washed there, too. In the Music Salon, now called the Conference Hall, Mussolini convened the 1935 Stresa Conference. During the hot months the Borromeos used to take refuge from the weather in six grottos downstairs. They are crypts incredibly decorated with white pebbles from the lake and black lava stone from Vesuvius. Among the furnishings are an alabaster vase, a statue of a sleeping Venus, and a prehistoric boat found on the bottom of Lake Maggiore. There is a fee for visiting the palace, and when the tour ends the guide ushers the party to the edge of the garden where he rings a bell. Then he announces in four languages that the admission fee does not include the tip. The ringing bell which signifies farewell, also summons a new guide (who will want a new tip) to usher you through the palace gardens. The unabashed shakedown may peel some of the romantic glamour from the palace, the gardens and Isola Bella itself, an island which Goethe himself once testified was one of the most beautiful spots in all Italy.

Besides the tour of the islands, there is a Three-Lakes bus trip from Stresa which visits Locarno, Lugano, Porlezza, Cernobbio, Como and Varese. It leaves at 8:30 A.M. and returns at 8:00 P.M., costs 3,300 lire. CIAT has excursion service to Maggiore, Lugano and Como leaving at 8:30 A.M. and returning at 7:30 for 2,800 lire. Traveling on the regular CIAT route you can come up from Milan to Stresa in little more than an hour, stay in Stresa as long as you like, then pick up the same bus on another day and continue on to Pallanza on the other side of the lake. The tour goes on to Como, and eventually back to Milan.

The Number 1 sometime citizen of Pallanza is Maestro Toscanini who rents San Giovanni, the fourth of the Borromean Islands, scarcely fifty yards offshore from the Grand Hotel Majestic. The fifty yards of water and rock separates Toscanini from the outside world of gawkers, autograph hunters, impresarios and newspapermen. He has been renting the island since 1925. Every May to September with his driver, cook and chambermaid, he takes refuge in his fortress of twelve sleeping rooms, and six baths, a plain plaster palazzo set in an unkempt garden of overgrowth and underbrush.

MAGGIORE'S SAN GIOVANNI
Number 1 citizen: Toscanini

Once when Toscanini was besieged by a pair of journalists
from Milan who were determined to get an interview, the maestro
locked himself inside his fortress. "They want to see my face,"
he thundered, "they will see my rear-end." At other times he has
been known to be more affable, and occasionally bridges the moat
that separates him from the world, and appears for dinner in the
dining salon of the hotel. Proud of his age, Toscanini at 82 likes
to say, "I'm still going strong — just like Johnny Walker."

To the Grand Hotel Majestic the maestro has brought renewed fame. During ten years of war the hotel was successively
a barracks for the German Organization Todt, a hospital, a partisan headquarters and finally a headquarters for South African
troops. It re-opened in April 1949 as a first-class establishment,
with its own bathing beach and golf course. It has an even hundred rooms, but since it is not exactly of new construction, only
thirty-two baths. A single room with bath and full pension during

the high season costs about 2,900 lire, plus about twenty percent for tips and taxes.

A ferryboat from Intra which is spittin' distance from Pallanza will take you across a short neck of water to the east side of Maggiore. From there the road runs through Lago di Varese on one side and Lago di Lugano on the other to the Lago di Como, the most famous — and some say — the most beautiful of the Italian lakes. If you have lunched in Pallanza it is an easy drive to Como by teatime. There is also fast train service up from Milan, or you can cover the thirty miles by regular bus, riding over the autostrade between rows and rows of mulberry trees and billboards (which are smaller perhaps, but no less numerous than what you'll find on Route 1 between Maine and Florida). Since the days of the rambunctious Romans, Como the lake has been a retreat for sophisticates. Virgil and Claudian both sang of it, not to mention Pliny the Elder and his nephew, Pliny the Younger, writers and orators. Como the town, where both Plinys were born, is the great silk center of Italy. In lofts all over town you can watch the bobbins bob and the spindles spin, weaving rich cloth that will eventually be sent to Milan for distribution and sale. For retail sale Como offers the tourist perhaps the widest and least expensive assortment of silk goods in the whole country. See Moretti for piece goods and Ravasi on the Piazza Vittoria for ties, scarves and shirting. If you buy it by the meter, tie silk costs 2,200 lire. Fine cravats that would bring $6 to $8 in New York are on meticulous display in plastic cases at Ravasi for 1,000 lire, or less than two dollars. Woven designs cost 200 lire more. If you can still get excited about a cathedral by the time you hit Como, the local duomo is celebrated. Built of marble, it was begun in Gothic design in the late fourteenth century, and completed in Renaissance in the fifteenth century. The dome was added by a Sicilian in 1731.

THE LAKES

During the pleasant days from April to the end of October the Milanese and some rich internationalists — like the wealthy Romans long before them — take to their villas on the hillsides around Lake Como. The transients of the international set take refuge at the famed Villa d'Este on the shores of the lake at Cernobbio, five minutes from the town of Como. The Villa d'Este is a hotel with a bizarre past and an elegant present. Those who come now to sip cocktails on its lakeshore terrace, to play golf on its eighteen-hole course, to play tennis on its clay courts, to swim in Como's clear waters, to eat by the light of its northern Italian moon are mostly Americans, Europe's dollar aristocrats. Next come the English and the Egyptians, followed by a smattering of assorted Europeans.

Enough Continentals and enough Americans of Continental caste come to Como to lend to the afternoon cocktail hour the sharp atmosphere of flirtation, intrigue and chic on the grand scale. An ordinary summer's day might turn up one of Aly Khan's former American girl friends who is forgetting him with an Egyptian with whom she periodically appears at Europe's best hotels. A few tables away a six-foot, five-inch Dane in a white linen suit is dabbling in foreign exchange over tea and pastry. An American lady in a pink dress speaks alternately in French and Italian, returning every now and then to read snatches from a serial story in the new *Cosmopolitan* which she holds on her lap. A pair of American businessmen, traveling on an Olson Tour, bend over the bar, looking incredulously at a bottle of John Jameson. The inevitable *femme fatale* sweeps in on the arm of an ascotted Englishman who smokes a Turkish cigarette from a long holder. She wears a printed sports dress of many colors which dips low in front in salute to the male population. On the subject of her the gentlemen of the many nations are united. She puffs great clouds of smoke from a holder half a foot long, sips gin and orange

SILK MILL IN COMO
bobbins bob, spindles spin

AT THE VILLA D'ESTE
over the rail, feet

juice, talks American in carefully nurtured British syllables. There are those at the hotel who insist her speech slips now and then into plain New Yorkese. Two Egyptians and an Englishman are trying to raise a pair of seats for a Toscanini concert in Milan. And over by the edge of the lake a fat, florid-faced man from New Mexico in a bursting blue suit from Montgomery Ward sits in his shirt sleeves, his cowboy Stetson on his lap. On the all-expense tour of which he is a member, the pace is fast. It's hot, and he is hanging his feet over the railing to cool.

There is a marble statue in the hotel depicting a man bent over holding his side. The wags have it that the statue represents a departing guest who has just paid his bill. Actually by American luxury hotel standards the rates are not particularly high. A two-room suite with glass-enclosed bath which, wall to wall, could probably accommodate a convention of the Rotary International, costs about $14 a day per person with food. Add to that the customary charge for service and tax which comes to twenty percent. But there are rooms for less. The average room rate with pension figures somewhere between $8 and $10 a day per person.

For this tariff the guest has the pleasure of living in the sixteenth century Villa d'Este, a palace on which have been superimposed the rich trappings of the Renaissance, and the modern structure of a great hotel. By the lake he can indeed, on fine days, have tea, then supper, and finally he can dance there until midnight when the orchestra moves inside to give retiring guests with lakeside rooms a chance to sleep.

Villa d'Este can trace activity on its site all the way back to 1442, when the grounds were occupied by a convent. Activity on the property hasn't been so circumspect since. The Villa, which was built many years later, was the home during the early nineteenth century of General Pino, an Italian fighting in the forces of Napoleon. Pino's last campaigns took him to Spain where he successfully stormed a series of medieval castles. When he returned to his home on the shores of Como, Pino discovered that his wife had built for him, as a home-coming present, a replica of his conquered castles in Spain. He was so elated that he invited the entire cadet corps of a Milan military school down for the day, and had them put on a mock attack against the castle walls. The ruins of Countess Pino's home-coming gift to the general still stand on the heights above the hotel.

Shortly afterward Villa d'Este was purchased by Carolina Amelia Elizabeth of Brunswick-Wolfenbut, otherwise known as the Princess of Wales. A lady of uncertain moods, she ditched the Prince of Wales when she was forty-six and came to Como to start life over. That's when the party first started at Villa d'Este. Her gay court-in-exile was the object of extreme censure in London. When the Princess visited Vienna the British Ambassador and his entire staff put on their monocles and stalked out of the city. And when George III died in 1820 and the Prince of Wales was to be crowned she suddenly — and without invitation — appeared at Westminister Abbey. She was royally rebuffed, and as the uncrowned Queen of England she died the following month.

Aside from journeying up to the golf course, seven miles away, where one may lunch on the terrace instead of at the hotel, or strolling in the gardens which were begun by Pino and improved by the Princess of Wales, there are a number of excursions by steamer and speedboat to the romantic villas around the lake. Villa Carlotta between Tremezzo and Caden, once owned by a German prince, has a beautiful tropical garden now open to the public. And General Butler Ames of Boston lets parties wander through his Villa Balbianello at Tremezzo. You can sail up to Isola Comacina, an island given to the King of Belgium after World War I. He later gave it to an art museum in Milan, but it is open to tourists and has a lovely restaurant. Greta Garbo

COMO'S GOLF COURSE
Garbo was entranced

was particularly entranced by the sentimental legend of the Villa
Pliniana. In a not-so-brief encounter some years ago a beautiful,
prominent lady of Milan high society left her husband and went
to live with another man. The lovers closeted themselves inside
the Villa Pliniana and didn't reappear for seven years.

There are trips, too, up to Bellagio, Cadenabia and Menaggio
whose eighteen-hole golf course is the oldest in Italy. The Grand
Albergo Villa Serbelloni in Bellagio is classified de luxe, the Belvedere in Cadenabbia and the Victoria and Grand Albergo Menaggio in Menaggio are all first-class, not to mention the Regina Olga
in Cernobbio and the Grand Albergo Tremezzo in Tremezzo. From
any of these lakeshore retreats the most sportive excursion is the
night trip to the gambling casino at Campione on nearby Lake
Lugano. Completely inside Switzerland, Campione is nevertheless Italian territory, although the play is in Swiss francs.

The biggest gamble in the lake country during recent times
was made by none other than Benito Mussolini. He lost.

On April 23, 1945, when the Fascist cause in Europe was falling apart like a stale crumb cake, Mussolini sped from Lake Garda west across the highway to Milan. Through the cardinal he tried to make a deal with Italian partisans which would insure his personal safety. The partisans would have nothing short of Mussolini's head, so on April 24 the erstwhile Duce with his mistress Clara Petacci and twelve Fascist henchmen decided to make for Switzerland. They spent the night of April 24 at Como, and the next day joined a German truck column which, with a light tank in the van, was heading for the Swiss border only a few kilometers away. With Mussolini decked out in a German helmet, goggles and the uniform of a Nazi corporal, the column roared through Como, through Cernobbio and up the west shore of the lake until they got to Dongo where they were halted by a partisan roadblock. The German SS colonel in charge of the column gave the patriots Mussolini, his mistress and his aides, and in exchange the partisans let the Nazis continue north to the border.

Mussolini and his mistress were taken to a small house above Dongo which is near the northern end of the lake, and here they spent their last night together. The following day, April 26, a Communist band picked them up at the house, brought them down to Dongo and shot them against the wall of a villa. On April 27 the bodies were taken to Milan and strung up feet-first in the Piazza Loreto.

The Fascists were carrying a huge hoard of cash at the time of their capture, and the disappearance of the money began a lengthy litigation which is still continuing in the Italian courts. Since it was Italian Communists who shot Mussolini, the money is believed to have been appropriated by the party and used for election campaigns. The story of the "Dongo Treasure" has become an Italian *cause célèbre*, particularly because the original partisans involved in the capture and assassination appear to have been liquidated by the party. At least they have never been seen since.

Lake Garda, the largest of the Italian lakes, is a key-shaped body of water running generally north and south over a distance of some thirty-two miles. As has been stated early in this thesis, it lies east of the rest of the Lombard lakes, about midway between Milan and the Adriatic.

The most fashionable of the resorts scattered the length of Lake Garda is Gardone, on its western shore. It is comparatively an easy ride over good roads from Milan, or, if you're coming down from the Dolomites, it is a morning bus run from Merano over roads that cut in and out of tunnels, now giving you a view of the lake, now plunging you into darkness.

Garda has had a nasty reputation about storms handed down from the Latin of Virgil who had plenty to say on the subject. Out of the north as if it had been blown through a tunnel, comes the Borea (sometimes called the Suer). Out of the east comes the Ora which turns north when it hits the water. For all of this, the western and southern shores of Garda grow a rich, tropical vegetation. The climate has proven equally nourishing for tourists, and the lakefront around Gardone is known as the Gardone Riviera. All along the shore are garden flowers, lemon and fig trees, open-air cafes, big hotels and a broad, pleasant promenade. The hills rise rather suddenly out of the water, craggy on the east shore, silver-green with olive trees on the west. Such hotels as the first-class Grand and the Fasano which used to deal almost exclusively in Italians, now cater as well to English and a few Americans. The crowd, like the atmosphere, is not at all flashy. One sails, one swims, one sits. One of the most famous of its recent visitors was Winston Churchill. He stayed at the Grand, took walks along the flower-bordered lakeside promenade, and sat among the crowds in the lakeside cafes. He went his way completely un-

MILAN'S BROADWAY
while Rome eats

disturbed, and in the words of an Englishman who was there at the time, "no one ever even asked him for an autographed cigar butt."

Milan is the commercial, financial, publishing and manufacturing center of Italy, and very proud of it. The streetcars are packed, you hop to get out of the way of cars, traffic becomes snarled, people on foot move quickly, and the tempo reminds you a little of New York. At night in the cathedral square electric signs, smaller than on Broadway, but startling all the same, flash out "Sarti," a brandy, "Cinzano," a vermouth, and the inevitable "Coca Cola." Everyone of the million and a half Milanese knows the bromide about indolent southern Italians, and they make sure no visitor leaves without hearing it. "Milan works," they say, "and Rome eats."

The history of Milan goes back to 408 B.C. when it was founded by the Gauls. During the fourth and fifth centuries after Christ, Milan and Rome were equally important. Milan was the

THE DUOMO
a pile of points and needles

seat of the Western Empire. Through the ages the city has had a bloody history. The invasions first by the Franks and the Burgundians, and later by the French under Louis XII reduced the Roman remains to dust. Although it is one of the oldest cities in Italy, there are virtually no ruins in Milan.

In March 1450 the first of the Sforzas, a famous Italian family, became Duke of Milan and between him and his son Lodovico the Moor, there was a brief intellectual flurry in Milan. Lodovico was a patron of Leonardo da Vinci who during this period painted the famous "Last Supper" in what was then the dining room of the Dominican Monks in the Church of Santa Maria delle Grazie. Using *tempera* — an oil coloring mixed with the white of eggs — da Vinci painted on top of the plaster, finishing the masterpiece in 1497 after two years work. Napoleon used the hall as a stable in 1805, but the Allies in World War II did worse. They bombed the church, collapsing three walls. The fourth wall, the only one left standing, was the wall with the painting. The church has since been rebuilt, the painting is intact and is again on public view.

Milan's cathedral is a massive pile of points and spires, like a pincushion with all the pins and needles carefully stuck in perpendicularly. The main spire with a gold statue of the Virgin atop it, is 354 feet high. Begun in 1386, the church was consecrated in 1577, but it was not until 1809 that the facade, begun four years earlier on Napoleon's order, was finally completed. Napoleon crowned himself in the cathedral, with the famous words: *"Dieu me l'a donné, gare à qui la touche."* ("God gave it to me, beware the one who touches it.") The crown was used by Frederick Barbarossa and Charles V among others. The iron rim inside is supposed to have been made from a nail of the true Cross brought from Palestine by Empress Helena. Known as the "Iron Crown" it reposes in the Cathedral of Monza in Lombardy.

Third largest cathedral in the world (next to St. Peter's and St. Paul's), Milan's duomo can hold 40,000, or more than everyone who lives in the capital of Oregon, which happens to be Salem. It is made almost entirely of marble which was quarried near Lake Maggiore, and it is supported by fifty-two columns each representing a week of the year. Counting large and small statues, there are about 2,000 figures in the cathedral, but the ceiling, which looks carved, is actually painted.

The duomo sits in its own broad square facing the battery of electric signs. On the right, as you come out of the church, is the Galleria Vittorio Emanuele, a long arcade covered with an immense canopy of glass panels. It was built in 1867, completely shattered by air attacks during the late war, and has since been restored. The stores and restaurants inside are among the best in town. Milan makes silks, shoes, and among other things, cars — Alfa Romeos, Isotta Fraschinis and the Lancia.

Milan is the home of one of the world's most famous opera houses, La Scala. It seats 3,600 people, and next to the San Carlo in Naples, is the largest in Europe. La Scala was built in 1778 on the site of a church which had been founded by one Beatrice della Scala who thus gave the opera her name. During the early years it augmented its earnings from ticket admissions and the sale of refreshments, by operating a gambling house on the premises. Many of the world's great composers performed in person at La Scala, among them Verdi, Gounod, Bizet, Wagner (at the first presentation of *Lohengrin* on March 8, 1888), Puccini, Mascagni (at *Cavalleria Rusticana*, January 3, 1891), Saint-Säens, Tchaikovsky, Richard Strauss, Debussy, Rimsky-Korsakoff and untold others. The highlights of the recent seasons have been summer concerts by Toscanini.

When they die Milan's citizens are buried in the city's famous monumental cemetery. If they are rich their grave will eventually be adorned with a monument, often gigantic and heroic. Some monuments have got so big they would be befitting as a municipal war memorial in a fair-sized town. Those pieces of sculpture which have been cast in bronze are considered the most important. Established in 1865, the cemetery covers four square kilometers, and includes burial grounds for Protestants and Jews which are separated from the Catholic section and from each other by walls. A similar, and perhaps even more elaborate cemetery is in Genoa.

Of Milan's million and a half citizens, only about ten percent are true Milanesi. There is a Milanese dialect which has many words of French, Latin and German. There is also a Milanese way of cooking which can include any of these dishes:

GALLERIA VITTORIO EMANUELE
a maggiolina *is a ladybug*

Minestrone alla Milanese: A thick soup of mixed fresh vegetables and rice.

Risotto alla Milanese: Rice cooked in fine chicken broth.

Ossobuco alla Milanese: Knuckles of veal with marrow
browned in white wine, and stewed in a sauce of onions, celery
and tomatoes, garnished with chopped parsley and grated lemon
rind. It is usually served with *risotto alla Milanese*.

Costolette alla Milanese: Breaded veal cutlet fried in butter.

Milan is also famous for its *panettone,* a high-domed fruit
cake once baked only for Christmas, but served now all the year
around.

Among the best restaurants in town are the Campari and the

Biffi, both substantial and popularly priced, located next to each other in the Galleria Vittorio Emanuele. One of Milan's gayest places is La Maggiolina where in summer there is dining and dancing on a huge outdoor terrace, formerly a German anti-air-craft station. In winter the festivities move inside to a recondi-tioned old Milanese inn. The place isn't exactly cheap, and the address, Via Torelli Viollier No. 28 is not easy to find. Since a *maggiolina* is a ladybug the management hands out ladybug pins which you will see on the lapels of tourists the length and breadth of Italy.

There are four hotels officially classified de luxe in Milan, though none is a Waldorf-Astoria. Perhaps the best is the Excel-sior Gallia, near the railroad station, the others being the Grande Albergo e di Milano, the Continental and the Principe e Savoia. One of the best bets in the city is the brand new Cavalieri. Offi-cially classified as first-class, it was built after the war, is com-pletely air-conditioned, and furnished in Italian modern, a rather unique decor.

If you're leaving town by the railroad station, have the cab driver make a short detour to the Piazza Loreto where Benito and Clara came finally to such an undignified end. There is no mem-orial, of course, to the place where the Duce and his mistress hung by their feet. The traffic is heavy now with little Fiats, with bicycles, with motor bikes, ancient lumbering trucks and shining new tourist buses. The posters that exhorted Italy to Fascism, like Mussolini's body, have long since been removed. A big bill-board advertises Nescafé. There is a gleaming-white gas station with a familiar red trim. An oval sign hanging from it, with a white background and red and blue lettering, is the sign of the new times. It says "Esso."

THE RIVIERA

PORTOFINO
from chi-chi to sensible

9. THE RIVIERA

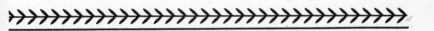

The international border between France and Italy that comes tumbling down from the Alps to fall into the sea just north of Nice, is the line that divides the chi-chi from the sensible. Those who come to the Italian side are not altogether interested in burning their insides at night and their outside by day. The Italian Riviera is never as frenzied, as frantic, nor as full of folde-rol as are things across the border. The privilege of lying on the sand during the day, or visiting the casino at night, and some-time between then and when it is time to lie on the sand again, of occupying a hotel room, is considerably less expensive a prop-osition on the Italian Riviera.

Officially the Italian strip, which until 1860 included Menton and Nice, is known as the Ligurian Riviera because Ligurian tribes settled it first some 700 years Before Christ. The soft curve of the fringe lies like a long question mark, horizontal, backward and face-down, along the edge of the Mediterranean. Down where the dot should be is Ventimiglia, on the border of France. Deep in the hollow of the gulf is Genoa which splits the Riviera into an eastern and a western section known respectively by the Italians as the Riviera di Levante and the Riviera di Ponente. Far on the end of the hook is La Spezia.

The western, or *ponente* side, is hot, overgrown with lush vegetation, especially in winter. The local dialect which runs from Nice to Genoa is similar to the Nicois of southern France, A *pizza* of southern Italy is called a *sardenaira* in Liguria. But the Ligurians also have their own dishes, particularly *farinata*, a cake made of chestnut flour, milk and water; and *panizza*, made of a flour ground from dried beans called *ceci*, and fried in boiling olive oil.

The highway, and less fortunately, the railroad track, runs along the shoreline from Nice and Monte Carlo through Ventimiglia, Bordighera, Ospedaletti and San Remo. Coming from France by rail you will be required to change trains at Ventimiglia and go through customs which, in view of the intricate border-crossing regulations with regard to such incidentals as cigarettes and money, can often be a bother. Not as detailed an inspection is made of those who come by road. Should you be entering Italy by bus, Italian border guards wearing Alpine caps with feathers will collect and examine passengers' passports, but seldom will they force the driver to unload the baggage for inspection.

Bordighera, with a number of second- and third-class hotels, and one first-class establishment, has developed into a middle-class British colony. Ospedaletti, just three kilometers from San Remo, ringed by a range of hills, is supposed to have the best weather of the western coast. It has, at any rate, attracted hundreds of villas which have changed the town from a fishing village into a residential resort.

Largest of the Ligurian retreats is San Remo where the grass burns up in the summer heat, is reseeded in the fall and grows during the winter. Climate has made San Remo a popular European winter resort since the days when Czarist royalty was in flower. A Russian orthodox church still pushes its mosques and turrets up among the palm trees, a holdover from the days when the socialites came down from Moscow in November leaving the Russian winter to the proletariat. The Queen of Montenegro, mother of the last Queen of Italy, is buried in the church.

A bulletin issued recently by the local chamber of commerce says, "San Remo is singularly free from dust particles and aqueous vapours; this favours the irradiation of ultraviolet rays." It is also a nice place to visit. For some fifteen years San Remo has employed a climatological expert to observe the local weather. He has come up with the fact that San Remo enjoys a total of 180 hours of sunshine every month, a commendable average that looks good against the 117 sunshine-hours registered at Merano and the 86 at St. Moritz. San Remo is shaded only by Los Angeles which racks up 234 hours and Miami with 219 hours. Both of these spas also record quite some humidity according to this climatological man, a department in which San Remo never registers more than 64 percent. Khartoum, Egypt, no resort, rings the international sunshine bell with a total of 265 hours a month, but the tropical heat over there will wilt you like a ten-cent rose in a steam-bath.

Aside from cultivating tourists, San Remo and the surrounding countryside also cultivates flowers, an industry which has given the area yet another name, the Riviera dei Fiori. The mountains which rise out of the sea along the Riviera have been stepped, reinforced with stone walls and planted everywhere with fields of carnations. In San Remo the flower market runs from November through May, and there is a huge flower show held every other April in the Villa Comunale, a municipal estate once owned by a Swiss cigarmaker. In the palm gardens of the villa, India figs grow on the cactus, the bougainvillea trees bloom rich and purple, and

SAN REMO'S CARNATIONS
tourists blossom too

BORDER GUARD
money can be a bother

the soft winter air brings on the mandarin and orange trees. The Riviera's richest flower market is Scandinavia whence carnations by the cargo-load are shipped by air.

Incubator temperatures are also responsible for the great palms that grow along the seaside. A less believable opinion fixes the responsibility for the growth of palms on St. Ampelio who landed on the coast near Bordighera seeking a sanctuary from the Barbarian hordes. As he knelt on the rocky coast to thank God for his deliverance one solitary date which he had brought from Africa fell out of his pocket. A palm tree, like Jack's beanstalk, sprouted between the boulders, followed, in more legitimate course, by others until today the Ligurian coast has become renowned palm country.

Through curious circumstance San Remo is by official appointment, palm-supplier to the Church of Rome. It happened during the raising of the obelisk in St. Peter's Square in 1586. To solemnize the ceremony Pope Sixtus V ordained that any who spoke during the raising would be killed forthwith. As the heavy monument was being lifted into place the strained guy ropes suddenly began to smoke. The crowd was not only silent but breathless. Finally a sailor from San Remo blurted out "Water the ropes!" a theoretically sound, if undiplomatic suggestion, which was immediately followed, saving the day. Not only did Sixtus spare the sailor, but he awarded to his family in San Remo an eternal franchise for supplying palms for Palm Sunday.

San Remo has all the accoutrements of the typical European luxury resort — casino, cable car, beach, golf course and a number of good hotels. The Municipal Casino has an outdoor terrace for summer shows, and a winter garden for galas. There is also a complete theater on the premises, and in the gaming rooms you'll find virtually every device for losing your lire with the possible exception of whist and slapjack. The crowd at the tables, in summer anyway, leans to the shirtsleeve side.

From behind the casino the cable car rises some 4,000 feet above sea level to the top of Mount Bignone which they like to call the highest mountain in Europe near the sea. It takes forty minutes to rise from the winter flowers at the base to the winter snow at the top. The golf course, which can also be reached by road, is the first stop on the upward cable-car route. Called the Golf degli Olivi, the course is probably one of the few whose fairways are separated by olive trees. Summer sun burns the grass to an ugly brown, and the course remains closed from June to November. The clubhouse is built in typical English manor house motif, a formal style not at all respected by the Germans during the late war who trotted horses into the main salon and set up a stable.

San Remo has a beautiful tennis club carved out of the side of a hill. For 300 lire, or less than fifty cents a day, you can play on one of the eight clay courts until you drop, an economic fact that might prove interesting to tennis court proprietors in Manhattan who charge $3.75 an hour of a Sunday afternoon. Jack Kramer, Frank Parker, Pauline Betz and Henri Cochet have all played exhibition matches on the courts. The annual tournament is held in March. For the same 300 lire you also get a locker, and use of the immaculate shower room. Pounding by the itinerant masseur is extra. Drinks are served on the terrace under the drooping pepper trees, in the shade of whose soft bending branches the local bridge club also holds its outdoor meetings.

With 450 yards of frontage, San Remo is in short supply of sand beach. The Morgana, a public beach club occupies some of those yards. Still bearing shell holes from the invasion, the Morgana has reopened and offers bathhouses, dining and dancing. Some hotels, notably the first-class Miramare, have beaches of their own, but more often hotels have built their own pools. The Lido Mediterraneo Hotel has an outdoor olympic pool adjoining its out-door restaurant. The Royal, probably the Riviera's best hotel, has built its entire guest life around a free-shaped pool landscaped into a hill overlooking the sea. More like a natural lagoon, the pool winds under the palms, is bordered with a flagstone walk, crossed by small bridges and illuminated at night by underwater lights. There is a bar at the regular water level for swimmers who are prone to develop a sudden thirst in the midst of an Australian crawl. Another waterside bar is only for underwater swimmers. They must dive under a tunnel and emerge in

POOL AT THE ROYAL
sometimes they swim in it

a grotto where drinks are fed to them with a long-handled tray. Diving boards are built into a particularly stout palm tree which has a crow's-nest on top. The olive trees are fitted with bird cages to keep the effect as al fresco as possible. The Royal's guests loll around the pool in the morning, take tea alongside it in the afternoon and dance beside it at night. Sometimes they swim in it. This kind of life costs about $10 a day for room, bath and meals. Rates at San Remo's other de luxe hotels, the Savoy and the Excelsior, are about the same. But the Riviera regimen is available — all meals included — at less than five dollars a day at places like the Morandi, one of the cleanest and neatest of the smaller hotels.

Most of the hotels in San Remo were closed during the war

at least until the Allies invaded Southern France. A German line was established along the Italo-French border and the Germans occupied the hotels until the Allies broke the Bologna line. The Germans evacuated with some haste, pursued as they were by Senegalese troops of the French Colonial army who first entered San Remo. Americans followed, and finally the resort was occupied for awhile by South Africans. By the fall of 1945 the hotels were being restored to order.

Should you be staying on the European plan in San Remo you'll find pleasant eating at the Rendezvous, the Castel D'Oria, the Pastorino and La Lanterna, on the port. The Candle Bar, brand new and right by the sea, offers dancing under the pines by moon and candlelight.

If you're in the mood for a minor expedition, take a ride down to La Mortola on the Via Aurelia, the seaside road, at the very edge of the French frontier. An excellent restaurant, famous on both sides of the border for its hot *hors d'ouevres*, it overlooks the famous gardens of the Villa Hambury. Established by a Briton named Sir Thomas Hambury, the grounds of the estate, which is now open to the public, are planted with some two thousand varieties of plants and flowers. Not far from the St. Louis Bridge, near the gardens are the dens of the Red Cliffs, a Stone Age Hotel inhabited by Neanderthal vacationists. Excavations undertaken between 1892 and 1902 uncovered six dens in the cliffs, and the skeletons of an extinct but gigantic race of men. The Romans who conquered the Ligurian tribes left the remains of a Roman theater at Ventimiglia, and the Saracens who invaded from North Africa left a tower at Bordighera. Up on the cape over San Remo is a weird abandoned village called old Bussana. In 1887 it was wrecked and killed by an earthquake which shuddered through villages from Marseilles all the way to Genoa. New Bussana rises over the sea, and old Bussana is a crumbling ruin, used now and then as a setting by moving picture companies. Perhaps the twentieth century will leave to the twenty-first the ruins of San Remo's Municipal Casino.

On the seaside road to Genoa it's a morning ride to Alassio which has, hands down, the finest beach of the western Riviera. Flanked by two capes, and sheltered by hulking mountains that all but push it in the sea, Alassio stretches for two miles along the water's edge. Once primarily a winter resort that attracted English and Germans, Alassio now is crowded during the summer bathing season as well, mostly with Americans and Italians. Winter temperature, too cool for swimming, averages about 51 degrees. There is an eight-court tennis club in town and all manner of craft are available for hire at the ocean. The Mediterraneo, classified as first category, is excellent, and the Bel Soggiorno, on the east end of the beach, with a waterside dining terrace and good cuisine deserves better than its official second-class listing.

A northern seaport, Genoa has that scraggly, unkempt, unwashed look of the southern Italian city. The streeets are narrow and crowded, and the air is agitated by the cries of the vendors who sell fish and lemonade and Palmolive soap for that schoolgirl complexion. On the Via Prè there is a bustling black market in cigarettes, both American and Swiss, by the pack or the carton. When the ships from New York are in port and the supply is heavy, the price is down. When the waterfront is tied up in political strikes and the supply is short, the price is high. Above the heads of the crowds that inch through the alleys hangs the wash of the Genoese. The women scrub the laundry in *truogoli,* the public open-air washing houses provided by the city in several wards. A tough waterfront saloon is named for Joe Louis, and the town's favorite son is Christopher Columbus.

CIGARETTE MARKET   *a city of merchants*
when ships are in, prices are down

It is the character of the Genoese to work hard and to make honest deals which are sealed with a cup of coffee and a handshake. The harbor moves the largest amount of tonnage in the Mediterranean, all of it handled by the *scaricatori,* the burly longshoremen of which there are 2,000. They hand down their trade, like fine watchmakers, from father to son. All wear, as a sort of uniform, a blue wrap-around apron, and most of them can walk up a gangway with a sack of meal under each arm. Many have migrated to harbors all over the world, and as a consequence the Genoese dialect has become something of an international language of longshoremen. Portuguese is said to be a derivative of Genoese and Spanish. The sentence, Give me a glass of wine (apparently a popular one with the Genoese anyway) would be *Dammi un bicchiere di vino* in Italian. In the Genoa dialect it becomes *Damme un gottu de vin*. It's like a fellow from Aroostook County in Maine trying to make himself understood in Yazoo City, Mississippi.

A city of merchants, Genoa got that way during the Crusades when, like Venice, it became engaged in outfitting expeditions bound for the East. Supply ports were established along the Barbary Coast, and as far afield as the Black Sea, a bit of imperialism that piqued both Venice and Pisa and provoked continuous conflicts with both powers. When the Genoese fleet sailed the seas its galleys flew a white flag with a red cross. The sailors of the white flag with the red cross enjoyed a respect for battle that made them immune from attacks by pirates. The ensign has since been adopted as the official flag of the British navy, which admired Genoese gallantry.

After the Crusades, Genoa found a new customer in the Spanish crown for whom it did banking and prepared expeditions which were beginning to probe into the New World. Had Genoa been more sympathetic to its own native son, Columbus, the first rights to the new continents might have been hers instead of Spain's. To Genoa goes the credit for first establishing many early banking systems that are still in basic use today. The first check was drawn in St. George's Palace, a building that was damaged during World War II, but still stands.

Lying at the edge of the sea, Genoa is locked in the collar of the Ligurian Alps. As the city prospered and became cramped for space, there was nothing left to do but climb the nearby hills. As recently as 1940 Genoa expanded in another direction — straight up. It built two skyscrapers — *grattacielo,* they are called, the most famous of which is crowned with the Capurro, the highest restaurant in Europe. Thirty-one stories above Genoa, the Capurro draws the homesick American colony who dance and eat outdoors and perhaps dream of the RCA Building in Manhattan or the Top of the Mark in San Francisco. Damaged by bombs in 1943, the Capurro was reopened in 1945. In the same square is the Porta Soprana, an old city gate which dates from 1155. It is covered nowadays with bright Communist posters exhorting the *lavoratori* to awake. In front of the *porta* are the remains of the childhood home of Columbus. At least Christopher's father, a wool comber, was a tenant there from 1460 to 1467. Experts in such matters believe the house was knocked down during the French bombardment in 1684, and rebuilt with the same stones. Elsewhere in the square is the Genoese agency for Kaiser-Frazer, and the Caffè Columbus which advertises its presence with a likeness of the Santa Maria in neon lights.

Sightseers should also take in Genoa's Cathedral of San Lorenzo begun in the ninth century and rebuilt in the fourteenth. It is a mixture of Gothic and Romanic, and in its striped marble effects shows some Pisan overtones. One bell tower was completed in 1552, but the traditional second one was never begun. The ceilings were never finished either. The cathedral was slightly altered on February 9, 1941 when, during a naval bombardment by the British a shell tore through a wall. The shell, easily five feet high, stands in the church and a tablet marks the place and the occasion.

Nobody should miss the city's famous Staglieno Cemetery which has over 3,000 monuments to deceased Genoese citizens, many of them magnificent marble tributes. The marble is never washed so that the dust may give a sense of relief to the stone figures. Begun in 1835, Staglieno has four kilometers of arcades each of which contains four layers of graves. Wealthy citizens often posed for the monuments long before their deaths. Sometimes the statues were decorated with fanciful allegories — a butterfly representing the soul upsetting an hourglass representing

the stoppage of time. Sculptors worked for glory rather than re-
ward, and many of them died to be buried in the free plots where
the graves are maintained for seven years with a simple headstone
before being exhumed. Families who want to retain such remains
an additional thirty years can buy a small plot on the roof of the
gallery for the equivalent of about ten dollars. Should the family
be unable to afford the new grave, the bones, at the end of the
seven-year period are piled in a pit and covered with lime.

For the rich Genoese there is eternal rest under the great
carvings. One unoccupied mausoleum was begun in flashy futuris-
tic style by the ex-captain of the transatlantic liner *Rex*. Before
the memorial was finished, the captain was overcome with a wave
of superstition and decided that to finish the construction would
mean his certain death.

One of the finest memorials, oddly, commemorates a poor
pushcart peddler of the city named Cattainin Campodonico. Called
paissanna by those who knew her well, the old lady sold nuts and
cakes in all kinds of weather until she accumulated enough money
to call in a sculptor. She posed for her own monument, lived to
see it completed, and died six months later, in 1881. A lifelike
statue of an old lady, the memorial bears an inscription written
in Genoese dialect as she might have said it. It says, in effect,
"Anyone passing my statue who wants to pray for me, I thank
them very much." The day I passed *paissanna* there were flowers
at her feet.

Some 6,000 German soldiers who died in World War II share
the cemetery now with the people of Genoa. The war even sought
out those long dead. One of the eighty-five raids which the Allies
visited upon the city hit the cemetery which is near the municipal
aqueduct. English-speaking guides are available for about a dollar
an hour at the entrance to the cemetery where you can buy flowers,
not to mention post cards and ice cream.

The hotel with the fastest turnover traffic in Italy is Genoa's Columbia Excelsior, the only de luxe category hotel in town. One block from the railroad station and the bus terminal, the hotel has a handsome new bar which it badly needed, and many of its rooms have been completely refurnished since the war. It is managed by F. V. Cochis who once managed Claridge's in London. Among the other hotels the Astoria Isotta is recommended, and most anyone should find the Bristol Palazzo on the Via XX Setembre old but decidedly good.

As you may have suspected, the Genoese, a rather partisan citizen, has his own ideas on eating too. They sprinkle everything not with tomato sauce, or grated cheese but with *pesto,* a green dust composed of basilic leaves, Sardinian goat cheese, olive oil, garlic, pine seeds and walnuts. The local restaurants are famous for:

Trenette col pesto: Curled noodles served with the aforementioned seasoning.

Ravioli alla Genovese: In case mother never told you what *ravioli* are, they are small squares of pasta stuffed with finely chopped white meat of chicken, veal, brains, sweetbreads and bread crumbs which are dipped in milk or cream cheese, boiled and served with heavy gravy.

Zuppa di pesce: A sort of local *bouillabaisse,* which means it's a mishmosh of all the fish foods, shell and otherwise, in sight.

Minestrone alla Genovese: Thick soup of vegetables and macaroni sprinkled with *pesto.*

Calamaretti: Tiny octopus, breaded, fried, and served with lemon.

Risotto con le Seppie: Boiled rice with ink fish.

Cappon magro: Boiled fish and pickles covered with mayonnaise.

Torta Pasqualina: A flaky tart filled with beet-root leaves, diced artichokes, junket, fresh cream, eggs, butter, cheese and pepper, oven baked.

The most famous restaurant in Genoa, the Grande Italia, went with the war, but you should be able to obtain any or all the delicacies delineated above by presenting yourself at one of these restaurants: Angela's on the Piazza Banco S. Giorgo No. 47, at the waterfront — a white-tiled place the decor of which may be somebody's idea of a john. It is in fact a restaurant, one of the best in town, supervised by Angela herself, a lady who is nothing if not informal. Bedin, on Via Dante No. 56; it specializes in fried foods. Gheise, on Via Boccadasse No. 12, has an out-door arbor fifty yards long, covered completely with vines. Americans camped in their yard during World War I, a fact which may make you feel at home. Anyway the restaurant people are still talking about it. San Pietro at Viale Brigate Partigiane No. 19, is near the sea, has dancing, is elegant and comparatively expensive. Later you can stroll along the Via Roma, the seaside road which, with the Piazza della Vittoria, were the two improvements bequeathed to the city by the Fascist regime.

Officially the eastern Riviera begins with the statue of Garibaldi on the Via Roma. Erected to honor Garibaldi's expedition which sailed from Genoa on May 5, 1860 with 1,070 volunteers to liberate Sicily, the statue, because of the peculiar technique of the sculptor is known familiarly as "the forkful of *ravioli*."

On the eastern side, the Riviera seems to possess a more tangible character. Ligurian villas are built square, with vaulted ceilings, and houses often have false windows painted on the outside. On days when there are local celebrations, the young and the agile dance the *tressette*, which involves a gymnastic jump, and a scissors-kick in midair. *Tressette* means "small braids" which is more or less what one makes of one's legs during the dance. The accompanying music, on accordian and clarinet, is called the *peli-*

ANGELA OF ANGELA'S
in the kitchen, green dust

gordin. What is left of the local costume is largely the *mezzaro*,
a long scarf falling almost to the knees which is worn by women. When their men are off fishing the local ladies occupy
themselves by making merletti lace. Tablecloths and runners are
made and sold on the streets of the eastern Riviera. Although no
Christian holiday passes without due pomp and celebration, St.
Joseph's Day which falls on March 19 is not only marked, but
solemnized by the eating of apple and raisin fritters.

Completely blockaded from the north by surrounding heights,
Nervi is a handy resort only five miles from Genoa. Connected
to the city by a trolley car line, Nervi is near enough to be considered a suburb. Chiefly, Nervi is a weather station, a European

CAMOGLI
"the houses of the wives"

refuge most popular from November until May, particularly in March, April and May. The temperature average from fall until spring is 51 degrees, but even during January and February the thermometer hardly ever bobs below 47. Most popular pastime in Nervi is strolling along the *Passeggiata a mare*, a pleasant seaside walk built high over the rocky cliffs. Nervi has no beach and those who swim there in summer go in from the rocks. Once a winter retreat for creaky Germans, Nervi now draws mostly Swiss and Italians. It has two first-class hotels, the Savoia-Beeler, which is Swiss-run, and the Vittoria.

The railroad follows the shoreline, and somewhere near the tiny town of Recco, east of Nervi, it crosses a bridge. Allied planes made twenty passes at the railroad bridge before they got it. Ninety percent of Recco was bombed in the bargain. The worst raid came after the armistice of 1943. As a warning the Americans sent over a solitary plane. But the curious people of Recco, instead of diving for a bomb-shelter came out to gawk at the aircraft. The bombing squadron bent on business, which followed the single plane, wreaked a terrible death toll. After the war the railroad bridge was rebuilt in record time at no cost to the government and dedicated to the original builder. It was constructed by his son and is called the Lodigiani Bridge.

Camogli, fifteen miles from Genoa, is built up the side of Portofino Mountain. At the edge of the sea there are cafes, bath-houses, a mixed fleet of pleasure boats and fishing craft, a mixed crowd of vacationers and fishermen. Camogli means "the houses of the wives" because here the women stayed home alone while their husbands who were either sea captains or fishermen went to sea. Like old Salem, Camogli has a reputation for making sea captains of its citizens.

Of the whole Italian Riviera, west and east, the purest concentration of chic and charm has been converged on a short peninsula, twenty miles from Genoa. Along the eastern cape, reading from the mainland to the sea, are Rapallo, St. Margherita Ligure and Portofino Mare.

Rapallo is built like an amphitheater opening on the sea. The seaward fringe is decorated with an almost continuous ring of open-air restaurants where you can sit under the palms and con-template donkey carts filled with children trotting along the road. In between the sidewalk cafes are half a dozen night clubs which have no cover or minimum charge, but make up the deficit by overcharging on drinks. A couple who order two Scotches apiece in the course of an evening will be in the ditch for eight dollars. Brandy is three dollars a slug, and a beer or a Coke is about a dollar even. Even at these prices there are those who dissipate until dawn. The clubs are often open until six a.m. If you are still game the most interesting in Rapallo are La Taverna Azzura which has both a satin-lined Bebi Bar, and an upstairs Bambu Garden. Hanging over the Tigullio Gulf near the Excelsior Hotel is the Dinghy Club which plays romantic spotlights on its um-brella pines, has customers enter through an arch of bottles, a not unsymbolic device.

There are no fewer than five hotels officially classified as first-class, of which the Excelsior is probably the best. It has an ex-cellent location by the sea, bathing facilities, dancing in an adjoin-ing casino and one of the best kitchens on the Riviera. Public rooms are one flight up. The Savoy and the Europa, like the Ex-celsior, are open all year around, charge about $2.50 a night for a single room with bath, or about $6 a day with meals, plus twenty percent for tips and taxes.

In the lovely harbor of St. Margherita, a few minutes up the shore, the yachts, the sailboats and the rowboats lie lazily at anchor; boys sit silently, their bare feet in the water, a fishing rod in their hands; and grizzled old veterans of the sea sit mending nets, a task in which they employ their hands, toes and teeth.

The best hotel in St. Margherita is probably the Miramare from whose terrace Marconi made the first successful tests of shortwave in 1933. There are four first-class hotels which are, be-sides the Miramare, the Eden Guglielmina, Imperiale and Laurin.

RIVIERA FISHERMEN
hands, toes and teeth

One wall in the Miramare is decorated with a photo of the American warship *Coral Sea*, signed with thanks from the captain who stayed at the hotel in July 1949. Rex Harrison was there the same month. Opposite the *Coral Sea* is Myrna Loy who dropped anchor at the Miramare for six solid weeks during the 1949 Easter season.

Meals are served in summer on the terrace overlooking the sea, and there is a pebble beach for swimming across the street. Paraggi, nearby, a sort of alcove on the sea, has a sand beach, and for that matter, its own hotel, all cramped at the foot of a range of hills that drop like a roller coaster down to the sea.

St. Margherita also harbors the Capo di Nord-Est, most

RAPALLO
Bebi bars and Bambu gardens

fantastic night club on the Riviera. In winter the club entertains
its guests in a subterranean grotto. In summer things are moved
outside to a series of flagstone terraces by the sea, all on different
levels. Aside from providing food, drink and music, the club plays
a searchlight on the water for those who want to take moonlight
dips. Recently Gregory Ratoff brought in a whole movie company
headed by Edward G. Robinson and Peggy Cummins, and used
the Capo di Nord-Est as a background for night-club scenes. The
management hired a special Brazilian orchestra for the arrival of
the company, a pleasant surprise for which Robinson reciprocated
by publicly playing the maracas. For the gambling scenes roulette
wheels and croupiers were imported from San Remo (the east
Riviera has no casino), and a torrid love scene was filmed in front
of the grand stairway near the club's mast which stands by the
sea wall. Maybe Hedda Hopper would like to know that Edward
G. Robinson and Gregory Ratoff didn't seem to get along at *all*.

Portofino is one of the most romantic little corners of the

world. Its tiny harbor has known such swashbucklers as Richard Coeur de Lion who sailed for the Holy Land from there in 1190, and Tyrone Power who romanced Linda Christians there some seven hundred and sixty years later. Part of its harbor is a bulging curve lined in symmetry with four-story houses whose roofs dip toward the sea. Residents tie their dinghies to a mooring right outside their door. Across the water, on the transients' side, fat yachts flying the flag of every registry are bumper to bumper.

Up on the heights is the Splendido Hotel where the terrace doors seem to open out on a new, fragrant world full of palms, bougainvillea, olives, cypress trees and pines. For Christmas there is fruit from the orange trees, and by January everything is yellow with mimosa. Summer or winter there is lunch on the open terrace looking down on the cove of Portofino. Tennis is a year-around sport, and in summer there is bathing at Paraggi, and picnic lunches which the hotel will pack, for walks up into the mountains. There is swimming from the rocks, too, if you wish, and deep sea fishing for *sagaro*.

Down in the harbor expensive little restaurants like the Delfino and the Nazionale who employ shirt-sleeved waiters, make a specialty of things like *carne all' uccelletto* which is chopped veal stewed in butter, tomato sauce and laurel leaves. At Delfino where Tyrone Power has eaten *twice*, there is a clock which, when wound for special customers, sets mechanical birds to flapping their wings and sends them flying around papier-maché trees. The thing to order is *frutti di mare*, a cold *hors d'oeuvre* of clams and tiny pink octopi flavored with vinegar and oil. Tastes rather like bicycle tire dipped in French dressing.

THE ROAD
SOUTH

ALONG THE LOWER SHINBONE
some of the best resorts — such as Capri

10. THE ROAD SOUTH
NAPLES — POMPEII — CAPRI
AMALFI — SORRENTO

Down from Rome toward the toe, the road winds through a part of Italy that is sad and sunny. The weather is hot, steaming the moisture from the land, leaving the earth dry and exhausted. The peasants have the hot country character. They carry baskets on their heads, wear no shoes on their feet. They are poor and they are many, and they crowd the streets and choke the highways. They are also dark and they look pretty much like what anyone might have expected of Italy before taking a trip there.

The plight of the southern Italian is a problem which the people themselves fail to find as distressing as does the tourist. For the tourist must take his shiny American car and plough it past the basket-topped heads and the unshod feet if he wants to get to some of the country's best resorts which lie along the lower shinbone of the boot.

Just east of the main highway, fifty miles south of Rome is Fiuggi, a well-spring of bottled water and a spa. Fiuggi is one of Italy's most popular table waters because it is healthful and it is still. After filtering through porous volcanic rock, the water issues from a pair of springs at a tepid temperature of fifty degrees. Purer than Ivory Soap, although absolutely tasteless, the water is radioactive as all get-out and contains a minimum of salts. All these fine attributes, as any M.D. will attest, make life pleasanter for anyone with gout, gravel, renal disorders and urinary catarrh. The water is excellent, what is more, for anyone who is thirsty. The cure season opens on May 1, a process that has been popular since the thirteenth century. Two of the most famous Fiuggi drinkers were Pope Boniface VIII and Michelangelo. Mountain-cured ham and walks under the chestnut trees are what Fiuggi is otherwise famous for. There is one de luxe hotel in town, the Palazzo della Fonte, and a broad assortment of second-class accommodations. It is not far to the snowfields of Campocatino (5,400 feet), which services Rome's skiers.

Perhaps another fifty miles distant, on the main highway to Naples is the hilltop monastery of Monte Cassino. Climbing to the top of the hill to establish the monastery in 529, St. Benedict found a temple dating back to 8 or 9 B.C., and an old Roman tower. He founded what was to become one of the most famous and richest sanctuaries of the Benedictine order. During the Middle Ages the monastery became a repository of art and culture collected from all over the world. All the possessions were at one time listed on bronze doors which had themselves been made at Constantinople, and the abbot was the overseer of nearly forty parishes. The abbey became a fount of monasticism, and during the dark years the solitudinous life of poverty, chastity and obedience practised at Monte Cassino was embraced by men all over the continent.

During the ages, Monte Cassino, on an undistinguished hilltop roughly midway between Rome and Naples, has been destroyed four times — first by the Lombards, second by the Saracens, third by an earthquake and fourth by 453 tons of bombs dropped by 229 Allied aircraft during seven of the twenty-four hours that comprised the fifteenth of February, 1944.

The bombing of Monte Cassino has emerged as one of the major controversies of World War II. During the bitter fighting in the sector of the Rapido River north of Naples that winter of 1943-1944, the mixed international elements of the Fifth Army arrived finally before the town of Cassino defended by the First Parachute Division among other crack German units. Although the Germans and the monks have earnestly insisted that the monastery was never used as a military observation post during the first days of the fighting, the attackers had evidence to prove differently. It was decided to bomb the monastery and attack again. Of this maneuver here is what Lieutenant General Jacob L. Devers, Deputy Allied Commander wrote General Marshall on March 22nd:

> We used air, artillery, and tanks, followed closely by infantry. I witnessed the attack from across the valley. It got off to a start with excellent weather. The bombing was excellent and severe, and the artillery barrage which followed it and lasted for two hours was even more severe and accurate with nine hundred guns participating. Two groups of medium bombers, followed by 11 groups of heavies, followed by three groups of mediums started . . . coming over every ten minutes up to 9:00 o'clock and thereafter every 15 minutes. In spite of all this and with excellent support all afternoon with dive bombers and artillery fire, the ground forces have not yet attained their first objective. . . . These results were a sobering shock to me.

What had happened was also a sober shock to air warfare. The planes had literally pulverized the town. When the bombing started the Germans merely withdrew. When it stopped they first took up positions behind the rubble fortifications provided by the bombing and managed to hold out for another ninety-nine days. Four hundred civilians were killed, 70,000 books were lost, 350 seventeenth century frescoes were destroyed. Nobody mentions how many soldiers were killed at Cassino, but on a slope opposite

MONTE CASSINO
*"We used air, artillery,
and tanks ..."*

CASSINO'S CHILDREN
in the dining room, flowers

the monastery, a Polish cemetery, built like a huge cross is a re-
minder that the Third and the Fifth Polish Divisions attacked
from the north and west. The 13th British Corps came up from
the south.

Not a monk was killed during the battle. Entombed for three
hours by one bomb, they were freed by another. The next day
they fled to Rome. When they came back the place was a wreck
but they found the statue of St. Benedict and those of two angels
intact. In the course of restoration which is taking place now at
full speed, nearly 1,000,000 cubic feet of rubble have been removed. The dining room has become a museum with fragments
of marble and pieces of sculpture gleaned from the wreckage. A

sign over a picture in the museum spells out the fury of the most recent destruction of Monte Cassino which put the efforts of the Saracens and the earthquake in the shade:

142 Fortress bombers dropped 287 tons of 500 pound general purpose bombs and 66½ tons of 100 pound incendiaries followed by 47 B-25's and 40 B-26's which dropped another 100 tons of H.E. (high explosive) bombs.

The town of Cassino which once occupied part of the hillside looks like bombed-out ruins which have been bombed again. What is left has been abandoned, and the town begun anew in the flat valley. The road to the abbey is in good condition, but the cable car isn't operating. There's a neat little hotel in town at the foot of the road. It is called the Excelsior, and in the dining room there are always flowers on the table.

Half-hour out of Naples is the great Royal Palace of Caserta, 830 feet long, 134 feet high, a tremendous memorial to the erstwhile Neapolitan monarchy. The palace, which has thirty-seven windows in each story, was first occupied by Ferdinand IV in 1774 who reigned over the Kingdom of Naples with his imperious wife, Maria Carolina, daughter of the Empress Maria Theresa.

Maria Carolina ran the wobbly kingdom, and dedicated herself to a continuing war against the revolutionary French. In this campaign she enlisted the aid of Horatio Nelson and part of the British fleet fresh from victory at the Nile. Dallying alternately with Lady Hamilton in Palermo and Queen Maria in Naples, Nelson seems to have come under the influence of both ladies. Although he had instructions from London to support the Neapolitan monarchy, he usurped his power and his position often to gain the Queen's favor.

The Caserta palace was purposely built twenty-two miles out of Naples so that it would be beyond the range of an invader's guns. It was originally planned to have part of the approach a waterway so that the nerves of a fretful monarch might be soothed by the time he arrived home.

Caserta's magnitude, many years later, also attracted the brass of the invading Allied armies in World War II. They established Mediterranean headquarters in the palace, and there received the surrender of the German troops in Italy on April 29, 1945.

Caserta is on the Rome-Cassino-Naples railway line, and you can also reach it out of Naples in twenty-five minutes on the fast train.

The approach to Naples, down a flat highway bordered with tall trees, is majestic and dignified, but the city itself is the urban equivalent of the vast overpopulation and poverty so prevalent in the southern countryside. It isn't altogether clear how the man meant it when he said "See Naples and die." The point is that the city isn't much of a place to visit and I wouldn't like to live there, but it is a handy place in a storm for anyone en route to Sorrento, Amalfi, Pompeii, Capri, Ischia, Paestum or Sicily.

Nobody can take away the fact that Naples has a lovely location, nestled along the curve of the Bay of Naples, with the massive hulk of Vesuvius in the background. The Greeks were the first ones to appreciate the climate and the view at Naples, but the colony they established there was overthrown by the Romans in 326 B.C. The noble Romans, however, who looked up to Greek literature and manners the way we have at times embraced the culture of the French, sought intellectual refuge in Naples which for a time maintained its Greek language and its Greek ways. Virgil wrote most of his *Georgics* in Naples, and was buried there. Nero, Titus and Hadrian, all Roman emperors, maintained villas in the city. When the Roman Empire fell, Naples came variously under the control of the Goths, the Lombards, and later the Nor-

NAPLES
the Greeks had an appreciation

mans. With Sicily it became part of the Kingdom of the Two Sicilies, and at one time or another it was the capital city for eight different monarchies. Garibaldi with his thousand followers sailing from Genoa to conquer Sicily finally stormed Naples and unified it with the rest of Italy in 1860.

Tourists coming to Naples will find themselves living in their own quarter located by the sea in the western part of the city. Coming by car from Rome the route through the maze of old Napoli lies along the broad Via Roma, still called the "Toledo," which virtually splits the city. The big hotels overlook the bay, near the big restaurants on the Porto Santa Lucia.

There is only one de luxe hotel in town, the Excelsior, which has been overhauled since the war. It was an elegant place in the days of peace when it was managed with no little suavity from 1927 until 1943 by M. Masprone, now manager of the elegant Gritti Palace in Venice. Ninety-six percent of the clientele in those days was British and American, Masprone recalls. People used the city as a terminal en route north from the ships that brought them from America, or on their way south to Capri or Sorrento. In the meantime they stayed in Naples long enough to have a *pizza*, hear the strumming of a Neapolitan harp, visit Pompeii and climb Vesuvius. A favorite story of the Excelsior involves an American woman who registered at the hotel and was duly ushered to her room. Ten minutes later she flew downstairs and stormed into the manager's office. "What do you mean by giving me this room?" she demanded. "Why it doesn't even have a view of Fujiyama!" The Excelsior also had a little difficulty with Serge Voronoff, the Russian proponent of continued virility through monkey glands. The register records that Voronoff came to the Excelsior with his wife on March 29, 1929 at which time he was 63. He liked his room all right, but insisted that the management remove the twin beds, and put in a double bed in which he would feel more at home.

First-class hotels which, like the Excelsior, are on the Partenope, the seaside drive, include the Santa Lucia at Nos. 46-47, the Continental, No. 44 and the Vesuvio, No. 45. Parker's Hotel Britannique on the Corso Vittorio Emanuele is considered in the upper city, although it does have a view of the bay and of Vesuvius. The Terminus at the railroad station has been completely re-done. In midtown you'll find the Londra on the Piazza Municipio, the Napoli on the Corso Umberto I, the Oriente on Via Armando Diaz, and the Turistico, Via Marconi, all officially classified as first-class establishments.

Eating in Naples is an experience which involves the combination of the seaside foods you always get in a port city, with all the Italian culinary staples — *pasta,* cheese, garlic, and tomato sauces. In the first place there is the *pizza* which as most everyone knows by now is a doughy discus — a sort of pie — made with fresh tomatoes, *mozzarella* cheese, anchovies, and sprinkled on top with *origano*, a mintlike herb. *Pizzas* are served everywhere, even in the Bronx, but especially they are served in *Pizzerias* which are temples given over to the adoration of the *pizza*. No other oven product except the doughnut and the hamburger was ever accorded such special treatment.

Here is a glossary of other things you may run across:

Cannelloni all' Amalfitana: A three-inch square of macaroni paste rolled and stuffed with fresh milk cheese, *mozarella* cheese, and ham, and cooked in tomato sauce.

Vermicelli alle Vongole: Fine spaghetti with clams, garlic and fresh tomatoes.

Vermicelli alla Napolitana: Fine spaghetti covered with a sauce of tomatoes and gravy, and covered with grated Parmesan cheese.

Zuppe di Vongole: Clams stewed in a sauce made of olive oil, fresh tomatoes, and *origano*, that herb again.

Mozzarella in Carozza: *Mozzarella* cheese on toast, dipped in the yolk of an egg and fried.

Costata alla Pizzaiola: Steak stewed in a sauce of oil, garlic, fresh tomatoes, and sprinkled with *origano*.

Seafood restaurants may be found in profusion on the Santa Lucia dock across from the big hotels on the Partenope. The tables are outdoors or indoors depending on the season, and you will surely be serenaded by strolling musicians. The Transatlantico, far out on the pier along the route of other fish houses, is one of the best restaurants at Santa Lucia. Zi Teresa, nearer shore, is equally good, and for that matter, draws the largest crowd.

Elsewhere in town you can do well at Falstaff on Via Simonelli No. 14, at Al Pappagallo at Via Carlo de Cesare No. 14, and at a place called Est! Est! Est! which is on Piazza Carita Nos. 7-8. On the hill there is Al Giardino degli Aranci at Posillipo Alto — reachable by cable car, auto or carriage — which has an orange grove and dancing; Paradiso on Via Manzoni; and D'Angelo on Via Aniello Falcone. Among the *pizzerias* look up Al Barile d'Oro, Via Serra No. 4; Da Ciro, Via Brigida No. 71, and Mattozzi on Piazza Carita No. 2. One of the best known tea rooms in town is the Grand Cafe Gambrinus which has a Neapolitan assortment of pastries, candy and ice cream. It's on the Piazza Trento e Trieste and the Via Chiaia. The via leads to the Riviera di Chiaia (they say KEY-AYA), a calm quarter in a stormy city.

The two great intellectual attractions of Naples nowadays are the Museo Nazionale and the San Carlo Opera. The museum has probably the greatest archaeological collection in Europe containing many of the articles of first century everyday life, and a fine collection of bronzes found in the ruins of Pompeii and Herculaneum. Many statues are Greek, dating from five centuries Before Christ.

San Carlo, one of the largest opera houses in Europe, was built by Charles of Bourbon in 1737. Burned in 1816, it was rebuilt in the European tradition with five gilded tiers, 184 boxes, and two galleries, an ornate, acoustically perfected theater in which Italian opera can perform with pomp and assurance.

Of new interest in Naples is the old Galleria Umberto finished in 1890. It received unprecedented notoriety with the publication of John Horne Burns's fine war novel, *The Gallery*. As a gallery, it has many fine shops which dispense among other things, excellent leather goods.

Vesuvius, the smoldering volcano which has been responsible for both the scenery and the drama around Naples, can be reached by the Circumvesuviana Railway which connects at Pugliano to the Vesuviana Railway. Naples to Vesuvius takes about an hour and forty-five minutes. By car take the highway to Torre Annunziata, then switch to the road up Vesuvius. It's twenty miles to Torre Annunziata and the whole trip will take about two hours.

POMPEII

under a lava blanket, a long sleep

The cable railway or a footpath will bring you up the last lap, and with the help of a guide you can, if you're nosey, step right down inside the crater. That Neapolitan classic, "Funiculi, Funicula," incidentally, was written for the inauguration of the funicular.

Vesuvius erupted as recently as 1944 and lava carried most of the funicular away. On April 4, 1906, the volcano began to belch streams of lava and later sent stones rolling down the 4,000-foot mountainside. Boscotrecase was completely destroyed, covered with six feet of lava. The torrent stopped short of Torre Annunziata, but smoke and black dust rolled in great clouds as far as Naples.

Pompeii was just recovering from the disaster of an earthquake which struck it in 63 A.D. when on August 24 of the year 79, Vesuvius erupted with a terrible roar. The eruption was the first ever recorded in the history of Vesuvius, and people knew the landmark only as a peaceful mountain covered with vineyards and forest. Those who stayed in Pompeii were asphyxiated by the poisonous gases, those who fled were killed on the roads. Pompeii, and Herculaneum as well, were laid to rest for fifteen centuries under a twenty-foot blanket of lava and ashes.

Engineers working on a land reclamation project in the sixteenth century first discovered Pompeii, but most of the early excavations were begun under Charles of Bourbon in 1748. From 1806 until 1832 excited archaeologists hopped about uncovering most of the public buildings, but from 1860 the work was conducted according to an orderly system, block by block. Pompeii, with a population of 25,000, offers one of the few examples in the world of a first century city stopped dead in time. The entire pattern of the metropolis remains — roads, houses, stores, forums, works of art, mosaics in the floor, election posters cut into the walls, flour mills, advertisements for coming spectacles in the amphitheater. There are even plaster casts of some of the bodies of Pompeiians who were suffocated. When the corpses decomposed they left hollow forms in the lava stone. Excavators filled the forms with plaster, and the casts that were made enclose the original bones. The agony of asphyxiation is clearly visible on some faces. Slaves can be identified by their belts.

Three sets of public baths remain in Pompeii, one dating from 2 B.C., and one so comparatively recent that it was never finished. Citizens came to meet and talk and bathe, passing all the while between the frigidarium through the tepidarium to the steamroom. The frigidarium has an open skylight, the tepidarium, where the temperature was kept warm by a bronze brazier, is still fitted with its original bronze seats. Steam was manufactured in the steam-room by boiling water in a bronze boiler and conducting it under the floor in terra-cotta pipes.

Opposite the baths is a winery where the wine was ladled to customers from earthenware jugs. Grooves for the shop's sliding doors can still be seen. Most streets, for that matter, which are paved with lava stone bear the ruts of chariot wheels. Stepping stones at street corners were installed by the Pompeii municipality to help pedestrians cross the avenues.

Largest residence in Pompeii is the House of the Dancing Faun, named for a small statue in the courtyard, the original of which now rests safely in the Naples Museum. Sleeping rooms open off the courtyard. There were four dining rooms, one for each season, arranged so that in spring and summer diners faced the blooming garden, and in winter the courtyard. All the walls were insulated with sheets of lead nailed to the stone and covered with plaster. The reception room once contained a precious mosaic depicting a battle between Alexander the Great and the Persians which has since been placed in the Naples Museum.

One of the best examples of Pompeiian life is the House of the Vettii which has been partly reconstructed to save its amazing collection of murals. It was the home of two bachelor brothers, apparently merchants, each of whom had his own sleeping room, and outside of it, his own safe. Marble basins and tables have been left where they were found. The bronze pipes and taps are original. Many of the paintings employ Pompeiian red, which although akin to Chinese red, is a pigment which has never been reproduced exactly. Some of the murals show the use of third dimension, an artistic trick entirely forgotten during the Middle Ages. Water color reproductions wrapped in aluminum tubes for safe transport can be bought for a few dollars.

The obscene room, which is kept under lock, contains a detailed marble statue of an amorous male, once used as a fountain. The walls are decorated with a number of frescoes depicting lovers in various phases of *amour*, documentary proof that for versatility Kinsey had nothing on old Pompeii. On an outside wall is a painting also covered and locked, showing Priapus, an early Greek god of male procreation, weighing his virility on a scale. Men are ordinarily readily admitted to the obscene exhibits, but women, especially if unaccompanied may run into a moralistic snag. There is nothing like a small tip to render a prudish guide amoral. It is still the subject of continued annoyance to a lady of my acquaintance who, on a recent trip to Pompeii, watched the men being ushered into the obscene room free of charge, while she had to pay.

Pompeii's Basilica, the remains of which stand near the end of the city forum, was the forerunner of the modern church basilica. Used as a law court and as a financial center, it has been likened by historians to a stock exchange. It was built in the second century Before Christ on foundations that date from two to three centuries before that.

Guides who can explain the ruins in a broad variety of languages can be hired on the premises at Pompeii, and there is enough to see to keep you on hand for an hour or a day. The place is open from nine until sunset, and in spring and autumn the ruins are open and illuminated at night. If your feet begin to sag you can hire a sedan chair at about 2,000 lire, and be hauled about by a pair of porters in what the Pompeiians used to call a *letiga*.

From Naples the Circumvesuviana Railway leaving from the Corso Garibaldi Station makes Pompeii in about thirty-five minutes; the State Railway leaving from the Central Station takes five minutes more. There are many trips every day. It's a quick fifteen-mile trip over the *autostrade* by car.

Herculaneum, less than five miles from Naples, hasn't been excavated with the same success which the archaeologists encountered at Pompeii. Herculaneum was covered with a layer of mud which solidified, whereas Pompeii's blanket was mostly ashes and pebbles. Most of Herculaneum still lies buried under the town of Resina, but the parts of it which have been unearthed reveal an intimate aspect of the early life around Naples. Furniture, household goods and whole houses have been recovered, and it is possible to walk through a door still mounted on its first hinges, climb the original stairs and examine life as it was lived 2,000 years ago. The express train of the Circumvesuviana Railway makes it to Herculaneum (which the Italians call Ercolano) in about fifteen minutes. Trolley car (number 55 will get you there) leaving from the Piazza Municipio every ten minutes takes almost an hour.

It's a lovely thirty-one mile drive around the fringe of the Bay of Naples to Sorrento. Eighteen miles en route is the ancient town of Castellammare di Stabia where you can take the waters internally or externally. It has a bathing establishment and a spa with twenty-four mineral springs gushing five million gallons of water in assorted flavors every day.

The wily Romans were quick to attach themselves to an unusually handsome neck of the woods, and vacation habits in Italy have really changed very little in twenty centuries of holidays. The Romans were the first to find Sorrento where they built villas and lolled through the warm weather months. Orange blossoms, silver olive trees, the sea, the serenity, and a tinkling music-box song called "Come Back to Sorrento" have been drawing people almost ever since. Many of those who have come have been creative artists, among them Richard Wagner who worked on *Parsifal,* Goethe, Byron, Walter Scott, Alexander Dumas, and Henrik Ibsen in 1861 and again, sick and poverty-stricken, in 1867 when he finished *Peer Gynt.* Verdi, Longfellow, Oscar Wilde, all came, not to mention Nietzsche who failed to be calmed by the calm-

IN THE FORUM
Kinsey had nothing on Pompeii

ness of Sorrento, and while at the resort revolted against his erstwhile friend Wagner, calling him a musician of decadent emotionalism.

The train, the highway, or the Capri boat will all bring you to Sorrento where most of the hotels are perched on a cliff 160 feet over the sea. Any way you do it, the trip shouldn't take more than an hour. There are four first-class establishments in town, the Cocumella, Vittoria, Tramontano and Reale, of which the Vittoria is the largest and probably the most famous. It is one hundred years old and was first called the Hotel Rispoli after the grandmother of the present owner. Its register is a diary of peregrinations, royal and renowned. Among those who have signed it were Marconi in 1916, Masaryk in 1921, the King of Siam in 1922, Petain in 1930, the Maharajah of Tipur and the Maharajah of Indore in 1930 (a banner year). Alfonso of Spain, Umberto of Italy and Queen Victoria of Sweden all stayed at the Vittoria in 1934. John D. Rockefeller, Jr. put up there on April 23, 1935 and wrote "With pleasantest memories of Sorrento and the Hotel Victoria."

During the war, from October of 1943 until 1945, the Vittoria was a rest center for officers of the Fifth Army. Mark Clark came many times during the war and during the peace. Most recently he came with his wife and later wrote, ". . . what a flood of memories was prompted by familiar sights and soil on which just a few years ago we had such heartbreaking struggles and then victory. Sorrento is such a beautiful spot and one of which I shall always have happy memories."

The event of 1948 at the Vittoria was the discovery of Roman columns buried in the hotel's garden; and the event of 1949 was the arrival for a three-day stay of Margaret Rose who, as everyone must know by now, is Princess of Great Britain and Northern Ireland.

Sorrento's best weather runs from the middle of February through the middle of November. It is not as hot in winter as Amalfi, and in the days before the war it was a place for a spring vacation. Now the crowd comes in summer. Rates for a single room with bath and all meals runs about $7 a day in first-class hotels, perhaps a dollar higher in summer.

Laces, embroidery and inlaid woodwork are the products of Sorrento. Music boxes, tables, and frames inlaid with bits of ebony, mahogany, and ivory are made in the home by artisans and then sold in the shops. Gallone has fine laces, and Sannuzzi has original laces, embroidery, silk underwear and woodwork as well.

SORRENTO BY THE SEA
tinkling music boxes called

At the Tamburello night club you can usually see a performance of the Tarantella, a coquettish boy and girl dance of courtship owned and patented in Sorrento. The dancers are dressed in folk costumes, and everyone joins in old Sorrentine songs. Sometimes the hotels invite a troupe to perform on the moonlit terrace by the sea.

The Amalfi Drive from Sorrento to Amalfi is one of the most beautiful trips in the world. It is also one of the twistiest, turniest stretches of road ever conceived, much less engineered. Running along the sea midway up the mountainside, it often seems pasted against the rocks. Although it is narrow, it is well-paved, and protected from a sheer drop into the Gulf of Salerno by a stout retaining wall.

You'll find Amalfi — and you'll be happy to reach it — a tiny stone city chopped out of the face of a cliff. Pushed to the very edge of the sea, and jammed back among the rocks, Amalfi gives the impression of a man scrambling up an embankment to escape the tide, yet never being able to find a foothold. The town has had a firm grip on itself for quite some time, however, and for awhile in the sixth century, even extended its power on the high seas. During the ninth century it shared some of the eastern trade with Venice, and once sent its fleet against the Saracens in support of Pope Leo IV. One of its citizens, name of Flavio Gioia, a navigator, is said in reliable circles to have invented the compass. For a time Amalfi flourished as a republic with no less than 70,000 people. But King Roger of Sicily clouted it into submission in 1131, and four years later the Pisans hove into the harbor, and the future of Amalfi for all else but a resort was sealed.

As a resort, its success seems assured. The cliff which prevents its expansion on the ground, also protects it from the northern winds. Since it faces the southern sun Amalfi can offer swimming in every month except January, February and part of March.

To reach the Cappuccini, Amalfi's best hotel, it is necessary to leave your car on the highway, and — when the electricity is running — take an elevator up the side of the mountain. Peace and quiet is what Amalfi trades on, and since the Cappuccini was the twelfth century sanctuary of Capuchin monks, it comes by both naturally. As a hotel it has such diverse advantages as a broad terrace looking out in the general direction of the Sicilian hills, and the original Moorish basement chapel of the monks in which services are still held every Sunday. A room and bath with three meals at the Cappuccini comes to about $5 a day during

June, July and August, and December and January. At other times the tariff comes down slightly.

One of the hotel's most famous guests was none other than Henry Wadsworth Longfellow, a man known to have been inspired by the sight of waves breaking on a stern and rockbound coast. Amalfi was no exception, and he wrote a ten-stanza poem about the resort which he produced on February 18, 1883. Said the first stanza:

> Sweet the memory is to me
> Of a land beyond the sea,
> Where the waves and mountains meet,
> Where, amid her mulberry-trees
> Sits Amalfi in the heat.
> Bathing ever her white feet
> In the tideless summer seas.

In town you might have a look at the cathedral which was built with a Byzantine front in 937, later restored along the same lines in 1891. The bronze door was made in Constantinople in 1066 when Amalfi was still a power. The *campanile* is a three-story tower in bright yellow, red and green. Amalfi's famous naval code, one of the first ever devised, has been reclaimed from the Museum of Vienna where it once reposed, and is on display now in the town's civic museum. From ten until four any day you can visit the Republic's Arsenals where Amalfi shipbuilders constructed the galleys that plied their way to the East.

Ravello, four miles up in the hills over Amalfi, was founded as a smart suburb for noble families of the maritime republic. Its cathedral has a fanciful pulpit covered with mosaics, and handsome twelfth century bronze doors. Palazzo Rufolo built in the eleventh century in perfect Alhambresque style, inspired Wagner to inscribe in its guest book, *"Richard Wagner mit Frau und Familie — Klingsor's Zaubergarten ist gefunden! — 26 mai 1880."* Or, "the enchanted garden of Klingsor (in Wagner's opera *Parsifal*) has been found."

THE ROAD SOUTH

Salerno anchors the east end of the dramatic seaside road. Aside from the cathedral which has an ornate, mosaic-covered pulpit similar to the one in Ravello, Salerno would hold little interest for the American, British or Canadian tourist. Events on the ninth of September 1943 changed things completely. Sicily had just fallen in a record campaign, and the Italian Fascist government had collapsed. Now the Allies were pushing onto the boot. Under Mark Clark the American 36th and 45th Divisions and Ranger units with the British X Corps and Commando troops landed along the Salerno beaches. The Germans got wind of the plan and opened the bidding with some tank thrusts. By September 13 the entire German XIV Panzer Corps had joined the party, and the Anglo-American situation on the beachhead was critical. As General Eisenhower wrote General Marshall at the time, "We are very much in the 'touch and go' stage of this operation." He put it mildly. The Air Forces were ordered to fly in reinforcements in twenty-fours. Before the time had elapsed 90 aircraft had dropped 1,300 paratroopers in an area 1,200 yards by 800 yards. The next day 131 planes dropped 1,900 troops. To seal off the Salerno area 3,000 sorties were flown, and planes dropped 2,150 tons of bombs. In the first eighteen days the Navy and Army service forces put ashore 108,000 tons of supplies, 30,000 motor vehicles and 189,000 troops. That was Salerno in the fall of '43.

Paestum, twenty-five miles south from Salerno along the Gulf (and fifty-nine miles from Naples) was a Greek city founded some twenty-five centuries ago. The metropolis has entirely disappeared except for three classic temples. All that remains of the basilica built in the sixth century B.C. are its stout Doric columns. The Temple of Ceres from the fourth century B.C. has all its columns and some of the roof supports, but the Temple of Neptune, also fourth century B.C. is virtually intact. Have a look at the lonely desert beach of Posidonia, two kilometers away, where on a clear day anyone with normal vision can take in a panorama from Punta Licosa, on the southern tip of the Gulf of Salerno, northwest to the Isle of Capri.

The pleasure islands of Ischia and Capri flank the entrance to the Bay of Naples like the lions in front of the New York Public Library. Ischia, the larger of the two, is a volcanic isle overgrown with pine forests, undermined by mineral springs and surrounded by sea. The combination makes it one of the healthiest places in the world east of Battle Creek, Michigan. There are six villages on the island, all connected by a twenty-mile road. Largest of the settlements is Porto d'Ischia which draws most of the tourists. It has fine beaches if you want to swim, a thermal station in case you have arthritis or rheumatism, and fine pine groves should you just want to go off in the woods and lie down. There are two second-class hotels to choose from — the Lido and the Regina Palace, two third-rate hotels — the Floridiana and the Ischia, and two first-class boarding houses — the San Pietro and the Villa Belvedere. There are enough restaurants around in case you don't like the hotel food, and you'll find dancing every night May to September, at the Pro-Ischia Club and the Monkey Bar.

No matter how you slice it, the steamer still takes two hours to ply the eighteen miles from Naples, a fact which makes Ischia something of an isle of isolation. Mussolini's wife, Donna Rachele, fled there with her two younger children Romano and Anna Maria after the war, but the family has since returned to a small apartment in Rome.

Capri, as you must have heard long before now, is sort of a plushy Provincetown with palms. The isle has a way of working on inhibitions like four martinis, particularly when it comes to dress. Richter's *Capri Guide* for 1949-1950 says that visitors have a way of losing their national individuality on the island, and become " 'Capri types,' donning exaggeratedly brief shorts, wearing brightly yellow slacks rolled up on their shins, indescribable shirts and wildly-colored scarfs." On the mainland, says Richter's, "there can be seen some individuals who are immediately classified as 'just back from Capri' — but it would not be as easy to determine their country of origin, nor in some cases even their sex."

The boat from civilization to Capri takes about an hour and a half, and you can get on board in Naples or Sorrento. It's a sleek white ship, and music screeches from the loudspeaker every time she puts into port. An arrival at Sorrento, I am sad to report, is no occasion in the opinion of the maritime music master, to play "Come Back to Sorrento." He chose, as I recall, the equally lilting, if less romantic composition known as "A String of Pearls." Ham sandwiches and cognac are both hawked aboard ship, the former, followed by a heavy sea, often inducing the need for the latter. The service at any rate is excellent and professional. An agent has reported to me, although I have never seen it, that some of the commissary staff on the Capri boats is Ethiopian. Some Negroes did find their way to Italy after the Duce's fiasco at Addis Ababa just before the professional phase of the war. The presence of a Negro waiter on a boat in far-off Italy was just too much for a pair of Memphis belles sojourning there recently. Bubbling with curiosity and theories about how the man had gotten there, they finally assumed that he was an expatriate from Dixie, and signaled him over. "Say, boy," they blurted out, "how these folks treatin' y'all over heah, ennahow?" The Negro bowed deeply, mumbled something in Italian, and made a hasty retreat aft.

Every visitor to Capri is welcomed to the island by twenty uniformed hustlers each of whom represents a local hotel. As the boat pulls in they line up in an orderly formation on the dock. When the passengers debark each solicitor, like a soldier counting off, recites the name of the establishment he represents. They say,

"Quisisana," "Cesare Augusto," "Morgano Tiberio," "Eden Paradiso," "Internazionale," until finally their voices are lost to other
hucksters who are selling boat trips to the Blue Grotto, carriage
rides up the hill and raw sea urchins to be eaten with a squirt of
lemon.

You give your baggage checks to the representative from your
hotel, and you take the funicular for the square of Capri village,
the heart of the island. Tables of the sidewalk cafes almost cover
the whole piazza. While an old tile clock in the tower clanks out
the quarter-hours the tourists loll in the chairs of the cafes. Facing
them on a flight of stone steps sit the barefoot boatmen and the
porters. One is bound to run across such Capri characters as Hans
Julius Spiegel, who is deaf, dumb and bizarre. He is usually
dressed in a red-stocking cap with matching tassel and blue
trousers. He wears silver bracelets and broad silver rings. Over
his shoulder he carries two oversized woven Sardinian bags. He
smokes a hooked Bavarian pipe, and underneath his blue sweater
he carries a tiny skull. He can say, "How do you do," and *"Auf
Wiedersehn,"* in a high falsetto voice, but if he likes you he will
uncover the skull, press it in your hand, and bless you with a
hocus-pocus sign. Then there is the Princess Pignatelli who wears
only black clothes, paints her nails with silver-black polish, and
has black window curtains in her villa on the Piccolo Marina. If
you want to know the weather tomorrow you look around the
square for Salvatore Panza, a retired fisherman who still wears
a blue cap and a walrus mustache, and maintains a respected reputation for meteorological accuracy.

They tell stories on Capri of German tourists who came before the war and rented villas while their wives were buying post
cards, and of Americans who caught the Capri fever and sold their
factories by cable. Augustus first came to the island by accident,
having been forced to take refuge on it during a return voyage

. . . facing the tourists sit the barefoot boatmen

from Sicily. He used it as a royal Roman playground for many
years. Tiberius, his stepson, settled on Capri when he was sixty-
eight, and during the last ten years of his life he ran the Roman
Empire while leading a dissolute existence tucked away in a clifftop castle. Those who incurred his disfavor were tumbled over a
balcony into the azure sea. From his vantage point he could watch
the approach of a hostile force which, if he expected one, never
came. Three times Tiberius set out for Rome, but each time he
changed his mind and made for the physical and emotional security of the island. He never saw Rome again.

The ruins of Villa Jovis, Tiberius's lofty retreat, still remain
and you can visit them aboard one of the four donkeys that are
kept in town for such excursions. One of them, out of deference,

is named Tiberius, the others being Michelangelo, Raphael and Ulysses. From the heights the Sorrento Peninsula, of which Capri was once a part, stretches out a yearning arm; to the left is Vesuvius wearing a cloud for a cloche.

Aside from the donkeys the principal means of transportation on Capri are the horse and carriage and the taxi. Capri's cabs are vintage-model touring cars, and since many of the streets are blocked off to vehicular traffic, they ply mainly between the square, the neighboring village of Anacapri, and the bathing beaches of Piccolo Marina. When taking out parties of sightseers the driver sometimes employs a small boy to watch the car whenever the touring party decides to proceed on foot. At other times, while the car is rolling along the Capri roads, the watchboy may hang on the running board and sing such lusty arias as "Santa Lucia," his purple veins bulging black beneath his olive skin.

The traditional trip on Capri, even for one-day excursionists over from Naples, is the Blue Grotto, a magnificent water-level cave. You make your deal with the boatmen at the Marina Grande, the main dock. The grotto is on the north coast near the west end of the isle, and to reach it you can climb aboard a party motorboat and ride for 250 lire, to the mouth of the cave. Here you have to pay an entry fee of 150 lire (100 on Sundays) to a floating cashier, and, since the motorboat can't fit into the grotto, you have to switch to a smaller craft. If you have the time it is much pleasanter to hire your own rowboat for something between 1,500 lire (asking price) and 1,000 lire (usual settling price). You still have to pay the entrance fee but you don't have to switch boats.

Boats, boatmen, tourists and floating photographers swarm around the opening to the grotto, like a crowd trying to get into a hit movie in Venice. You may have the feeling that you're being taken, just like a tourist, but it's worth the shakedown. When it's

BESIDE THE BLUE GROTTO
floating cashiers

your turn to go inside you lie flat on the bottom of the boat or
you'll leave your head on the Capri cliffside. The entrance is five
feet high, and impassable in rough weather. The boatmen will
yank the chain at the entrance — one quick lurch and you are
through. Since the grotto walls don't extend to the sea floor the
reflection of the sky turns the waters inside an intense aquamarine,
a color that will become apparent as your eyes become accus-
tomed to the darkness. It is said, but not proven, that Tiberius
had a tunnel bored from the top of the island from which he could
descend directly into the grotto.

If you would rather have terra firma under foot there are land
trips to see the Villa San Michele in Anacapri, made famous by
Axel Munthe, the Swedish physician and author of *The Story of
San Michele*. Since Munthe's death recently, the house has become a museum of the relics he collected, and rather odd and
tasteless they are. There is an ancient Roman skull which had a

gold coin in its mouth when found, a Byzantine mosaic table which was being used as a washboard by some Sicilian women when Munthe saw it, and an Egyptian sphinx which was discovered in a Calabrian cave. The sphinx sits on a terrace of his villa now, looking out to sea. They say if you touch its rear-end with your left hand and make a wish it is sure to come true.

On foot you can walk behind the Quisisana Hotel to see the gardens built in 1902 by Krupp, the German munitions maker. Italy's position in World War I left the gardens with the embarrassing name of the German, and they were subsequently called the Augustus Gardens. Krupp also built the walk that winds down the side of the cliff to the Piccolo Marina. The white villa by the water seen from the observation point at the beginning of the walk belongs to Gracie Fields. During the war Allied officers swam from the private beach, and used the house as a kitchen and locker room. Gracie was singing for the troops in India at the time, and when she returned the boys were good enough to give her back her house.

The walk to the beach down Krupp's pathway will take at least twenty minutes, and you'll need a swim at the end of it. An easier way to go is to hire a carriage or a taxi near the square and take the back road. Capri's beach is nothing but hard stones, and walking on a bed of nails can't be more painful. One way of avoiding the torture is to hire a boat, tether it to a rock offshore and swim from there. Or wear sandals. As for beach costumes, if you forget your bathing suit on Capri, a band-aid will do.

To see the Faraglioni, three huge rock formations sitting offshore (*faraglioni* means lighthouses), follow the signs along the Via Tragara. They will bring you eventually past the Tragara Night Club, an officer's club during the war, and the Vismara, next door, where the brass stayed, among them Spaatz, Montgom-

CAPRI'S BEACH
most everyone wears sandals

ery, Eisenhower and Smuts. The house has been used many times as a movie location.

Of the three Faraglioni, the roof of the *Scopolo*, the farthest one out, is the home of a particular species of blue lizard found nowhere else in the world.

If your arches hold out, at sunset you can climb up to the Castiglione, a medieval fortress built on the ruins of a Roman villa. It was defended by both French and British forces. The route to the fort passes the villa of the late Count Ciano, a two-story stucco house which was first used after the occupation by the British naval forces. So many Americans married Caprese girls,

THE FARAGLIONI
on top, blue lizards

after the Yanks took over the island as a rest center, that the army requisitioned the villa as a honeymoon retreat. Nine couples could be accommodated at a time, having their breakfast in the solitude of the villa, and taking the rest of their meals at the La Palma.

You may never wear anything more dashing than a starched collar and a bowler at home, but on Capri everyone succumbs to the extent of affecting Capri sandals. They are brightly colored, eminently chic, beautifully made and cost $1.50. Raffia shoes with crepe soles are about $2. City shoes and evening slippers for women in original, fanciful designs are handmade by cobblers who often work in the street. They sell at $10 to $20 a pair. Handmade embroidered silk blouses are $5, a price which authoritative feminine sources inform me would be quadruple in New York. The collection of smart stoles, shawls, skirts, rainwear and sportswear is the most concentrated grouping of original Continental designs in Italy. Although most of the goods are displayed on racks outside the shops, you might pay particular attention to the Via Camarelle which winds to the right as you come out of the Quisisana Hotel. See G. de Martino at No. 23 for shoes, La Tessitrice at No. 67 for spectacular gold lamé shawls and sporty skirts, and the Snobberie which has blouses, sweaters, belts, skirts and dresses.

Despite the number of outlanders who have turned Capri into virtually an international settlement, the island does offer some culinary dishes that are purely local. There is, in the first place, *spaghetti si totani*, a *totani* being a boneless fish; *quaglie con piselli*, quail with peas — lots of quail on Capri; and a local version of *ravioli* stuffed with *caciotta* cheese. Island vineyards produce both reds and whites.

At the Pizzeria Gemma, under the Moorish colonnades, everyone sits around an old-fashioned oven and watches the chef bake *pizzas*, custards, apples, and in season, chestnuts. They also make a *pizza calzone* (trousers) of tomato, cheese and ham.

The Gatto Bianco, or White Cat, serves magnificent *crepes al formaggio*, which as you can probably determine, are cheese pancakes; *cannelloni;* and *riso al curry con Gamberi* — or curried rice and shrimps. There's an out-door terrace and the tariff is inexpensive.

Hosteria degli Amici is run by one Ermanno F. de Saint Rémy, an Italian despite the camouflage, who came out of the army and opened Capri's plushiest restaurant. It used to be a coffee shop for baggage porters, but Signor Saint Rémy, a man of considerable Continental charm, who happens also to be the U.P.'s Capri correspondent, whitewashed the walls, installed a live grape arbor for a ceiling and a piano player who plays the

PIZZERIA GEMMA
under the Moorish colonnades,
calzone

BERGMAN AND ROSSELLINI
a fateful summer

scores from the current New York musical comedies. The formula is an outstanding success. Not cheap.

Of Capri's hotels the Quisisana, probably because it has sheltered everyone from Bergman and Rossellini during their fateful summer of 1949, to the United States Army's headquarters during World War II, is doubtless the best known. It is in the village of Capri five minutes by sandal-shod foot from the square, and has sheltered among many others, Tyrone Power, Myrna Loy, Alexander Korda (who rolled in on his yacht), Peggy Cummins, Bob Considine and John Gunther who said of Capri's population, it is "the most fascinatingly debauched and corrupt set of Displaced Persons above the rank of baron ever known." During

debauched? corrupt? displaced?

the height of the summer season a room and bath with all meals costs about $8 a day per person at the Quisisana. Having been under American requisition for three and a half years they are rather used to Americans by now.

The most beautiful hotel on the isle is the Caesar Augustus which opened in the spring of 1949. It is perched on the edge of the cliff 900 feet over the sea in the village of Anacapri. It has a terrace looking out on the water for lunch, lights in the trees at night, a bar with pastel purple stools, natural panelled wood and indirect lighting. For couples who want to be alone there is a chalet built on a promontory hanging out over the sea. It has one bedroom, living room and bath, faces water on three sides, and can be reached by a mountain stairway. Room, bath and full pension at the Caesar Augustus starts at 4,500 lire ($7.20) during the summer, and 4,000 lire ($6.40) during the rest of the year, plus the usual twenty percent. The Eden Paradiso, also in Anacapri, has a dining terrace overlooking its gardens of lemon, orange, tangerine and persimmon trees. All rooms face south, and most any winter day (average temperature: 50), you can sit on your brightly-tiled balcony and bask in the sun and the warm winds out of Africa. Life in *paradiso* costs between five and six dollars a day, ambrosia included.

Is the reason social or meteorological?

II. SICILY

A hurly-burly isle overgrown with children and orange groves and olive trees, Sicily squats in the Mediterranean Sea, two miles from Italy on one side, a hundred miles from Africa on the other. The northern corner of its trangular shape stretches toward the tip of the Italian toe like a new-born calf reaching for its mother.

Four and a quarter million people live in Sicily, a parcel of land slightly smaller than Maryland. Sicilians tend the orchards, spin rope in the street, love ice cream, drive hand-painted carts pulled by plumed donkeys and horses, eat tasteless pit-laden cactus fruit called *fichi d'india*. The men are given to caps and bandannas and the village women to black dresses covered by black shawls.

A Sicilian puts all his effort, his ingenuity, his talent, and more money than he can afford into his cart. The dominant colors represent different localities — red and yellow for Palermo, blue and red for Catania, Prussian blue for Agrigento. The sides of the wagon are frequently painted with murals depicting scenes

from everyday life. Subjects for cart art have included such ex-
cerpts of Americana as Buffalo Bill and Al Capone whose demise
in Miami amid an aura of palms was depicted on a cart observed
recently in Palermo. Bright plumes sprout like fountains from the
back and the head of the horse. Invariably the farmer's dog trots
under the wheels of the wagon, protected from the traffic and the
sun but still not worth a seat upstairs.

As a stepping stone between Africa, of which it was once a
geographical part, and Europe to which it was connected by
legend, Sicily has been shuttled around between the Phoenicians,
the Greeks, the Romans, Carthaginians, Saracens, Normans, Swa-
bians (German), Aragonese (Spanish) and Bourbons, not to mention the Italians, and later the Germans. On January 23, 1943,
General Eisenhower received a message from the Casablanca Conference. It read:

> The Combined Chiefs of Staff have resolved that an attack against
> Sicily will be launched in 1943 with the target date as the period
> of the favorable July moon.

Combined American and British troops landed along the
south shore on July 7, 1943. Although it had once taken the Saracens thirty-one years of siege to conquer the town of Enna, and
the Normans were holed-up for a quarter of a century around the
same target, the Allies in a whirlwind, thirty-eight day campaign
had chased the last German from the island by August 17.

Shortly after the war in Sicily ended in 1943, a twenty-one-
year-old Italian named Salvatore Giuliano was arrested for in-
dulging in black market activities. Salvatore's parents had arrived
back in Sicily from their home on East 74th Street and First Avenue in New York just one month before he was born. In his
Sicilian boyhood Salvatore was normal, religous, good in school
But when policemen tried to arrest him that day in 1943 Giuliano
shot one dead. The other cop fired at Salvatore, but the boy

part Arab ...

... part Greek ...

... part Roman ...

... and a little sad

escaped, wounded in the side, and joined the guerrilla bands roaming the hills.

Since then Giuliano has become not just an outlaw, but a legend. He is often called the Robin Hood of Sicily. Certainly he has stolen from the rich, and certainly he has given to the poor, although there are many who question the altruism of his intentions. He has dabbled occasionally in politics, and once sent President Truman a request for arms and ammunition, promising to deliver Sicily to America as a forty-ninth state. Roaming the hills around Palermo with a small gang, Giuliano robs, kidnaps and murders. The first two crimes he is careful to confine to Sicilians. The latter is reserved for police and oppressors of the poor. Thirty-seven hapless murder victims have fit that category so far.

To combat the growing legend and the growing death list of Giuliano the authorities have sent a task force of 1,500 Carabinieri — all bachelors — to Sicily, equipped with fighter aircraft and a detachment of paratroopers. They have posted a bond of 3,000,000 lire — some $4,800 — for his arrest. And they have issued nearly 150 arrest orders.

Some say Giuliano will never be caught because he is an agent of a foreign government. He has been credited to America, Britain and Russia. Others connect him with highly-placed Italian politicians. Despite his atrocities his popularity cannot be denied. Not long ago a reporter and a photographer for the Italian magazine *Oggi* (*Today*) obtained an exclusive interview with him. The magazine published a special Giuliano edition, and although the editor, the reporter and the photographer were all clapped in jail for "glorifying crime," the edition sold 1,200,000 copies in a country with a forty-five million population.

Although Giuliano is bringing notoriety to Sicily, he is playing hob with the tourist industry. Skitterish travelers, they say, have been avoiding Palermo like the plague. Carabinieri on the lookout for Giuliano sometimes set up roadblocks and examine identity papers on the roads leading out of Palermo, but the chances of getting caught in a bandit war are mighty slim. Besides Giuliano simply *loves Americans.*

For some social or meteorological reason lawlessness has always flowered in the warm Mediterranean islands. The bandits of Corsica took a back seat only to the fierce Mafia, the secret society rampant in Sicily during the last century. It took a trial by duel to get membership in the Mafia, and in the code of the society it was considered downright dishonorable to take a complaint to the law. Offenders were actually hidden from the authorities so that one could reserve for one's self the right of visiting proper vengeance.

When feudalism collapsed in Sicily, in 1812, the feudal troops, with nothing left but arms and ammunition, took to the hills around Palermo and became brigands. During the decades that followed Sicilian authorities tried to throttle the Mafia, but they only succeeded in spreading the society to other countries. In 1890 the Chief of Police of New Orleans was murdered by the local Mafia which had come to the United States in 1860. The officer had interrupted a gang war between the Mafia and a rival society. Eleven Italians were rounded up for complicity in the chief's murder, but other Mafia members visited the jury and six defendants were let free. That was too much for the good men of New Orleans who broke open the city jail where nineteen Italians were residing, and lynched all but eight of them. In more recent days, the nefarious activities of Al Capone were said to have been linked with the Mafia, American branch.

All of Sicily's conquerors have left some bit of imprint on the island, particularly the Greeks, many of whose temples after twenty-five hundred years still stand majestic in the hot Mediterranean sun. Those who come to Sicily to see its ruins and

ON A SICILIAN SIDEWALK
in garbage can, deep fat

THE MONDELLO ROAD
rope spinners in the sun

escape the weather of the north can cross on the ferry from Messina. But most tourists fly the 169 miles from Naples to Palermo, or take the night boat. The boat pulls out of Naples at nine in the evening, arrives in Palermo at about nine the next morning. It's a quick, comfortable trip and the accommodations are clean and pleasant. Most cabins have two-decker berths, and rooms for single occupancy are difficult to obtain. A persistent concierge or travel agent can turn the trick, however.

Palermo, capital of Sicily and its largest city, is half metropolis and half resort. Founded by the Phoenicians 700 years Before Christ, Palermo, aged and well-ripened, sits in the center of a graceful bay known as the Conca d'Oro — the Golden Shell. Nobody has more cousins in Chicago than the people of Palermo. During the nineteenth and early twentieth centuries the Palermitans built a bridge of emigrants to the New World.

If you come to Palermo to live a resort life probably you will stay at the Villa Igea, a beautiful two-hundred-room hotel at the foot of Mount Pellegrino away from the center of town. What imported shipyard workers billeted in the hotel didn't ruin during the war, nine bombs in the gardens helped to finish. Everything has been restored now, and the gardens, shaded with palms slope gently down to the Palermo Bay. The southern exposure faces the sea, and there is bathing, yachting and tennis.

The Grand Hotel and des Palmes, on the other hand, is right in the center of things on the Via Roma. A substantial, commercial hotel, des Palmes proved inspirational for Richard Wagner who lived there while completing *Parsifal,* which he finished in January of 1882. The hotel has a Wagner Salon in honor thereof.

Palermo's charm, aside from the usual churches and palaces, is in the singular habits of its people. At noon the street laborers stop work for an open-air lunch, as do road workers of Sicilian extraction all over the world. Those who practice their native Sicilian talent in the home country, eat *rascature e panelle,* potatoes fried in deep fat in a garbage can set up on the sidewalk. They sell for five lire each, and nothing served in the Villa Igea tastes better. Also on the usual menu are dried shrimp, bread and grapes.

Don't miss La Piazza, the incredible open-air market of Palermo, a teeming mass of humanity dealing in broccoli that looks like cauliflower, dolls made of sugar, whole skinned goats, dry milk powder still in GI tins and Camay soap. There are piles of *pepperoncini* — red paprikas; bunches of *settembrina* — September flowers; piles of shocking pink candy; racks hung with pungent *salsiccia* — Sicilian sausage; bakery windows full of huge *sfincionelli* — pizzas the size of cartwheels loaded with oil, tomato sauce and anchovies. Above the din is the cry of the man who sells boiled polyps. And mingling with the crowd is the *acquavitoro*, the lemonade salesman; and the pickpocket whose favorite trick is to flash a picture of Mussolini in front of a foreigner while a stealthy confederate does the dirty work.

Palermo's cathedral was built on a location once occupied in the ninth century by a Christian basilica, a building which later was altered into a mosque by invading Arabs, and finally changed again into a Catholic church by the invading Normans. The present building was begun in 1169 by an Englishman, Walter of the Mill, an archbishop who served as tutor to William II of Sicily. Changed many times through the centuries, the cathedral reflects Sicily's conquerors, especially the Normans and Saracens. The Florentines got a finger in the works when an architect named Fuga added the dome and the battlements, improvements about which the Sicilians are not very enthusiastic. Among the famous figures buried inside are King Roger, the first king of Sicily; his son-in-law, Henry VI; Henry's wife (Roger's daughter), Catherine; and their son, Frederick II, the vital, warlike intellectual under whose patronage Palermo produced poets and became, in fact, the cradle of Italian literature.

But one of Sicily's most interesting churches is the Norman cathedral in Monreale, five miles from Palermo. You can reach it in twenty minutes aboard trolley-bus Nos. 8 or 9. The walls inside are literally covered with mosaics — some 70,000 square feet of them — decorated here and there with palm motifs. The tomb of William the Evil, of red stone, lies alongside William the Good, of white. Adjoining the church is a cloister of the Benedictine monks which enclosed a palm garden. The cloister columns are decorated with strips of mosaics many of which were dug out by invading troops. A fountain in the corner of the yard is decorated in typical herringbone design representing African palms. The outside walls, made of lava stone brought from Etna, are partly Norman and date from 1100.

To cool off from Palermo's heat, head for Mondello, on a cape six miles north of town. There is service by de luxe bus or trolley. The Stabilimento Balneare has a restaurant looking out on the green sea, offers bathing from a sand beach and cabañas. All around Mondello mountains rise almost straight out of the sea, forming a wind-screen for the beach. En route from Palermo you are sure to see the teams of rope spinners, working under the broiling sun by the side of the road, twisting strands of hemp by antiquated methods into cord. Men, women and boys — the whole family — join the operation.

After work is over there is nothing a Palermitan would rather do than eat ice cream. A banana split is child's play in Sicily where ice cream is spiked with candied fruits, marshmallows and cake. One of the best places in town to imbibe is the American Bar, which is neither American nor a bar. Try *caffè imbottito* which has a base of coffee ice cream; *cioccolata imbottita*, mainly chocolate ice cream; or *cassata alla Siciliana*, mostly vanilla.

For a new thing in restaurants try the Spano on the waterfront twenty minutes ride from downtown Palermo. Tables are set up in a wooden shed built on pilings out in the water. Inside the shed everything is decorated with the same abandon with which the local painters beautify Sicilian carts.

A last word about Palermo would be to warn you that no burnished veteran of the Mafia is more a brigand than the city's cab drivers. The rates are high to begin with, and there are extra charges for such incidentals as extra passengers and pieces of luggage. Anything that won't fit in your pocket automatically becomes a valise.

During the winter season CIAT operates its excellent bus

system on a week-long circular tour of the island. The service is the same as offered on the mainland — two drivers, English-speaking hostess, and coach equipped with bar, radio and sliding roof.

One of the most fascinating stops on the CIAT route is Agrigento, on the south shore, once one of the great Greek cities of the world. By car it's a three-hour trip across the island through brown hills, parched, barren and uncultivated. A round trip in a chartered car will cost about 24,000 lire (roughly $40). The diesel express train makes it in two hours and a half, and from the depot you can get a bus or hire a carriage out to the ruins.

Present-day Agrigento, a city of some 30,000 people, sits on the acropolis of the ancient Greek city, looking down on the Greek temples and the sea beyond. The famous Hotel dei Templi, outside the city, has been closed since the war, leaving a choice between the Grand Bretagne e Gellia (second class) and the Belvedere (third class). The best restaurant in town is the Giugiu, and if you like muscatel, Agrigento is famous for it.

When they founded the city in 582 B.C. the Greeks called it Akragas. It became the richest city in Sicily, second in size only to Syracuse. Early sources place the population between 200,000 and 800,000 people. As a voluptuous metropolis, full of temples and monuments, Akragas, on a haughty plateau commanding the sea, became an international prize. It fell in 406 B.C. to the Carthaginians, was retaken in 330 and rebuilt. Then it fell to the Romans, was taken again by the Carthaginians, and finally, in 210 B.C., succumbed to the Romans. Vandals, Goths, Byzantines and Arabs all ravaged it. The Normans changed its name to Gergent, which became Girgenti, and finally Agrigento.

All that remains of ancient Akragas are a few lemon-hued temples rising out of the dusty soil. They all face Greece. Toward the end of January or the beginning of February, the whole pla-

SPRING IN AGRIGENTO
lemon-hued temples and pink blossoms

teau breaks out in white and pink almond blossoms, like an eighty-year old lady in a frivolous new dress.

The Temple of Juno marks the south end of the city. Destroyed once by fire (in 406 B.C.) and later by an earthquake, it still has a complete line of columns along one side. The Temple of Concord, a perfect example of Doric architecture, is one of the best existing Greek temples in the world. Concord can ascribe its state of preservation to the fact that it was adopted as a Christian church. The Christians cut arches in the walls of the original pagan temple, but after the last mass 120 years ago the Christian traces were removed and the Greek ruins preserved. Christian tombs outside the temple still remain. Classical dances are often performed in front of the ruins. All that is left of the Temple of Castor and Pollux are four dramatic columns and a bit of the cornice.

Amid these ruins of antiquity American forces were encamped for three months following the Sicilian landings of 1943. The road from Agrigento along the more fertile south shore en route to Syracuse, passes Licata and Gela, two of the three Anglo-American invasion points.

Syracuse, which once had a population of half a million, whose city limits measured fourteen miles across, was once the greatest Greek city in Sicily. Founded in the eighth century Before Christ, the city flourished then crumbled before a Roman invasion led by Marcellus who laid siege to the city in 214 B.C. Syracuse was greatly aided in the fight by the the new-fangled war machines of Archimedes, the physicist who discovered the principle of the lever and sent projectiles hurling among the Roman ships. After two years the city fell, and in the melee of the occupation, Archimedes was killed.

There is much to see in Syracuse, and good hotels in which to stay. The weather is hot, nurturing citrus fruits and green cactus bristling with red *fichi d'india*, and causing the hotels to close between May and October. Three are officially-registered first-class hotels — the Villa Politi, the Grand and des Etrangers. Villa Politi, one of the smartest before the war, was taken over by the Italian Army at the outbreak of the hostilities, then given to the Germans as an air force headquarters. English troops took over after the invasion, the Americans moved in for a spell, and the hotel finally reopened for civilians in December 1948. Like the other first-class hotels in Syracuse, the Villa Politi charges about 3,500 to 3,800 lire for a single room and bath and full pension. In front of the hotel is Paradise Quarry which has supplied stone to Syracuse since the fifth century Before Christ. Carthaginian prisoners of war worked in the pit, quarrying stone from the bottom up, leaving stone pillars to support the stone roof. In the earthquake of 1562 the roof collapsed.

The Greek theater that still exists in the old city is one of the greatest in the world. Unlike the yellow temples of Agrigento, the theater is soft gray. It was hewn out of solid rock and sits on a hillside that looks out to sea. Ten thousand can be seated in the theater. The audience through the ages has included Plato who sat with Dionysius, the Syracusan tyrant, and also, on one occasion, the people of Syracuse who had come to see the final naval battle when Syracuse repelled the fleet of Athens on the nearby seas.

Beginning in 1914 until the outbreak of the war, the Instituto Nazionale del Dramma Antico offered an annual spring performance of classical Greek plays in the theater. The plan was begun again in May 1948 with the *Orestea*, a trilogy by Aeschylus, performed in 458 B.C., about the time the theater was built. It includes The Agamemnon, The Choephorae and The Eumenides. The Greek theater will perform at Syracuse every three years and on Holy Years, as things stand now. Hotels remain open through the period of the performances.

Although the Greek theater is acoustically perfect, the oddest acoustical phenomenon in Syracuse is the far-famed Ear of Dionysius. A narrow grotto, 71 feet high, it reverberates from the slightest whisper. The door knocker rapped at the entrance sounds like the concussion of a sixteen-gun salute to anyone inside. Cicero wrote of a grotto where Dionysius kept his prisoners so that he could overhear their conversations from the clifftop above, an early job of wiretapping. To a painter who visited the "speaking grotto" as it was called in 1642, the cave looked like an ear, and so for double reasons it became known as the Ear of Dionysius. The adjoining cave is occupied by a family of rope spinners whose ancestors are supposed to have begun plying the craft in the same cave during Grecian times.

The cathedral of Syracuse was constructed from a Greek temple built in the fifth century B.C. In the seventh century A.D. the original columns were enclosed and arches cut in the interior walls. The children of Syracuse are baptized from a Greek vase found in the Capuchin catacombs.

Sicily's oldest cathedral is underground in the catacombs where St. Paul is believed to have preached. His altar is preserved in the dank caves. A monk will show you through the catacombs noting the Greek inscriptions on the walls, and explaining how vials of blood of the saints were found in the underground cells. There were bones in the crypts until World War II, when the catacombs were used as an air-raid shelter. It was found more sanitary and less nerve-wracking to have the skeletons removed.

The superstitious and the adventuresome often came to Syracuse to bathe in its Fountain of Aretusa, a fresh water spring which bubbles up at the edge of the sea. The fountain's reputation derives from a legend which involves Aretusa, the daughter of a goddess and Alfeo, a young king of old Greece. They fell in love, and one day during their courtship, while Aretusa was blithely gathering flowers in the meadow, overanxious Alfeo advanced on her with a look in his eye that unmistakably said, "rape." Aretusa cried for help, and her mother who was a goddess, and therefore possessed of influence in such matters, turned her into a river. Alfeo pleaded to be turned to water, too. He was, and as luck would have it the two waters met in Syracuse and became a spring known as the Fountain of Aretusa. Local experts insist the fresh water of Aretusa passes through the sea water and yet remains unsalted.

Generals who believed in the magical powers of the water always bathed here before a battle. Horatio Nelson not only

THE GREEK THEATER
on a stone seat, Plato

FOR THE BOYS FROM SYRACUSE
outlandish colors

bathed here, but took on water for his fleet. He later wrote Lady Hamilton, "I am sure I will carry the day since I have bathed in the Fountain of Aretusa." Papyrus plants thrive in the water, one of the few places outside of Egypt where they grow. After the Allied landings a foundation was sunk in the fountain and a platform built over it to facilitate the unloading of ships. Much papyrus was ruined, the Syracusans say.

One of the best ways to see the city is by carriage; one of the most novel is by outsized rowboat which the boys from Syracuse paint in outlandish colors, like Sicilian carts.

Catania, Sicily's second city, on the east coast road to Messina, lives in the shadow of Mount Etna and is subject to its whims. Etna, as the beautiful mountain, has brought many visitors to Catania; as the unpredictable volcano it has ruined the city; but then it has deposited lava which has enriched Catania's soil. Although it is a stop on the route of the Italian airline, Catania loses the bulk of the tourist trade to Syracuse on its south and glamorous Taormina on its north. There is one first-class hotel in town, should you nevertheless want to stay there — the Centrale Corona on Via Etna 218.

Mount Etna reaches 10,742 feet into the Sicilian sky, so dominating the nearby skyline that the people have given it a mystical human personality, as a ventriloquist comes to treat his puppet. "How does she look this morning?" they will say. "Smoking?" "Her head in the clouds?" "New snow on top?" She covers a total of 460 square miles and measures ninety-one miles around the base. There have been some 135 recorded eruptions of Etna, as long ago as the eighth century B.C. and as recently as 1947. Of modern times Etna has been averaging upward of seventeen eruptions a century, and at that rate has about twelve to go before the year 2000. One of the worst was the eruption of 1166 when Catania was virtually inundated.

TAORMINA
across from the lighted windows, Etna

The top of Etna, should you want to reach it, is eighteen miles northwest of Catania. A good motor road has been built up the mountain, and the bus will take you as far as the 5,500-foot level where there is a hotel. It's a good three-hour hike from there, and recommended to Alpinists only. Along the lower levels of Etna the houses are built of black lava stone, there are gardens of cactus, and vineyards that grow a black grape which give an inky wine. The warm temperatures and the lush soil grow orange, lemon, pear, crab apple trees and olive trees. Gradually the trees become chestnuts and evergreens, and the houses are few. Finally there are birchwoods, and then there are shrubs. The snowfields which last almost all year around have become popular with skiers. See the Italian Alpine club in Nicolosi, nine miles northwest of Catania for the last word on mountaineering.

Magnificent Taormina, high on a cliffside between Catania and Messina, was settled by the Greeks and popularized by Kaiser Wilhelm II. It sits, horseshoe-shaped and happy, four hundred feet above the sea, a winter refuge both chic and secluded. From the open-air Greco-Roman theater where spectacles are performed in season, you can look up to the snowfields of Etna, across to the lighted windows of the hotels and down to the beach of Mazzaro.

Twice during its history Taormina was wrecked by invading Arabs, but that was long before it was a resort. No slower than any other military machine to find a pleasant location in which to carry a fight, the Nazis chose Taormina as a headquarters during the late war. Word of this decision reached Allied ears, and the first bombing, oddly enough, interrupted a conference of high German brass. Ten generals were killed.

Thirty-five hotels are back in business, the notable absentee being the Castello e Mare which never re-opened. The beautiful San Domenico Palace, once a convent, completely refurnished, is back in business. It offers drinks to guests in a stately, panelled bar. The glassed-in lobby is built around the erstwhile garden cloister. The arched windows of its rooms face the hillside cypresses and the sea. Among the smaller establishments is the Timeo on the Via Teatro Greco, which has a cliffside terrace, the Miramare and the Excelsior, all first-class.

Shopping in town you will find Taormina's second industry, after tourism, to be embroidery. Handmade blouses run about 5,500 lire, luncheon sets for six about 15,000 lire, smart sandals, comfortable for local excursions, are 1,400 lire.

The oldest coffee shop in town is called, contrarily, the Caffè Nuova (new). In winter it offers besides coffee, dancing. Taormina's newest night club is the fashionable Villa la Palmara, across the street from the San Domenico Hotel. The Kaiser's villa before the First World War, Palmara became a night club in the fall of 1949. Decorated like an elegant private home it has soft piano music for cocktails, a restaurant, and dancing.

To me, Taormina is one of the loveliest resorts in all Italy. That is, to me and the late Kaiser Wilhelm II.

INDEX

INDEX

INDEX

INDEX